CATASTROPHE

CATASTROPHE

LAW, POLITICS, AND THE HUMANITARIAN IMPULSE

Edited by
AUSTIN SARAT and **JAVIER LEZAUN**

University of Massachusetts Press
Amherst & Boston

Copyright © 2009 by University of Massachusetts Press
All rights reserved
Printed in the United States of America
LC 2009039768
ISBN 978-1-55849-738-2 (paper); 737-5 (library cloth)

Designed by Jack Harrison
Typeset in Scala
Printed and bound by Thomson-Shore, Inc.

Library of Congress Cataloging-in-Publication Data
Sarat, Austin.
    Catastrophe : law, politics, and the humanitarian impulse /
edited by Austin Sarat and Javier Lezaun.
        p. cm.
Includes bibliographical references and index.
ISBN 978-1-55849-738-2 (pbk. : alk. paper) —
ISBN 978-1-55849-737-5 (library cloth : alk. paper)
1. Disaster relief—Law and legislation—United States.
2. Emergency management—Law and legislation—United States.
3. Disaster relief—Political aspects—United States.
I. Lezaun, Javier. II. Title.
    KF3750.S27 2009
    344.7305'348--dc22
                                        2009039768

British Library Cataloguing in Publication data are available.

To Benjamin Sarat,
with hope that he will grow up in a more humane
and compassionate world (A. S.)

To Agustina Ortiz Marañón,
who survived with fortitude a tragic century (J. L.)

Contents

Acknowledgments

We are grateful to our colleagues in Amherst College's Law in
Science/Science in Law Project for their intellectual companionship
and their support for this project. We also thank the college's
President's Initiative Fund for generous financial support.
Finally, we appreciate the skilled research assistance
of Tovah Ackerman.

CATASTROPHE

Introduction
The Challenge of Crisis and Catastrophe in Law and Politics

Austin Sarat

Javier Lezaun

From the September 11, 2001, terrorist attacks to Hurricane Katrina, from the Darfur tragedy to the Minnesota bridge collapse, ours is an "age of catastrophe." In this era, catastrophic events seem to have a revelatory quality: they offer powerful reminders of the fragility of our social and institutional architectures, making painfully evident vulnerabilities in our social organization that were otherwise invisible. By disrupting the operation of fundamental mechanisms and infrastructures of our social order, they lay bare the conditions that make our sense of normalcy possible.

A catastrophe is thus a moment of manifestation, an opportunity to take in and discern what had previously been veiled. This opportunity is also a challenge, a challenge to human resilience and optimism in the face of disaster. Legal, political, and humanitarian responses are premised on the deep-rooted assumption that we can at least decipher the meanings of disaster, at best correct its causes and prevent future occurrences. Whatever explanatory theory one holds, whether the devastation is attributed to God, nature, or society, catastrophic events test our legal, political, and humanitarian resolve and resourcefulness.

This testing is particularly salient with respect to the law. That is the case not only because the breakdown of legal order is one of the clearest signs of a catastrophic disruption, but, more importantly, because the law plays a crucial role in drawing lessons from disaster, in providing relief and redress to victims, and in correcting the vulnerabilities that caused or compounded the destruction. Catastrophes, in other words, put the law to the test of demonstrating its capacity to mitigate or reduce human suffering.

At a time when our societies are directing an unprecedented level of resources and ingenuity to anticipating and mitigating catastrophic events, this book, *Catastrophe: Law, Politics, and the Humanitarian Impulse*, examines the tests that catastrophe poses to politics and humanitarianism as well as to law. We want to explore legal, political, and humanitarian responses during times when the sudden, discontinuous, and disastrous event has become, perhaps paradoxically, a structural component of our political imagination. We understand our present condition as irredeemably shaped by past catastrophes, and we expect a future punctuated, if not profoundly affected, by disasters yet to come and barely imagined. We want to analyze whether law, politics, and humanitarianism live up to the challenges posed by disaster as well as the role each plays in creating a more resilient world.

Catastrophic Politics

The study of catastrophes and their political and legal significance has undergone a series of significant changes and turns over the past several decades. As a backdrop to the chapters that follow, let us take stock of some of the elements of this transition.

From Natural Disasters to Manufactured Risks

Any survey of the social-scientific literature on catastrophes and disasters will note a progressive shift of emphasis, from a consideration of natural disasters as "acts of God"—unpreventable and largely unforeseeable events that allow no useful preparation and produce no liability—to a growing perception of catastrophes as human-made affairs.[1] Perhaps not all the links in the causal chain that brings about a catastrophe can be attributed to human action (or inaction), but the patterns of damage and suffering that disasters generate follow fault lines with a distinctive social history.[2]

In parallel, there has been an evolution from approaches that emphasized, to the point of exclusivity, engineering solutions to natural hazards toward perspectives better attuned to the role that law and policy do play in reducing, or increasing, social vulnerability to disaster.[3] The social-scientific literature on risk illustrates this transition well. The "risk society" thesis argues, for instance, that we live in a world dominated by "manufactured risks" in which differential exposure to man-made hazards constitutes a new principle of social inequality.[4]

Disasters have thus been denaturalized, at least in the academic literature, less so in the assumptions and criteria of policy organizations.[5] Catastrophic events might introduce a radical level of discontinuity in everyday life, but the trajectory of their effect responds to the patterns and configurations of our social organization. If we accept that disasters have institutional and political genealogies, often with a distinctive national character,[6] and that there is thus a social distribution of the exposure, vulnerability, and suffering associated with catastrophes, we must necessarily highlight the significance of the law in shaping the preconditions, severity, and effects of catastrophic events.

The Politics of Disaster Inequality

Within this broad understanding of disasters as social events infused with politically and legally relevant meanings is a second, consistent thread in the more recent literature on disasters: the growing attention to the politics of inequality in connection with crises and catastrophes. As Kai T. Erikson wrote, "If one were to draw a map of places in which disasters are most likely to strike, we would also be sketching at least an approximate map of places in which the vulnerable are most likely to be gathered."[7] The recent warning from the United Nations Intergovernmental Panel on Climate Change that the poorest countries will be the hardest hit by the effects of global warming is simply a reminder that this nexus of social disadvantage and vulnerability to disaster only becomes more apparent as the time frame and scale of the problems and the afflicted populations increase.[8]

Not only do we know that exposure to catastrophic disruption is unequally distributed along lines of entrenched social disadvantage; we also have evidence that the responses of policymakers in the event of a disaster, and the relief they provide to victims, are often tainted by the same kinds of bias and discrimination that put certain populations in harm's way in the first place. Thus, disasters might end up exacerbating inequalities and discriminations, but, at the very least, they can serve to make the plight of vulnerable and underprivileged groups strikingly visible, by manifesting inequality in the rawest, most unadulterated way. They are powerful visualization devices.

One remembers the iconic photographs commissioned by the Farm Security Administration of victims of the "Dust Bowl" and the floods that afflicted farming communities in 1930s America, or the more recent video footage of New Orleans residents unable to flee Hurricane Katrina: the shock of discovery in many commentators was palpable. It seems that too often the precarious living conditions of deprived and discriminated groups only become apparent in the wake of their destruction. Whether that realization leads to action is another matter.

The capacity to correct the chronic inequalities exposed by catastrophic events depends partly on the public representation of disaster victims. Victims of disaster might be free of the stigma of blame that is often attached to disadvantaged groups, but this suspension of prejudice is not universal, nor, crucially, indefinite. The media play a crucial role in creating and sustaining long-distance and long-term compassion as well as in establishing a moral imperative to redress not only the immediate effects of a catastrophic event, but also the structural conditions that made certain populations particularly defenseless.[9] There is, though, much evidence that the policy processes that can lead from compassion to provision are convoluted, often specific to particular kinds of disaster and not others, and always susceptible to be short-circuited by antagonistic interest groups or sidelined by other priorities.[10]

The Ambivalences of "Reconstruction"

In his analysis of the "disaster writing" that followed the 1871 fire in Chicago and the 1906 San Francisco earthquake, Kevin Rozario notes a consistent utopian trope: the devastation inflicted upon these two great U.S. cities was conceived by many as an "instrument of progress," even a "blessing." At any event, it was seen as an opportunity to realize in their resurgence the ideal of a more perfect community: these cities would be rebuilt, bigger and higher.[11] Ideal visions of postcatastrophic regeneration were often little more than thinly disguised boosterism on the part of those who saw in the real estate *tabula rasa* created by the disaster an opportunity for speculative investment, but utopias of reconstruction have nevertheless been a key narrative in the efforts to cope with disaster and make sense of the future that ought to follow it. Catastrophes might at first vindicate the naysayer, but it is typically the visionary entrepreneur who provides moral comfort and stands to benefit most from the new situation.

Americans might have become irreversibly cynical by the recent experience of Hurricane Katrina and New Orleans—a city that, years after the fact, has hardly recovered, let alone been reborn, from the devastation that descended upon it—but it is fair to say that the contemporary literature on reconstruction offers a more nuanced and ambivalent picture of the state to which devastated communities are typically "restored." There is, for one, a more complicated view of the politics and economics of material reconstruction, a view that looks more closely at the interests that drive and benefit from rebuilding and those that are marginalized in the process, from Bhopal to Beirut.[12] Mike Davis spoke of "seismic Keynesianism" to describe how, in southern California, postdisaster economic aid has historically served not just to repair the damage inflicted by earthquakes, but to upgrade and invigorate the economic infrastructure of the region as well as reap the resulting political windfall.[13]

Beyond the politics and economics of *material* reconstruction, scholars are also paying more attention to the subtler repair of the social bonds and the individual and communal identities shattered by disaster. Objects of moral or emotional significance (what Erikson described as the "furniture of self")[14] are almost always irretrievably lost in the wake of a catastrophe. The complex fabric of social life is generally irreversibly altered, a fact that only becomes apparent, however, long after the emergency management operations are over and the relief organizations have left.

In Adriana Petryna's study of the Chernobyl "technogenic" catastrophe, for instance, we observe how the concept of "reconstruction" extends from the immediate treatment of victims (and their conversion to the long-term status of chronic disability) to the transition of the Ukraine to market economics and independent statehood.[15] As this and other studies suggest, rather than restitution (let alone heroic rebirth), the aftermath of catastrophe is typically a drawn-out process of social reconfiguration in which different forms of legal intervention are used to shape a future that usually looks nothing like the pre-catastrophe past.

The Value of "Resilience"

Discussions of social "resilience" have come to dominate much of the literature on catastrophes and crisis management, in contraposition to the earlier emphasis on anticipation and planning. Resilience refers to the ability of a community to withstand devastation and restore its fundamental operations on a relatively short notice, after a critical experience.[16]

"Resilience" and "anticipation" are obviously not mutually exclusive principles of action, but the emphasis on the former signifies a growing skepticism regarding the ability of societies to foresee and adequately plan for catastrophe.[17] There is an irreducible uncertainty as to the location, form, and scale of devastation. Moreover, the costs—economic and political—of effective contingency planning might be overwhelming. It is better, the argument goes, to build the decentralized capacities and redundancies that would enable a community to weather the crisis and return quickly to something resembling its normal state.

Resilience is a flexible notion, and as such it can be applied to a diversity of institutions and infrastructures.[18] It is difficult, but open to empirical investigation, to determine which features of the fabric of a given society give it a particular capacity to withstand breakdowns and disruptions. For instance, how does the particular distribution of wealth affect a society's ability to recuperate from a catastrophe? What is exactly the relationship between the degree of political decentralization and the ability of those most directly affected by a disaster to organize the first response? There is, moreover, a deficit in our understanding of how the legal system contributes to society's hardiness in the face of a catastrophic event, of how, in the first place, the law could augment its own resilience as an apparatus of social order in moments of widespread disturbance. What would a "resilient" law look like, and what trade-offs would we have to incur to achieve it?

Taking the Law to Task

As mentioned earlier, catastrophes put the law to the test. On the one hand, the emergency reveals its ability to operate under stress (or lack thereof) and the limits of its capacity to deal with extraordinary events and circumstances. The aftermath probes law's power to mitigate human suffering in the short term and to institute the kind of social change that would prevent or at least mitigate future occurrences. We can sketch here at least five dimensions along which the law is called upon to act in the event of disaster.

Maintaining Its Own Operability

The first demand is that the legal system preserves its own order, its ability to operate according to a pre-established set of rules, routines, and protocols. The disruption that catastrophes introduce in the routine functioning of the law serves to highlight the moral and material preconditions of a proper legal order.

Fighting "Lawlessness"

Perhaps the most studied dimension of legal ordering in the context of catastrophic events is fighting "lawlessness." There is an immense body of literature and public discourse on the lawlessness of catastrophe areas and on the necessity of ensuring a rapid prosecution of crime and disorder in disaster-stricken communities. The militarization of first-response operations (evident, for instance, during the Katrina crisis) is partly related to this fixation on the allegedly anarchical and alegal conditions of disaster zones. The sociological literature on disaster zones (see chapter 4) offers a counterpoint to the focus on criminality as the main way in which law is "broken" by catastrophic events.

Stabilization and Resettlement

Disasters are followed by settlements. In an immediate sense, displaced victims must be sheltered, and, depending of the severity of the damage, they might have to be permanently relocated. "Relief efforts risk turning survivors into dependents of the state," notes a recent report by the United Nations Special Rapporteur on adequate housing. Katrina has offered us plenty of lessons on the pitfalls of resettlement policies, from the disruption and destabilization of community networks, to the exposure of victims to toxic chemicals in government-provided trailers.[19]

In his classic study of the 1972 Buffalo Creek, West Virginia, flood, Erikson noted how the law had served to inadvertently stabilize the chaotic circumstances that followed the disaster by forcibly settling victims as they were found, without regard to the social units and neighborhood structures that characterized their life prior to its disruption.[20] The 2004 Asian tsunami left more than one million people in need of urgent resettlement, many of whom were still suffering inadequate nutrition and health conditions in makeshift camps months after the disaster struck.

Identifying Victims and Culprits

Disasters leave behind a mesh of liabilities and diffuse lines of responsibility. The law is expected to perform its traditional function of apportioning blame, disentangling the human and nonhuman factors that contributed to the disaster, and identifying those who are deserving of relief and those who are deserving of punishment. In other words, the law is to function as an instrument of forensic scrutiny and produce clear lines of accountability where there was only confusion.

Reducing Future Vulnerability

Drawing lessons from a catastrophe, let alone the right ones, is not an automatic process, and legal processes play a crucial role in deciphering the meanings of catastrophe and instituting the necessary changes. The academic literature demonstrates that some disasters have been more fruitful in terms of the amount of legal and policy innovations they have triggered. Earthquakes seem to provide, at least in the United States, the best example of a sustained effort to engineer into the landscape the legal and material changes that would mitigate the effects of future disasters. The evolution of building codes, the enshrining of "right-to-know" legislation for real estate transactions, and alert and evacuation protocols are all examples of how the law can be deployed to attenuate vulnerability in the long term.

The chapters that follow seek to locate catastrophe on various axes of law, politics, and humanitarianism. They present case studies, each of which is designed to help us understand responses to catastrophe in the domestic and international realms. Before we get to those case studies, though, Peter H. Schuck offers in chapter 1 a broad conceptual overview of the meaning of catastrophe as seen through the differing lenses of law, politics, religion, and science.

Schuck defines "catastrophe" as a sudden, very fatal disaster and explores six features he believes are present in a paradigmatic catastrophe: magnitude, pervasiveness, uncertainty, preventability, irreversibility, and crisis. He identifies other attributes of catastrophe that influence legal, political, and humanitarian responses: what he calls public recognition, community of concern, identifiable versus statistical victims (a phenomenon in which victims who can be humanized as individuals—like a little girl trapped in a well—often receive more resources for their rescue than statistical victims), telegenicity (dramatization and humanization of victims by the media), winners and losers (the unequal distribution of the costs and benefits of catastrophes), and buffering institutions ("By buffering institutions, I mean family, private and public relief efforts, religious consolation, a strong community, insurance coverage, and other legal remedies of repair or reparation").

Schuck discusses four frameworks for explaining catastrophes: religious, scientific, legal, and political. For each, he discusses its central values, the incentives and techniques, and the biases and orientations. He also explores how science, law, and politics are interrelated.

Religion: "In most religious traditions, catastrophes are the consequence of divine intervention or of human failure to abide by God's laws." Sometimes, though, catastrophes are so horrible and affect so many innocents that even devoutly religious people cannot accept "God's displeasure" as an explanation.

Science: "In its professional norms and aspirations, and to some extent in its actual performance, science is committed to a conception of truth . . . reached through a conventional methodology of proof . . . based on the testing of falsifiable propositions." Science, though, is not performed in a bubble."

Law: Whereas science claims to deal only in verifiable truth, legal principles are normative. They concern how the world *should* work rather than how it *does* work. Whereas science is the search for truth, Schuck argues, law is the search for justice. Although the law is in more of a hurry to come to a conclusion and is much less coordinated than science, it is also much more authoritative and definitive.

Politics: "Just as scientists often play politics, politicians also have many opportunities to exploit the prestige and symbols of science so as to fortify their empirical claims, legitimate and build public support for their decisions, and clothe themselves in the mantle of scientific truth." In politics, Schuck believes, three values are paramount: the participation norm (that in the interest of human dignity, individuals should play a role in political decisions), the accountability norm (that officials be held responsible for their actions and the conflict), and the conflict management norm (which says that the other values can only be achieved if social conflicts are kept under control).

Political culture, Schuck quotes Richard A. Posner as saying, has weakened the capacity of decision makers to use scientific understanding to prevent catastrophes. This weakening, Schuck suggests, results from a pervasive scientific illiteracy among the western elite as well as a paradoxical veneration of scientists that "accords more respect to their policy judgments than is warranted by their narrowly scientific expertise." Science, although allegedly valued as an autonomous sphere distinct from other disciplines, is inextricably intertwined with politics and law, especially when concerning catastrophes. Legal, political, and humanitarian responses to catastrophe draw on and deploy science instrumentally, and each is mediated and rendered legible through institutions or processes that effectively infuse institutional perspectives into public and private decisions.

In chapter 2, Michelle Landis Dauber takes up what Schuck called the *ex post* containment of disasters and discusses how a previously set social situation can sustain or exacerbate a catastrophe. She uses the history of federal disaster relief in the United States, especially the Great Depression and the New Deal, to illustrate the interplay of legal, political, and humanitarian concerns as well as the way policymakers mobilized various discourses to shape and sell particular responses to catastrophe. Crucial is their ability to draw an analogy between any catastrophe and a natural disaster.

Beginning in 1790, Dauber notes, the government started giving direct payment from the U.S. Treasury to relieve "sufferers." "These early appropriations quickly hardened into a set of legislative precedents that were repeatedly invoked both for and against proposed relief measures. . . . By 1827, disaster relief was already established as a nascent federal entitlement program that was seen as entirely constitutionally permissible." Throughout U.S. history, Congress has drawn on this early history of disaster relief to determine how to respond to crisis and catastrophe. "Ultimately," Dauber notes, "whether or not an event was a 'calamity' deserving of federal intervention turned on the ability of the claimants to argue that they, like those who previously received aid, were innocent victims of fate rather than irresponsible protagonists in their own misery."

Prior to the New Deal, responses to the catastrophic were largely uninhibited by constitutional objections because those objections seemed "irrelevant to the imperative to respond to blameless suffering." Indeed, starting in 1890, the long history of federal disaster relief was often cited in Supreme Court briefs and opinions and in policy debates as evidence that Congress had unlimited power to appropriate funds for the "general welfare."

Advocates of the New Deal drew on this tradition in arguing that the Great Depression was a disaster, like a hurricane or a flood, that deserved federal relief just as the government had provided it to disaster victims in the past. They worked to represent the victims of the Great Depression as morally blameless. "Once built," writes Dauber, "the Depression could appear in many arenas, including Congress and the Court, as a national disaster for which, Stanley Reed told the Supreme Court in 1936, it could be 'safely assumed' that federal relief was constitutional." Only by portraying the Great Depression as a disaster and the New Deal as a continuation of the governmental tradition of giving federal relief could such a revolutionary relief effort have occurred.

Recently, Dauber suggests, as in the case of Hurricane Katrina, circumstances can move people from one state of moral blameworthiness to another, "making the moral economy of disaster and relief vividly clear. . . . [Katrina] provided an abundance of such jarring moments, as reporters and politicians competed with one another to express outrage over the treatment of the same poor, black residents of New Orleans who had been the targets of popular and sustained cuts in welfare and public housing programs." President George W. Bush, Dauber argues, made the same mistake with Katrina that President Herbert Hoover did with the Great Depression. They both failed to recognize that people in desperate financial circumstances could be successfully portrayed as victims of a disaster that was not of their making. Because of his inability or unwillingness to address the Depression, Hoover, although very generous with federal aid in many circumstances, has come to represent an enormous failure in the history of the Republican Party. In the end, contrasting Hoover and Franklin Delano Roosevelt, Dauber suggests that disasters, although potentially perilous for politicians, can also be a source of enormous political benefit for those who can control them.

Susan M. Sterett takes up the legal, political, and humanitarian responses to Hurricane Katrina in chapter 3. For Sterett, the key fact is that "the American state is *disaggregated*. Caseworkers, courts, and executive agencies make decisions that are not tightly linked either with one another or with a decision set in principle from a statute." During catastrophes, states act based on individual decisions rather than on common norms. As a result, "a disaggregated state allows a claim to total control while ascribing failures of control and relief to others, sometimes to individuals and sometimes to particular units in the state, and sometimes to the force of disaster." Sterett suggests that

> the usefulness of thinking through exceptional governance in disaster would also be extended by conceptualizing the "catastrophic state" not as something that does or does not exist, but on a continuum. . . . Even when some part of the rules of state operation are suspended, if state actors have not wholly abolished every element that supported the practices of the state—interest organizations, lawyers, doctrine stating decision-making procedures—suspension could be brought within ordinary governance.

Thus, she argues, the state was able after Katrina to extend housing assistance for longer than it ever had before for any catastrophe. She notes:

> That the entire juridical order was not suspended and that the ordinary organization of interest groups, lawyers, and courts persisted allowed the administration of relief to be brought within the administrative state's due process during negotiations in court cases. The due process to which the courts held the central state responsible was continually violated, but the expectation that it should be available made it possible to bring suits and negotiate with the administration.

After Katrina, the state stood in a middle ground between total control and continued ordinary administrative procedures. Some rules were applied as a whole and then were broken in particular cases, and some rules were ignored. Writes Sterett, "It signaled that disaster relief could . . . [adopt] administrative due process without the court requiring it. Signaling the juridification of chaotic decision making could signal competence and accountability, but state organizations could follow procedures without actually distributing benefits to people, or without extending the mission to rebuild New Orleans or the competence of clients."

Federal relief after Katrina, Sterett reminds us, was patchy and inadequate. To handle a huge caseload, the Federal Emergency Management Agency (FEMA) hired 30,000 new employees, many of whom had no previous experience. Almost immediately, lawsuits concerning housing benefits were brought to court. The first major case was *McWaters v. FEMA*, in which "the complaint challenged FEMA's slowness in determining eligibility for individual assistance, the lack of notice about its policies, and its decision to require people to document how they had spent the $2,358 issued under the individual assistance provision soon after the storm." The *McWaters* trial delayed the end of FEMA's temporary housing assistance programs. The judge spent much of his opinion chastising FEMA for attempting to "evict" the victims for whom it had been providing housing. Here again, as in chapter 2, the decision to continue relief was based on the decision that these people were homeless "through no fault of their own."

As a result of the case, FEMA was required to clearly notify its aid recipients of all its decisions and policies concerning them. As Sterett writes, "No court ever made a direct order to extend payments," but by joining its pressure with public disapproval the courts nonetheless had a strong effect on FEMA. By merely reviewing FEMA's policies, the court was able to cause large-scale policy changes.

In Sterett's view, the legal, political, and humanitarian responses to Katrina combined elements of "generosity" and the "Kafkaesque impossibility of policy." As she writes, "Concessions, orders, and disaster-specific guidance allowed multiple norms to persist alongside one another: the state offered housing relief, but it policed fraud and protected budgets." Little was decided as a matter of principle. The courts provided some bureaucratic oversight, but made only very limited orders. Sterett concludes that "litigation and concessions in a climate of skepticism about public assistance and contempt for FEMA extended relief without requiring any institution to address in principle what people deserve after disaster and why, or when disaster and assistance for it ends."

Chapter 4 takes up the question of what catastrophes do to legal institutions themselves. Focusing on two case studies, the September 11 attacks and Hurricane Katrina, Thomas A. Birkland first examines myths that have developed concerning what happens to a society after a disaster. These myths, he suggests, have been internalized by researchers, decision makers, and the public at large and have led to bad policy decisions.

The first of these myths, the looting myth, holds that after disasters, people panic, act irrationally, and hinder one another's ability to get to safety. Many studies have proved that people in disaster situations often act calmly and reasonably, most often helping one another to safety. The second, the helpless citizen myth, suggests that "citizens are helpless and cannot be trusted with risk information; . . . this [myth] exists notwithstanding years of social science research that suggests that, when presented with sound information, citizens can make informed risk decisions." The third is the civil disorder myth, which indicates that in disaster situations, communities move into a Hobbesian state of nature. Although this myth is false, the news media, in an attempt to create a compelling story, focus on panic, looting, and assaults while portraying prosocial behavior as exceptions rather than the norm.

Fourth is the first-responder myth. First-response units such as the police or fire department are made into heroes in disaster situations and are portrayed as the perfect opposite of the panicked, criminal victim. Birkland cites Kathleen Tierney's observation that "social science research has consistently shown that community residents are the true first responders in both disasters and terrorist attacks, but homeland security initiatives ignore the vital role the public plays in disaster response." The fifth myth is that everything can be put back together. Disasters such as the September 11 attacks and Katrina, Birkland writes, cause widespread and pervasive changes in both our physical and political environments. The rebuilt area never matches the area as it was before. Everything cannot be put back together. Sixth is the myth of lessons learned. Here, Birkland suggests that one can only claim that a lesson is learned if the supposed lesson is implemented and if that implementation is more successful than prior implementations.

Research, Birkland writes, has revealed certain facts or failures common to a wide range of disasters: failures to plan realistically, failures to execute plans, failures of intergovernmental coordination, and failures to provide sufficient relief for disaster mitigation. Birkland focuses his analysis specifically on the court system after the September 11 attacks and Hurricane Katrina. In both situations, vital records were lost or damaged, cases were postponed, and communication between judicial institutions was patchy. Three issues require continued legal attention after disasters: the disruption of ongoing cases that began and were to continue had the disaster not disrupted normal proceedings; the question of insurance payments and other liability issues in disasters; and the legal problems attendant to postdisaster reconstruction, particularly regulatory takings of lands in hazardous areas.

Birkland concludes by identifying five questions that he believes need to be explored when thinking about judicial responses to disaster: (1) What are the most common threats to court security? (2) What are the most *consequential* threats to court security? (3) How do these threats vary by jurisdiction? (4) Is planning uniform within or between jurisdictions? (5) Are "lessons" really "learned" from past events? Or are lessons or aphorisms merely observed, without any fundamental action being taken? Only by answering these questions, he says, can we prepare our courts to effectively operate during times of crisis and catastrophe.

Kim Fortun begins chapter 5 by discussing the Bhopal disaster of 1984, when forty tons of toxic gas were released from a chemical plant over the city of Bhopal, India. No alarm was sounded. With no evacuation plan and with false information from the chemical plant, ten thousand people died within the first few days following the disaster. This catastrophe triggered inquiries in the U.S. Congress concerning information available to the public about chemical or nuclear risks in its area.

Although chapters 1 through 4 focus primarily on the institutional structure of disaster relief agencies, Fortun discusses the availability and importance of information in aiding grassroots disaster prevention. She is particularly interested in the environmental domain in which "information strategies are now relied on to address pollution, loss of biodiversity, climate change, and a range of other issues involving entangled social, technical, and natural systems." This initiative works on the assumptions that information in more hands is a good thing and that people will act more rationally if they have more information.

These "information strategies" for dealing with environmental risks are central to the so-called Community Right-to-Know Act. Under this act, high-risk facilities are required to provide information to local governments to plan emergency evacuations. The act also created the Toxic

Release Inventory (TRI), the first publicly available federal database in a computer-readable format. "The effects of distributing TRI data in the United States," Fortun contends, "have been enormous, sparking environmental initiatives within corporations, in the communities affected by pollution, and by national and international environmental groups." Similar initiatives have been passed around the world.

These initiatives raise questions such as what information is necessary to fulfill right-to-know requirements and how that information should be provided. A website called Scorecard, created by one of the largest environmental organizations in the country, is designed to make organized and categorized information readily available to the public. Scorecard, Fortun argues, facilitates a kind of scientific literacy.

Sometimes, though, information can be considered a threat to safety rather than a boon. In August 1999, President Bill Clinton signed an act blocking Internet postings of "worst-case scenarios" of high-risk facilities around the United States. These scenarios could show, for instance, the radius within which people would die without proper evacuation if there were a massive toxic release from a plant. They were banned because it was claimed that they could help terrorist organizations. Greenpeace and other environmental organizations have skirted these restrictions by providing the public with maps that make catastrophic risk potential visible without providing the kind of detail that could facilitate sabotage at the local level. Fortun sees value in these efforts because right-to-know initiatives and information technology can inspire action and provide increased safety for individuals, even if they cannot deliver complete information

This book concludes with a chapter by Peter Redfield and Edward B. Rackley that focuses particularly on humanitarianism in the "not-war-not-peace" phase of catastrophes. They note the growing importance of humanitarian actors in international responses to catastrophe. They also note that "the Red Cross lineage of humanitarianism conceived of suffering as an exceptional state and its response as an attempt to re-establish normal conditions appropriate for human dignity." Humanitarian aid, they contend, has long oriented itself in terms of short-term aid and urgent action. Now, though, the focus is more on long-term humanitarianism and alleviation of the "normal misery."

From the perspective of humanitarianism, Redfield and Rackley argue that, first, "crisis defines and justifies a milieu for action," and, second, "claims of crisis extend well beyond immediate moments of urgent action." Finally, they write that "crises do not simply end as much as fade from view, often displaced by other dramas elsewhere. In fading, they reveal a more complicated topography of time beneath the concentrated present of action."

It is this third observation on which Redfield and Rackley concentrate. Even in emergency situations, they contend, the end of a crisis is difficult to conceptualize, much more difficult than the identification of and initial response to the crisis, because even if a dangerous situation is contained, chronic concerns may still remain. To illustrate this point, they take up the example of child soldiers.

In this case, transnational humanitarian concern, "however parochial in its assumptions, does converge with a very real problem." They write: "Contemporary child soldiering represents a sort of living crisis." Humanitarian intervention around "children associated with armed conflict" has focused on disarmament, demobilization, and reintegration. This process has been used in postconflict reconstruction in Afghanistan, Haiti, and Africa. In the disarmament phase, weapons belonging to both combatants and civilians are collected and disposed of. During demobilization, groups are formally disbanded. Reintegration is the assistance, including vocational training or cash payments, offered to ex-combatants to facilitate their move back into civilian life. This third phase is the least developed, but contemporary movements in humanitarianism have started to stress long-term reintegration.

Others have tried to combine legal instruments with "evidence-based advocacy." Thus, in April 2004, the United Nations Security Council called for countries where the rights of children were systematically violated as a result of conflict to develop concrete plans to monitor and report child soldier recruitment in an attempt to end it. The resolution even outlined six core violations of children's rights, including the killing and maiming of children and sexual violence perpetrated against children. It recognized that the use of child soldiers requires close monitoring and long-term attention.

As Redfield and Rackley note, "The effects of a catastrophic event . . . can ripple through an extended family over time, affecting not only individual psyches but also the very fabric of their sociality. . . . From this perspective, it is an illusion to assume an event is simply contained in time." Like Birkland's myth that everything can be put back together and Sterett's argument that FEMA needed to be stopped from withdrawing support for Katrina victims too quickly, Redfield and Rackley argue that catastrophes reverberate through societies long after the initial shock dies down and urge that humanitarian intervention be judged by its attentiveness to the chronic aftermath of disaster.

Taking all the chapters together, we are asked to rethink our understanding of catastrophe and in that rethinking imagine new legal, political, and humanitarian responses. We are asked to see through and beyond the myths that surround catastrophe and our responses to it, and think about and through the consequences of disaster.

As this book suggests, the ways we respond to catastrophe are both structurally embedded and contingent, entrenched in the structures of our law and politics, but also amenable to change and reform. In the end, it is our hope that this discussion will spark attention to both the structural and the contingent, and to the adequacy of law, politics, and humanitarianism in the "age of catastrophe."

NOTES

1. Ted Steinberg, *Acts of God: The Unnatural History of Natural Disaster in America* (New York: Oxford University Press, 2006); E. L. Quarentelli, ed., *What Is a Disaster? Perspectives on the Question* (London: Routledge, 1998).

2. Barry A. Turner, *Man-made Disasters* (London: Wykeham, 1978).

3. See, for instance, Carl-Henry Geschwind, *Californian Earthquakes: Science, Risk, and the Politics of Hazard Mitigation* (Baltimore: Johns Hopkins University Press, 2001).

4. Ulrich Beck, *Risk Society: Towards a New Modernity* (London: Sage, 1992). See also Anthony Giddens, "Risk and Responsibility," *Modern Law Review* 62, no. 1 (1999): 1–10.

5. Mark Pelling, "Natural Disasters," in *Social Nature: Theory, Practice, and Politics*, ed. Noel Castree and Bruce Braun (Oxford: Blackwell, 2001), 170–89.

6. See Steven Biel, ed., *American Disasters* (New York: New York University Press, 2001).

7. Kai T. Erikson, *Everything in Its Path: Destruction of Community in the Buffalo Creek Flood* (1978; repr., New York: Simon and Schuster, 2006), 24.

8. United Nations Intergovernmental Panel on Climate Change, Working Group II, *Climate Change 2007: Impacts, Adaptation, and Vulnerability* (Cambridge: Cambridge University Press, 2008).

9. Luc Boltanski, *Distant Suffering: Morality, Media and Politics* (Cambridge: Cambridge University Press, 1999).

10. Thomas Birkland, *Lessons of Disaster: Policy Changes after Catastrophic Events* (Washington, DC: Georgetown University Press, 2006); Rutherford H. Platt, *Disasters and Democracy: The Politics of Extreme Natural Events* (Washington, DC: Island Press, 1999).

11. Kevin Rozario, "Making Progress: Disaster Narratives and the Art of Optimism in Modern America," in *The Resilient City: How Modern Cities Recover from Disaster*, ed. Lawrence J. Vale and Thomas J. Campanella (New York: Oxford University Press, 2005), 27–54.

12. Sheila S. Jasanoff, ed., *Learning from Disaster: Risk Management after Bhopal* (Philadelphia: University of Pennsylvania Press, 1994); A. Hashim Sarkis, "A Vital Void: Reconstructions of Downtown Beirut," in Vale and Campanella, *The Resilient City*, 281–97.

13. Mike Davis, *Ecology of Fear: Los Angeles and the Imagination of Disaster* (New York: Vintage Books, 1999).

14. Erikson, *Everything in Its Path*, 48.

15. Adriana Petryna, *Life Exposed: Biological Citizens after Chernobyl* (Princeton, NJ: Princeton University Press, 2002).

16. Aaron Wildavsky, *Searching for Safety* (New Brunswick, NJ: Transaction Books, 1988).

17. Lee Clarke, *Mission Improbable: Using Fantasy Documents to Tame Disaster* (Chicago: University of Chicago Press, 2001); see also H. Anheier, *When Things Go Wrong: Organizational Failures and Breakdowns* (London: Sage, 1999).

18. Arjen Boin and Allen McConnell, "Preparing for Critical Infrastructure Breakdowns: The Limits of Crisis Management and the Need for Resilience," *Journal of Contingencies and Crisis Management* 15, no. 1 (March 2007): 50–59.

19. See "FEMA Knew of Toxic Gas in Trailers," *Washington Post*, July 20, 2007.

20. Eriksson, *Everything in Its Path*.

1

Crisis and Catastrophe
in Science, Law, and Politics
Mapping the Terrain

PETER H. SCHUCK

Crisis and catastrophe loom dauntingly, even impossibly, large in science and law. (I use the plural because crisis and catastrophe are quite distinct phenomena, despite their potential overlap.) They are also words that we moderns use so casually and promiscuously that their meanings have lost whatever precision they may have once possessed, and have acquired that familiar fuzziness that marks so much of our popular discourse. Their capaciousness and imprecision, of course, furnish all the more reason—and enticement—for scholars to take them on and try to wring from them some drops of intelligibility, clarification, and perhaps even guidance for our inevitable encounters with them in the future.

This explains my challenge and motive. Here, I intend to map the broad conceptual terrains of crisis and catastrophe: the definitions, analytical distinctions, explanatory frameworks, institutional milieus, regulatory techniques, and perspectival interpenetrations (my clumsy term for the fruitful ways in which legal and scientific concepts bleed into one another). I leave to later chapters the hard thinking about their real-world implications and applications.

Definitions

The definition of crisis and catastrophe begins with the definition of *definition*. According to the always reliable *Merriam-Webster's Dictionary*, the first two definitions of *definition* are (1) the formal proclamation of Roman Catholic dogma, and (2) a statement expressing the essential nature of something. Let's jump to the second definition.

The *Oxford English Dictionary* defines *crisis*, in pathological terms, as "the point in the progress of a disease when an important development or change takes place which is decisive of recovery or death; the turning-point of a disease for better for worse; also applied to any marked or sudden variation occurring in the progress of a disease and to the phenomena accompanying it." More generally, a crisis is "a vitally important or decisive stage in the progress of anything . . . ; also, a state of affairs in which a decisive change for better or worse is imminent; now applied esp. to times of difficulty, insecurity, and suspense in politics or commerce."Two aspects of these definitions are notable. First, a crisis is a point in a dynamic process; it is not static. Second and related, it may mark a turning point for the better, not just for the worse. In this same encouraging vein, as I point out later, it has often been remarked (usually by the Panglossians among us) that the Chinese character for crisis also means opportunity.

The *OED* definitions of *catastrophe* seem much darker, referring more to end- states, and bad ones at that. The third definition is "an event producing a subversion of the order or system of things," and the fourth is "a sudden disaster, wide-spread, very fatal, or signal." The *OED* goes on to note parenthetically, and with gentle mockery, that "in the application of exaggerated language to misfortunes it is used very loosely."[1] Even here, however, there is some room for optimism. After all, subverting the order or system of things may be the prelude to progress. Or so all revolutionaries tell us, and some of them have been right. (Although it depends on one's time frame. Chou En-Lai famously replied to a question about the effects of the French Revolution, "It's too early to tell.")

Moving from canonical definitions to colloquial usages and picking up on the *OED*'s parenthetical observation, one need only listen to our colleagues or children, not to mention people on television or the subway, to know that we have normalized, and in that sense trivialized, both of these seemingly apocalyptic words. Why should that be? As an objective, historical matter, it is difficult to believe that we face more and worse crises and catastrophes today than our ancestors did. This qualification brings us to two other important points about these words, points also discussed later: crisis and catastrophe are to a considerable extent in the eye of the beholder, and they seem highly dependent on sociocultural context. This historical speculation reflects my perception that we moderns marinate in apprehension of imminent and painful death, obsession about mortal sin, fear of social exclusion, and bewilderment over God's inscrutable justice much less than our forebears did.[2] Although crisis and catastrophe are of course common in Third World societies, sharp declines in hunger, disease, and poverty have occurred even there in the last few decades.[3] Relatively prosperous Americans remain a very anxious, not to say neurotic, people preoccupied with imagined status differentials, Freudian struggles, the shipwreck of old age, and existential angst in an ego-centered world.[4] Nor do I deny our quest for spiritual consolation in almost any place where it might be found, as we seek desperately to fill the void of mystery left by society's secularism and disenchantment. Rising expectations suggest that we are more likely than before to be disappointed with our lot, which may make us more likely to think of these disappointments as crises and catastrophes. Whatever the truth of this cognitive supposition, it seems clear that Americans live more secure lives in almost all respects than ever before.[5] Objectively viewed (if such a thing is possible), crises and catastrophes, at least as our ancestors understood them, are fewer, farther between, and more easily weathered.

At this definitional stage of our inquiry, we might also proceed inductively. That is, we might ask which are the paradigmatic examples of social crisis and catastrophe and then ask just why it is that we consider them paradigmatic. Some of them will arouse little disagreement. The AIDS epidemic, the destruction of New Orleans by Hurricane Katrina, the Holocaust and other genocides, the Buffalo Creek disaster, Mao's Great Leap Forward and Cultural Revolution, famines, the attacks of September 11, 2001, and the vast incidence of asbestos-related disease are all iconic examples of catastrophes that only those with large ideological or selfish axes to grind would be brazen (and crazy) enough to deny.

The classification of other events is more debatable, for various reasons. The collapse of Enron, for example, is arguably different "only" in magnitude from a large number of other business failures, but at some point such differences are large enough to place the failure in a distinct category, catastrophe. Some undoubted catastrophes have been obscured in historical memory, perhaps because they were "folded into" what seemed like larger ones. Thus, the flood of the Mississippi and Ohio rivers in 1937, described as the worst natural disaster in U.S. history,[6] was subsumed in the Great Depression, whereas the catastrophic Spanish flu pandemic of 1918, which killed between 50 million and 100 million people worldwide in eighteen months, is less memorable than the holocaust of World War I, which was far less lethal. Why are some occurrences so universally considered to be catastrophes? Six features of the paradigm, which are present in varying degrees in different cases, stand out: magnitude,

pervasiveness, uncertainty, preventability and responsibility, irreversibility, and crisis. By putting these features together in some fashion, one
could (but I shall not) also create a scale of catastrophe.[7]

Magnitude

Catastrophes usually involve the death, severe disability, or serious dislocation of many people.[8] I do not mean that individuals do not experience
their isolated losses as catastrophic. On the contrary, we do. Indeed, the
fact that these losses are solitary and not shared (at least at that point in
time) may make them feel even more devastating. For present purposes, though, we are concerned with the subset of suffering that is widely
shared within a relatively fixed period of time.[9] The dollar losses (only a
subset, of course) from so-called natural disasters, it seems, have steadily
increased.[10]Does the magnitude factor mean that every large-scale military conflict is a catastrophe? The answer, I think, is no, and for a revealing reason. However tragic and bloody the carnage and chaos they cause
are, some wars (albeit very few) are nevertheless thought to be "good" by
most observers, World War II being the clearest and perhaps most recent
example. (The current campaign in Aghanistan is thought by many, including President Obama, as a good, or at least justified, war). Why good?
The answer is twofold: good wars are wars that could not honorably have
been avoided in light of the danger posed by an implacable enemy, and
they succeed in defeating that enemy and averting an evil even greater
than that entailed by the suffering of war's victims. These moral judgments, of course, may change over time and with historical perspective
and reinterpretation.[11]

Pervasiveness

A tragedy may affect a small number of people but devastate their community so deeply and completely that it qualifies as catastrophic. Consider
the Buffalo Creek disaster, chronicled by sociologist Kai T. Erikson. The
victims there were few in number (125 to 150 people) but made up virtually the entire town, which in turn constituted the entire domain in which
its inhabitants lived their lives.[12] As Erikson shows, the deluge literally
engulfed the whole social world of the community, creating irreparable
trauma and despair. Like the Buffalo Creek disaster, but on a much larger
scale, Hurricane Katrina effected a major destruction of the social, economic, legal, political, infrastructural, and even demographic systems of
New Orleans.

Uncertainty

Predicting the sunrise and sunset are easy, but predicting future contingencies is exceedingly difficult, perhaps especially for catastrophes, which are usually unique in some senses.[13] Predictions are notoriously unreliable even when the predictors can draw on mountains of data. (Economists, it is said, have predicted nine of the last five recessions). Predicting unprecedented natural processes—climate change or asteroid collisions, for example—may be the most difficult of all due to nature's infinite complexity and its dependency on poorly understood processes.[14] At the same time (and perhaps surprisingly), a catastrophic risk in nature is not "some freak outlier with no connection to more mainstream risks," but is instead a most unlikely conjunction of such risks.[15] These predictive difficulties reflect a number of factors, including our inherent cognitive limitations, our arguably more malleable cognitive errors, our psychological biases, and our normative attitudes toward risk.[16] Thus, Mary Douglas and Aaron Wildavsky have shown that conceptions of and attitudes toward risk vary not only among societies but also within a given society.[17] All humans tend to discount the future rather heavily. That is, we value a given benefit more highly the sooner we will receive it, while seeking to defer a cost for as long as possible. Even so, people (and perhaps societies as well) vary in their propensities to respond to uncertainty with denial, with worst-case scenarios, or with something in between.

Democratic political institutions reinforce these future-discounting propensities. Future generations do not vote, politicians' time horizon is relatively short, and we are all tempted to hope that costly problems will go away before we must face them. For this reason alone, the long-term challenge of climate change poses a harder political problem than the threat of future flooding of New Orleans. The latter, after all, just occurred, recurs frequently, and admits of familiar and less costly solutions.

In analyzing the accident at Three Mile Island and the risks of other technologies, sociologist Charles Perrow emphasizes certain features of such technologies that make accidents of this kind more or less predictable.[18] Particularly conducive to system failure (hence his phrase "normal accidents"), he argues, are interactive complexity (that is, where two or more discrete failures can interact in unexpected ways) and tight coupling (that is, where subcomponents of the system have prompt and major effects on one another). The important point of his analysis, for present purposes, is that the predictability of catastrophe—and hence preventability (discussed immediately below)—is a function, among other things, of technological and organizational complexity, interactivity, redundancy, and other design decisions. Societies also vary in how present- or future-oriented they tend to be and hence in their propensity to anticipate, plan for, and prevent bad outcomes.[19] For example, Americans appear to be less fatalistic than Europeans,[20] a factor that helps account for the greater robustness of the European welfare state. Relatively individualistic Americans are more likely than more fatalistic Europeans to think that people bring their poverty and dependency on themselves through bad choices, short time horizons, and poor planning.[21] For better or for worse (both are possible), people's attitudes about uncertainty, risk, time discounting, and future orientation are not fixed. Instead, they are influenced by many contextual factors and are mediated by cognitive prompts and biases that policymakers can use to facilitate more (or less) rational public deliberation about the risks of bad outcomes.[22] For example, the recency of Katrina triggers an "availability heuristic" that makes voters more aware of the risk of recurrence than an equally likely risk that has not received media attention. Very low probability events—for example, an explosion of a nuclear power plant—are particularly vulnerable to cognitive—and hence predictive—errors of both underestimation[23] and of overestimation.[24] Some other cognitive obstacles to rational planning for catastrophes, obstacles that are rooted in our political culture, are discussed later. Richard A. Posner takes note of several of these features—magnitude, uncertainty, and pervasiveness—in defining a catastrophe as an event that has "a very low probability of materializing but that if it does materialize will produce a harm so great and sudden as to seem discontinuous with the flow of events that preceded it."[25] In some parts of the world, however, certain undoubted catastrophes—floods and droughts, for example—are not all that improbable, at least judging from their periodic recurrence.

Preventability and Responsibility

Catastrophe's meaning is conditioned by—indeed, may be inseparable from—the distinctly modern notion of social control and its close cousin, preventability. Perhaps more than other people, Americans are inclined to think that bad things do not occur because of (in Einstein's words) "a cosmic roll of the dice," or because we have sinned, or because of random bad luck, or even because of contingent social policies and practices. Precisely because our knowledge of natural and social systems has advanced so far and our competence in engineering them has become so great, we tend to assume that when bad things do happen, we could have prevented them by adopting better controls and policies.[26] This assumption of control (if not omnipotence) and thus of moral agency and responsibility makes preventable catastrophes seem all the more devastating. After all, if they resulted from negligence, not necessity, they must have been our fault, at least when viewed in retrospect. (Decisions or omissions that seem negligent after the catastrophe occurred may not, in fact, have been negligent *before*, given what was then known.) This imagined responsibility for preventing catastrophes extends beyond the conditions that caused them to the desire to minimize the suffering that ensues. That is, even if the risk of a catastrophe cannot be prevented or much reduced, the magnitude and distribution of its bad consequences can nevertheless be managed in better or worse ways.[27] The catastrophic counterparts of what Guido Calabresi called the secondary and tertiary costs of accidents can be spread or reduced[28] through a variety of insurance and other buffering institutions, discussed below.

The economy of responsibility for catastrophes, then, is a variable, not a constant. It depends on what society considers blameworthy, which in part depends on the course and reach of science and technology. Many diseases—polio, for example—that were once considered outside our control are now eminently preventable, treatable, and thus unacceptable. Advances in genetic engineering will constantly extend this control, and this growing capacity for control will entail, arguably, a greater sense of social responsibility to exercise it. The same is true of engineering advances that affect floods, drought, earthquakes, and other geophysical calamities.[29] At the same time, however, other kinds of scientific advances are challenging traditional notions of causation, preventability, and responsibility with respect to many harmful conditions that have always been considered a matter of individual responsibility. Examples include substance abuse, obesity, various forms of incompetence, and susceptibility to certain illnesses and deviant behaviors. Growing genetic knowledge will surely magnify these challenges.

Irreversibility

Catastrophes may be preventable, but once they occur, they are essentially irreversible. That is, their calamitous consequences can only be coped with or managed, not undone. Cass R. Sunstein has carefully analyzed the problem of irreversible and catastrophic occurrences, exploring the distinctive ways in which we should think and decide about them. Sunstein notes, for example, that society may rationally manage irreversibility by "spend[ing] extra resources to buy an 'option' to protect against irreversible harm until future knowledge emerges. The value of the option is that of delaying the decision until better information is available."[30] The current debate over the "precautionary principle" in regulatory policy also highlights the difficulty of knowing how to deal with irreversibility and worst cases.[31]

Crisis

Each of the paradigmatic examples of catastrophe identified above precipitated a crisis (as defined earlier), and I suspect that this sequence from catastrophe to crisis is the norm, although not invariably.[32] The reverse, however, is not always true: many crises are not caused by, or even associated with, catastrophes. An example is the crisis over the future funding of Medicare and Social Security. Although the resolution of this crisis cannot long be delayed, few would refer to the demographic trends that have produced it as a catastrophe; indeed, the causes of the crisis—greater longevity and better health-care technology and access—are clearly social goods, not bads. Another example of a crisis that is not (yet) a catastrophe is global climate change. The magnitude of its bad effects, should they occur in the future, may well be catastrophic,[33] and the need to begin dealing with these possibilities promptly is critical. When and if these bad effects occur, they may, in fact, be reversible through some combination of behavioral and technological changes.

Some Further Distinctions

To sharpen, deepen, and clarify these definitional points, a brief discussion of some further distinctions is in order.

Public Recognition

Some catastrophes are accorded explicit public recognition. The most obvious recognition of this kind is the creation of a governmental program to prevent or remedy the catastrophe, as with the 9/11 Victims Compensation Fund or NASA's Spaceguard Survey program to avert asteroid collisions.[34] Some catastrophes, however, receive no such official recognition but are instead endured privately, for at least some period of time. Such was the case with the AIDS problem before it reached epidemic proportions and was finally viewed as such. My main concern here is with publicly recognized catastrophes.

Community of Concern

Societies differ from one another, and vary themselves over time, with respect to the temporal and spatial domains over which their sense of political, legal, and moral responsibility—of community, in other words—extends. Judging from public attitudes toward reparative justice for past injustices amounting to catastrophes for the victimized groups and for the larger society, our conception of community probably extends back no more than a few generations, within the scope of living memory. For example, claims for reparations to the descendants of American slaves have fallen on deaf ears,[35] whereas Congress has legislated compensation for the Japanese and Japanese Americans interned during World War II,[36] and governments at all levels have adopted affirmative-action programs for minorities thought to have suffered discrimination in the not-so-distant past.[37] It is the *spatial* dimension of the community of concern, however, that is most relevant to our conceptions of catastrophe. An immense literature in philosophy, political science, social psychology, and other fields addresses the fundamental questions of what moral (and legal) claims we have on one another, and whether and how the strength and content of those claims may vary depending on history, geography, religious values, political culture, leadership, wealth, visions of the respective roles of individual and state responsibility, philanthropic traditions, attitudes about the causes of misfortune, and many other contingencies.[38] The answers to these questions define the appropriate community of concern and, perhaps, of action (both preventive and remedial). For some individuals and cultures, the relevant community of concern or action is the primary group: self, clan, tribe, family, church, fellow ethnics. For others, the community is spatially wider: neighborhood, town, state, nation.[39] For a relatively small but growing number of cosmopolitans, it is Lifeboat Earth, the Global Village, or some other depiction of our universal ecological and moral interdependence and responsibility. Conversely, the causality of this mutual concern can move in the other direction. That is, the experience of catastrophe, like the fear of an external enemy, can construct a sense of community among people who were hitherto strangers.[40]

Identifiable versus Statistical Victims

Catastrophes make salient a classic distinction, developed by economist Thomas C. Schelling, between identifiable and statistical victims.[41] Victims are identifiable if we know something about who they are as individuals, even if we do not know their names or much about them other than their plight. Common examples are the little girl who falls into a well, the hiker who gets lost in the wilderness, and the worker trapped in a mine. (In a tragic variation on this last item, Congress spent $42 million to relocate a relatively small number of inhabitants of a Pennsylvania mining town after an anthracite fire burned for more than two decades.)[42] In contrast, statistical victims are known to us not as flesh-and-blood individuals but only as abstractions, as members of some group that may be defined only by their common, sometimes hypothetical victimization. Their harms would have been avoided had preventive resources been expended. Schelling asks why society is so much more willing to invest substantial resources to rescue identifiable victims than it is to spend the (typically) fewer resources that would have prevented such accidents from happening in the first place. This perceived proliferation of identifiable-victim catastrophes, however, often seems to lead to so-called compassion fatigue, the tendency of people exposed to so many humanized tragedies to gradually grow more accustomed to the suffering of others. As the number of these tragedies mounts, the observers are likely to feel increasingly helpless in the face of it all. In time, this helplessness may morph into indifference, even callousness. The psychology of compassion fatigue is doubtless complex, and it presumably affects different observers differently.[43] Mother Teresa's compassion, for example, seems to have been indefatigable, but fund-raisers for humanitarian groups take account of compassion fatigue in their planning. Such fatigue may plague efforts to reduce the suffering from catastrophes.

Catastrophe proliferation intersects with this identifiable-statistical victim distinction in another way, which may have mixed consequences for our thinking about catastrophes. Statistical victims are systematically disadvantaged organizationally and thus politically. As abstractions, they lack any obvious supporting constituency.[44] They are represented, if at all, only by proxy, and any arguments that these proxies make on their behalf are likely to be abstract and speculative, and hence less compelling to politicians and voters. One of the most serious challenges to just and rational government decisions is the tendency of policymakers to ignore statistical (or "invisible") victims and their interests and to focus instead on those that are more palpable and identifiable.[45] On the other hand—a reason for some hope—the high human and fiscal costs of responding *ex post* to the identifiable victims of catastrophes should lead rational policymakers to search for less expensive *ex ante* strategies. When policy planners analyze the costs and benefits of such catastrophe-prevention strategies, they are more likely to take into account the hypothetical cost-bearers and beneficiaries—including statistical ones—of the various policy alternatives under consideration.[46] Society reacts quite differently—and more to the point, with much greater sympathy and willingness to help—to identifiable victims than to statistical ones, even when identification provides absolutely no more information about the victims than that they are in danger. Perhaps we respond more emotionally to flesh-and-blood victims because we can more easily imagine ourselves in their situation.

Telegenicity

Whatever the psychology of this phenomenon, today's media vastly magnifies its effect by enabling us to perceive people as identifiable victims—often giving them names, faces, family members, backgrounds, and other identifying details—even though they otherwise remain perfect strangers to us. The media dramatize and humanize the plight of these victims. Moreover, in telling victims' stories, the media often search for evidence that their situation was preventable, that some individual, system, or institution was at fault. This striking telegenicity of almost all such situations, and the powerful incentives on the part of media to capitalize on this fact, means that catastrophes, hitherto abstract (if not statistical) to all but those close to the scene, seem to abound.[47] Indeed, the ability of victim organizations, relief agencies, and desperate governments in the geographical area of the catastrophe to recruit, mobilize, and service media by providing them with the images and stories they need for broadcasting may be crucial to their ability to attract wider attention and resources. The incentives created by this dynamic interaction between media and victims—their symbiotic, sometimes manipulative relationship—can lead to grotesque distortions and on-site confusion,[48] as apparently occurred during the immediate aftermath of Hurricane Katrina.[49] In contrast, ordinary poverty is seldom telegenic[50] or, when televised, may lend itself to widespread misrepresentation of the problem.[51]

Winners and Losers

Not all members of the catastrophe-enduring community suffer equally. The adage that "it's an ill wind that doesn't blow somebody some good" is true even of catastrophes. In any society, including very poor ones, there are always some individuals who are in a position—by luck, resourcefulness, or otherwise—to supply what victims desperately need (for example, food, spiritual support, building supplies). Meeting these needs may involve the most heroic generosity or the most despicable exploitation, and everything in between. More generally, empirical studies find that catastrophes, at least in the United States, usually produce a subsequent boom in the local economy due to an influx of insurance, public money, reconstruction projects, bargain prices for property, and so forth.[52] The ability of individuals in a community to take advantage of these post-catastrophe opportunities varies considerably. The distribution of the costs and benefits of catastrophes, then, is a very important variable. Politically, the distribution of winners and losers, even more than the magnitude of their gains and losses, affects their ability to form and maintain coalitions that can effectively promote their interests.[53] Emotionally, it may matter a great deal to victims whether they suffer alone or are part of a larger group of victims who can provide solace and community. Socially, the status of the losers within the culture may affect how the larger society thinks about and reacts to catastrophe.

Buffering Institutions

A catastrophe's convulsiveness is affected by the extent to which buffering institutions exist to palliate or ease the terrible human toll. By buffering institutions, I mean family, private and public relief efforts, religious consolation, a strong community, insurance coverage, and other legal remedies of repair or reparation. China's Cultural Revolution lacked any buffering institutions; it destroyed even the integrity of the family. In the United States, the response by governments to the Centralia, Pennsylvania, anthracite fire, far from buffering the disastrous effects, magnified them.[54] In contrast, the September 11 tragedy was buffered by a wide variety of institutional responses, including an unusually generous compensation program and an unprecedented outpouring of charitable and emotional support by a vast array of well-wishers throughout the nation and even abroad. The buffering institutions available to asbestos victims, also catastrophic by reason of their vast number and the other innocents caught up in the numerous corporate bankruptcies, are not as extensive as those available to victims of the September 11 attacks but are far greater than to, say, Katrina victims. A society's attitudes toward risk, preventability, and time discounting, discussed earlier, shape its demand for, and its design of, buffering institutions to deal with catastrophes.

Explanatory Frameworks

Attitudes toward catastrophes—the ways we explain and try to make sense of them—are surely numerous, but it is useful to focus on a small number of common frames—religious, scientific, legal, and political—for this understanding.[55] Each frame is an artifact of the distinctive culture—the patterned ways in which their members tend to perceive, think about, and find meaning in reality—that vivify them. In all of them, but to different degrees, the notion of causal responsibility figures prominently. I first discuss religion briefly and then devote more extensive analysis to science, law, and politics, focusing on their distinctive central values, incentives and techniques, and biases and orientations. Because I elaborate these explanatory frameworks at a metalevel, my discussion is by design general and schematic. More specific application of these frameworks to the techniques of actually managing catastrophes is discussed later, along with regulatory techniques and interpenetrations of the frameworks. Accordingly, readers more interested in such specifics may wish to proceed directly to those discussions.

Religion

In most religious traditions, catastrophes are the consequence of divine intervention or of human violation of God's laws. Noah's flood, the destruction of Sodom and Gomorrah, the enslavement of Israel, the afflictions of Job, and countless others are attributed to one or both of these causes, either expressly in sacred texts or by prophets or other religious interpreters who seek to understand the moral significance of catastrophes, past or impending. The need of believers to ascribe some reason or meaning to catastrophes is manifested in the practice of theodicy, a body of thought intended to justify the ways of God to humans, particularly in light of the existence of evil.[56] Often, religious observers (and even victims) of catastrophe find comfort in the notion that divine reason and will were at work. Nevertheless, the horror of a catastrophe is sometimes so great, the suffering of innocents so cruel, the punishment so disproportionate to any human transgression, that religious people simply cannot accept theodical justifications for injustice. This disproportion may precipitate a crisis of belief that results in their abandonment of faith. Many Jews, for example, have responded to the Holocaust in precisely this way.

Science

In a famous series of lectures in 1959, British writer C. P. Snow depicted scientists as optimistic and practical, concerned above all else with understanding nature and solving problems.[57] He maintained that they read few literary books and have underdeveloped imaginations. He noted, however, that the scientific culture was not monolithic, suggesting that pure scientists have little more in common with engineers and other applied scientist than with literary intellectuals. Snow surely exaggerated here, for whatever the differences among scientific subcultures, there is a core of beliefs, training, and techniques common to those who are recognized as scientists by the scientific community, at least as conventionally defined.

Central Values · What constitutes this common core? Peter Huber, an engineer-lawyer who is a militant scientific positivist and a caustic critic of the law's treatment of scientific evidence, asserts that "the scientific ideal stands in sharp contrast to the windy agnosticism of the modern philosopher, litigator, or social engineer." Huber holds that the modern scientist is not dogmatic but is instead "a credulous skeptic—skeptic in that he demands serious evidence and proof; credulous in that he concedes, not just offhandedly but very systematically, that every measurement, correlation, analysis, or theory may contain some margin of error, which may in turn conceal important but unrecognized new truth."[58] Science, Huber insists, is the domain of systematic verification to which social purposes are quite irrelevant. Other commentators, less tendentious than Huber, are also deeply critical of science's claim to detached, ahistorical objectivity, emphasizing instead the contingent, socially constructed, resource-constrained character of scientific paradigms and propositions, especially in areas of great uncertainty or in which dominant views are firmly institutionalized.[59] This critique is an important antidote to the more transcendent, universal pretensions of certain conceptions of science, but it would be equally wrong to conclude from the fact of science's social embeddedness that its culture is as flexible, indeterminate, and relativistic as those of law and politics. In its professional norms and aspirations, and to some extent in its actual performance, science is committed to a conception of truth (although one that is always provisional and contestable) reached through a conventional methodology of proof (although one that can be difficult to apply and interpret) based on the testing of falsifiable propositions.

Incentives and Techniques · What motivates scientists to behave as they do in their professional settings? Like other highly educated people, of course, they are driven by a desire for professional recognition, economic security, social influence, job satisfaction, and intellectual stimulation, among other things. Some of the goals that motivate them, however, are peculiar, if not unique, to the scientific culture. Perhaps most important, scientists subscribe to and are actuated by rigorous standards of empirical investigation and proof; to deviate from these standards is to be deemed professionally incompetent or worse.[60] Scientists also define themselves in part by their membership in larger scientific communities that both contribute to and are entitled to exploit the scientists' own work.[61] These principles of peer review invigorate and enforce their adherence to a norm of extreme caution (what Huber calls "credulous skepticism"). These values and incentives lead in turn to a distinctive set of scientific practices and techniques that have had to adapt to new conditions: widespread team research, the fragmentation of science into a large number of increasingly narrow technical specialties coupled with the cross-cutting nature of intricate research problems, vigorous competition for the necessary large aggregations of capital and talent, and the need to devise techniques for diversifying the risks of failure. In addition, science's time frame is relatively open-ended, tending to move in its own, largely autonomous rhythms dictated by the pace of technological development and dissemination, the availability of resources for further investigation, and the process of consensus formation among scientists.

Biases and Orientations · Like all cultures, science nurtures certain biases, blind spots, and predispositions. Most scientists receive an intensely technical training, face strong incentives to follow highly specialized career paths, and must keep up with voluminous research literatures that are often more specialized still. Generalist scientists today are few and far between. These conditions foster a decidedly narrow, technocratic perspective. Their hunger for the respect of other scientists, buttressed by peer review, causes the vast majority to shun advocacy of controversial positions on technical issues in the mass media or other nonprofessional public forums, including courtrooms and legislative hearings. Doubtful about lay understanding and fearful of being misinterpreted or misused, they tend to be far more comfortable reporting on their work in the precise, qualified, technical language of the peer-reviewed journal than holding press conferences to announce their latest findings to reporters whose scientific training may not extend much beyond a course in biology taken many years ago. Skittish about active involvement in politics and wary of lawyers and other professional advocates who do not subscribe to their distinctive canons, they prefer the familiar environments of the laboratory, the seminar room, and the specialized scientific meeting to the courtroom or talk show.

Experimental scientists are preoccupied with the process of unearthing hard facts; their goal is discovery, their master techniques are the analysis of data and the testing of theories. Unlike lawyers and politicians, there is little in their training, professional norms, or work environment that gives them a sophisticated understanding of social value conflicts or even equips them to address such conflicts. The political process that pits science against other normative systems is the bailiwick of specialized science bureaucrats. For most practicing scientists, however, politics is terra incognita. Scientists' uneasiness around politicians is actually a special case of their more general suspicion of populism. One defining feature of any culture is its orientation toward the roles of expert and lay judgments in conferring legitimate authority on decisions, and science is no exception. Its distinctive position can be illustrated if we imagine a spectrum along which attitudes about the sources of legitimate decision-making authority are arrayed, with professional autonomy at the left-hand pole and lay decision making on the right-hand pole. Science, with its technocratic commitments to rigorous method, objectivity, and expert judgment, would occupy the professional autonomy pole; pure science would be on the extreme left and applied science to its right. Expert bureaucracy would lie a bit farther to the right. Law—divided into nonjury and jury components—would lie somewhere near the middle, and political bureaucracy would be located nearer the lay-decision-making pole.

Law

If the scientific culture, with its emphasis on rigorous methodology and proof, is arcane and remote from public view and common experience, the legal culture—or at least much of it—is to the average citizen more conspicuous (for example, the imagery of trial), part of the vernacular (the language of rights), and numbingly familiar (the preparation of tax returns).

Central Values · Law's version of truth only dimly resembles the version advanced by science.[62] Indeed, the notion of verifiable truth to which scientists appeal in their experiments and research bears almost no relationship to the conception of truth ordinarily pursued in legal proceedings. Legal principles are normative propositions about which particular states of the social world *should* be sought, not positive statements about how the natural or social world *does in fact* work. Legal principles seek and find their justification in arguments derived from a bewildering array of social policy goals: fairness, efficiency, administrative cost, wealth distribution, and morality, among others. Legal decision makers balance these goals in nonrigorous, often intuitive ways that are seldom acknowledged and sometimes ineffable. Moreover, courts explicitly invoke other considerations in support of their decisions that are essentially social policies in disguise. Even the classic principle of *stare decisis*, for example, appeals to the policies of predictability, expectations, and decision cost minimization. The practice of analogical reasoning appeals to the policy of treating like cases alike. The principle of deference to particular institutions appeals to the policy of specialized, expert decision making.

This difference between science and law entails a fundamental distinction between the pursuit of "truth" (science's province) and the pursuit of "justice" (law's province). How much may law deviate from scientific truth before its legitimacy is jeopardized? Like conceptions of justice, a society's tolerance for legal error is a variable, not a constant. Changes in public attitudes, political discourse, and scientific opinion can alter the level of legal error that society, and hence the law, will accept. Today, the law seems to be demanding greater reliability of scientific claims before it will honor them, although evidence of this shift remains fragmentary. These convergences between the standards of truth in science and in law are noteworthy and on the whole encouraging, but the more general point remains that the two cultures characteristically pursue fundamentally different ends: verifiable fact for the one and justice for the other. This difference also implies that science and law have different orientations toward the distributive consequences their activities generate. Many individual scientists, of course, care deeply about whom their findings benefit and burden, yet the culture of science in principle must take a dispassionate stance on that question. The canons of science, after all, dictate that if research uncovers a new truth, scientists must not suppress it but instead should let the chips fall where they may. In principle, at least, how society ultimately decides to use (or misuse) scientific facts is a separate question about which scientists may feel strongly but usually possess no special expertise.

In contrast, the legal culture is anything but neutral about the distribution of outcomes, even in principle. It is normative to its core. The law, of course, defines rights and duties with desired substantive outcomes very much in view when it protects property, proscribes criminal conduct, exacts taxes, supports wars, demands equal treatment for similarly situated groups, and regulates social and economic relationships. Practicing lawyers are expected to advocate their clients' biases and implement their agendas; failure to do so may constitute professional malpractice. Academic lawyers routinely elaborate legal theories designed to promote values they personally prefer. Among those in the field of law, only judges are expected to put aside their normative goals when those goals conflict with the properly understood rule of law.

Incentives and Techniques · The incentives that motivate legal actors are varied but largely conventional. In this respect, the law is no different from other cultures. Some of the incentives that shape lawyers' conduct, however, are distinctive to their professional milieus. For practicing lawyers, the decisive incentive is the need, consistent with both self-interest and professional ethics, to represent the client's interests effectively, whatever those interests may be. Lawyers' income (if not always their psychic well-being) is enhanced by a willingness to subordinate their personal policy views to those of the client. Somewhat paradoxically, this substantive self-abnegation actually reinforces, and then rationalizes, the legal culture's singularly powerful normative thrust by ensuring that any clients who can afford to hire a lawyer can enjoy some access to the policy-making and adjudicative processes, where they can press their claims. Whereas the scientist's "clients" are verifiable facts waiting to be revealed and used, the lawyer's are social interests seeking gratification and advancement.

Lawyers' strong client orientation also colors how incentive structures in the two cultures treat uncertainty and complexity. Paradigmatically, science progresses by generating new data and hypotheses that often undermine the then-dominant theories. When that occurs, the resulting uncertainties and complexities may persist for a long time; although these uncertainties often contain the seeds for new progress, they must first germinate. Despite this tendency toward uncertainty and complexity, however, science's ultimate goals are precisely the opposite: it seeks the most parsimonious theory that can both explain all existing data and yield testable new hypotheses.

In contrast, legal actors are more agnostic about whether and to what extent certainty and simplicity are virtues in law. For practicing lawyers, it all depends on their clients' interests, which may militate in favor of certainty on one issue, uncertainty on another, and a shifting balance over time on a third. For judges, it depends on how they balance various goals of the legal system, such as the competing policies of having clear rules and of responding flexibly to equitable considerations in individual cases.

Legislators and bureaucrats, who also face countervailing incentives, will tend to favor legal complexity and uncertainty because it helps them both resolve intricate political and policy disputes and develop special expertise that confers autonomy, prestige, and power over decisions.

The law is usually in much more of a hurry to decide than science is. Ironically, however, law's findings, although less reliable and tested than those of science, are treated as more final and authoritative. Law operates under pressure to resolve particular disputes speedily and conclusively. Once it finds facts (and confirms them on appeal), those findings are considered *res judicata*: final for the law's purposes, however erroneous they may be in fact. Science, in contrast, seeks to develop a professional consensus on the truth of its propositions. This consensus often takes a long time to assemble, yet even then it is conditional, always open to revision on the basis of new data or theories.

Biases and Orientations · Law, like science, has its characteristic blind spots and preoccupations. The differences between the two cultures in this respect are fortified by their members' distinctive training. Scientific education is largely didactic and constructive; it emphasizes the transmission of information, the techniques of theory building, and the modes of empirical investigation. Legal education, in contrast, is essentially deconstructive and dialogic; it emphasizes the malleability of facts, the plasticity of legal doctrine, the indeterminacy of legal texts, and the power of rhetorical skill. Decades after specialty and subspecialty training became common for doctors, moreover, lawyers continue to be trained and to practice as generalists. Their mere admission to the bar usually entitles them to practice law in any field they like with no legal requirement for specialty certification. Most judges in the United States are also generalists, not only because of the nature of their legal education but also because of the general jurisdiction of their courts. Indeed, unlike their colleagues in civil-law countries, they receive no special training to be professional judges. The legal culture exhorts both judges and ordinary lawyers to have a broad, synthetic, social vision rather than a narrow, insular, technocratic one.

On the other hand, the central role of lawyers in the adversary system can foster a kind of truculent tendentiousness that can encourage them to take frivolous positions, overlook or obscure complexities, and give short shrift to other points of view. They can do so with the easy conscience of advocates who confidently assume that any extreme claims they make will be countered by others no less extreme and will then be resolved by judges who understand this exercise in hyperbole and routinely make allowances for it. Their professional penchant for advocacy and rhetoric, intensified by the financial interest that many have in disputes and litigation, often promotes conflict rather than resolving it. Commentators have noted that the adversary process is far better at deconstructing scientific claims than at reconstructing "the communally held beliefs that reasonably pass for truth in science."[63] Few scientists feel comfortable in this contentious milieu. Most find it particularly repugnant both as an intellectual process for seeking truth and as a matter of personal and professional style.

Finally, law is both authoritative and suppletive—it both legitimates official actions and facilitates private ones—which creates other biases. Because much law must be predicted, understood, and applied by many ordinary people with limited resources, simplicity is often a compelling legal virtue. Law cannot afford to be as nuanced as the realities it seeks to shape; it necessarily draws lines and creates categories that force many legal decisions into a binary mold; one is either in or out of the category, and it matters a great deal which. This rather arbitrary binary classification, so characteristic of legal thought, is utterly alien to science.

Politics

Politics—the pursuit and exercise of the coercive, prescriptive, and symbolic powers of the state—lies near the core of all social life, appearing in many forms and venues. Here, our principal interest is in how politicians approach those public policies whose legitimacy draws heavily on scientific authority and on scientific propositions about the natural world. As noted earlier, the paradigmatic examples are regulation of the safety of foods, drugs, consumer products, the environment, and the workplace.

Politics relates symbiotically to both science and law, but in different ways. Science has its own politics, often fierce and bitter, in which scientists pursue power, recognition, and resources from the government, the profession, and other sources. Just as scientists often play politics, politicians also have many opportunities to exploit the prestige and symbols of science so as to fortify their empirical claims, legitimate and build public support for their decisions, and clothe themselves in the mantle of scientific truth.

Central Values · Like all cultures, politics pursues a mix of values, some of which are unique to its particular way of life. In a liberal democratic polity like that found in the United States, which purports not to privilege particular visions of the good, they are chiefly process values, although they are deployed in pursuit of substantive ends. Three of these process values seem paramount. The *participation* norm holds that individuals should be empowered, in the interest of human dignity, to play some meaningful role in shaping decisions that affect their vital interests. The *accountability* norm demands that officials be held politically responsible to the public for their actions. The *conflict management* norm emphasizes that other values can be achieved only if social conflicts are kept within tolerable limits.

Incentives and Techniques · These values engender an equally distinctive set of political incentives and decision techniques. Virtually all academic models of politics, as well as many less systematic commentaries, posit that politicians are primarily, if not exclusively, driven by the need to build and maintain a winning electoral coalition. No sophisticated political analyst, of course, doubts either that most politicians' definition of the winning coalition is complex enough to accommodate other personal and ideological goals which they possess, or that politicians sometimes take positions on issues which cannot easily be explained simply in terms of conventional calculations of electoral advantage. Even when the electoral imperative is narrowly conceived, however, it explains their actions better than any other single factor.

From this preoccupation with election, certain behavioral strategies follow, most of which sharply differentiate the political culture from the scientific and legal ones. One important difference relates to the cultures' audiences and thus to the form of discourse that is possible. Unlike scientists and judges, who mainly address their professional colleagues and can employ technical and theoretical kinds of arguments, politicians speak to a lay and largely uninformed electorate. Often, they can only reach the voters through media that, although sometimes more sophisticated than the voters, are also severely constrained by space and the voters' limitations of time, understanding, and interest. Knowing that, politicians struggle to exploit the voters' limited attention span and comprehension, sometimes diverting their attention to particular problems rather than others.[64]

Instead of the nuanced, abstract arguments deployed in the scientific and legal cultures, then, political rhetoric is relatively crude and particularistic. Where both scientific and legal discourses are designed to pursue truth through the elaboration of principles, the ultimate point of political discourse is to persuade. Rhetorical strategies that would be professionally unacceptable in science and often in law—explicit appeals to sentiment, ideology, or interest—are standard tactics in politics, where the "mobilization of bias" is both normal and normative.

In addition to a distinctive audience and rhetoric, politics has its own time horizon. Especially when compared to science, but even when contrasted with law, political decisions tend to be spasmodic and impulsive, in part because voters' interests in catastrophe are spasmodic and impulsive.[65] Political decisions are also shaped by deadlines that seem highly arbitrary from almost any other perspective, especially that of a scientific model of decision making in which evidence is gathered, alternative hypotheses are considered, and a deliberate, rational judgment is reached. The political culture often demands swift action, and when it does it will not tolerate delay, even if prudence might counsel otherwise. The pace of mass democratic politics is driven by the insistent rhythm of public opinion, which will not be temporized.

Another distinction of the political culture relates not to discursive method but to decisional technique. In theory and largely in fact, scientific hypotheses are confirmed or refuted by experimentation, and judicial rulings proceed by reasoned elaboration of established principles. In contrast, the paradigmatic decision technique in liberal democratic politics is bargaining to a consensus, a process that is complex, amorphous, and continuous. Numerous participants form constantly shifting alliances and deploy a fluid mixture of rewards, threats, special interest claims, public interest ideals, and evocative symbols. Personalities can play an outsized role.[66] Because the process is so fluid and open-ended in time, participation, and issue-space, political outcomes are not merely unpredictable; they are also opaque and hard to identify. Even the enactment of legislation, itself a protracted affair, is only a shadowy guide to what it will become. Its meaning will depend on its future implementation. These defining features of political behavior, of course, shape the criteria for evaluating that behavior.

Biases and Orientations · Politics also has its characteristic blind spots. A notable one is its abhorrence of firm principle, which, of course, is seldom publicly acknowledged as such; instead, it is portrayed and celebrated as a benign commitment to consensus and compromise. This commitment is not merely inevitable and habitual; it is also *normative*. Another distinctive bias of politics is its populism, its appeal to the putatively superior virtues of common people. Although law is more populist than science, politics is even more populist than law. Our political culture maintains the principle that the legitimacy of public decisions must rest primarily on bases other than the professional status, esoteric knowledge, or special expertise of the decision maker. This principle applies regardless of whether the decision maker is a regulatory bureaucracy, corporation, or individual official. It affirms that however much technocracy can contribute to public deliberations, the popular will is the ultimate touchstone of policy.[67] It insists, sometimes to the point of outright pandering, that the people know best even when it is clear that they do not. This principle goes well beyond a grudging, realistic recognition that in a democracy the voters have the last word; it is also fundamentally normative. It elevates the wisdom of popular judgments, their superiority to those of the experts, and the independent integrity of the political process, to the level of central articles of the democratic faith.

Posner emphasizes certain other features of political culture that tend to undermine the ability of decision makers to deploy scientific understanding in an effort to prevent catastrophes. He attributes pervasive scientific illiteracy in part to a Western bias even among elites that favors philosophical, literary, and artistic traditions over scientific ones and in part to religious influences that challenge the authority of science. This ignorance of science, Posner says, "coexists dangerously with an uncritical veneration of science and scientists" that accords more respect to their policy judgments than is warranted by their narrowly scientific expertise. Finally, he posits that portrayals of natural and man-made catastrophes in films and other popular media as well as unrealized doomsday predictions by scientists may have caused Americans to grow apathetic toward catastrophic risks.[68]

Techniques for Regulating Catastrophe

Legal and scientific perspectives on catastrophe—and, indeed, on everything else—are mediated and rendered legible[69] through institutions, processes, and modalities that effectively infuse those perspectives into public and private decisions. Because each of the three broad categories of regulatory techniques—legal-governmental processes, market processes, and the use of social norms—exhibits distinctive strengths and limitations, different societies combine and refine them in ways that are characteristic of those societies. Here, I focus on how American society does so.

Legal-Governmental Processes

Conceptually speaking, the legal-governmental approach to catastrophe takes two forms: *ex ante* and *ex post*.[70] The *ex ante* approach consists of planning for catastrophes and seeking either to avert them or to minimize the harm that will occur if they cannot be averted. The *ex post* approach seeks to manage the consequences of those catastrophes that do occur.[71] Sometimes, particular systems operate in both dimensions. Tort law, for example, is designed both to deter risky activity that would otherwise cause or contribute to catastrophes, and also to compensate their victims. The same is true of other civil or criminal sanctions for conduct that may lead to catastrophes; they aim at both *ex ante* deterrence and *ex post* punishment. Structurally speaking, there are six legal-governmental institutions bearing on catastrophes. Three are predominantly *ex ante*: planning, research, and regulation. Three are predominantly *ex post*: tort law, social insurance, and postdisaster compensation.

Planning · Governments seek to anticipate and avert catastrophes. The U.S. Army Corp of Engineers, for example, conducts elaborate engineering studies and plans before building dams, levees, military fortifications, and many other forms of physical infrastructure in order to prevent or mitigate catastrophic outcomes. The U.S. Centers for Disease Control plans public health campaigns to reduce the incidence and severity of contagious illnesses. The FBI and state and local police departments have special teams designed to detect and defeat terrorist attacks.[72]

Research · The federal government subsidizes an enormous amount of biomedical, energy, agricultural, military, climate change, and other kinds of research directed at existing or potential catastrophes.[73] Some states are now sponsoring research on stem cells, pollution control, and energy conservation.[74]

Regulation · A ubiquitous technique of government planning for catastrophes is administrative agency promulgation and enforcement of regulations that require both private and public entities to do, or refrain from doing, certain things in order to deal effectively with catastrophic risks.[75] From plant location and design to the disposal of nuclear waste, the Nuclear Regulatory Commission, for example, comprehensively regulates the nuclear power industry. Federal and state banking agencies regulate with an eye to preventing failures by financial institutions affecting a large number of people. Private individuals or organizations often sue to compel government agencies to undertake certain preventive measures, but standing doctrine sometimes bar courts from hearing such claims. In a highly controversial decision in 2007, the U.S. Supreme Court held that states had legal standing to sue the Environmental Protection Agency in an effort to compel the agency to regulate climate change.[76]

Tort Law · Private tort litigation seeking monetary compensation is a predictable sequel to almost any catastrophe in which a solvent entity that may have caused the harm can be identified and sued. The best illustration is mass tort litigation, which includes cases involving widely distributed and allegedly toxic products like asbestos, Agent Orange, Benedictine, breast implants, Dalton Shield, and fen-pen. In the wake of Katrina, lawsuits have been filed against the Army Corp of Engineers, among other defendants.[77] The law often immunizes government officials and agencies from tort liability,[78] but some private defendants also receive immunity. For example, the U.S. Congress enacted legislation shortly after September 11, 2001, protecting the airline industry from liability beyond each airline's existing liability insurance.[79] Daniel A. Farber's recent study of the tort system's responses to catastrophic risks such as large-scale flooding, terrorist attacks, and climate change finds no consistent pattern of immunity for those who created the risks or failed to take precautions against them, and he advocates social insurance or tort compensation for such losses.[80]

Social Insurance · This post–September 11 legislation protected the airline industry from claims related to September 11 by replacing the tort system with a special statutory remedy against a new governmental entity, the 9/11 Victims Compensation Fund.[81] This remedy, which was hastily designed and then carefully regulated in light of the uniqueness of that tragedy, was a novel hybrid of tort and social insurance principles.[82] Social insurance against catastrophe has also taken more traditional forms, however, with less tort and more insurance. Examples include the Smallpox Emergency Personnel Protection Act of 2003[83] and the Price-Anderson Act of 1957.[84] In the case of Hurricane Katrina, initial declarations of a temporary state of emergency were soon followed by federal legislation approving $52 billion in aid to Katrina victims.[85]

Postdisaster Compensation · The 9/11 Victims Compensation Fund is unusual in providing government payment of monetary compensation to individual victims of a catastrophe that the government did not cause and for which it had not assumed financial responsibility in advance through a social insurance program. Legal historian Michelle Landis Dauber, however, has chronicled many examples of such compensation—to the victims of Indian raids, for example—beginning in the early nineteenth century.[86]

Markets

Markets play an essential role in harnessing self-interest, information, and incentives in the service of preventing catastrophes and, should catastrophes occur, of reducing and redistributing their costs. The shape of the law and of science about catastrophes reflects market choices, but it also influences those choices. There are many policy techniques for harnessing economic incentives to encourage the mitigation of catastrophic risks. Dennis S. Mileti mentions subsidies, low-interest loans for retrofitting, and tax breaks or relief for mitigation activities,[87] but there are many, many others. The role of contract in generating and economizing information about risk is particularly important.

The central instrumentality of markets, of course, is contract. Law prescribes the conditions under which contracts are enforceable, the consequences of breach, and so forth. For purposes of managing the risk of catastrophes, the most important feature of markets is the economy of information—here, information about future risks and about the costs and benefits of the activities that may produce these risks—that markets create. Markets economize on information by viewing it like any other good, entailing benefits and costs in both production and use. Whereas law must rely on centralized political institutions to gather, process, interpret, disseminate, and correct information, markets radically decentralize it to individuals and firms, minimizing what each of them must know about the complex world in order to make decisions that are individually rational and efficient, decisions that, *mutatis mutandis*, may (or may not) also be socially desirable. If property rights in information are well defined, assigned, and priced—important conditions given information's public good aspect and burgeoning social value—markets can produce information that is relevant, accurate, and almost instantaneously responsive to changes in facts and opportunities. Because feedback loops are as short as proximity to customers can make them, correction is constant and relatively cheap.[88]

For catastrophe management, the most important market mechanism is the insurance contract. In principle and often in practice, such contracts can induce those with the strongest incentives to accurately predict future risks—both the risk of occurrence and the costs of such risks, should they materialize—by mobilizing the best scientific and other information bearing on those risks, doing so by betting their own money on the outcome and acting in ways that maximize the probability of winning the bet. A strategy of improving risk information by developing robust but unconventional insurance markets—for example, bets on the outcomes of future elections—holds considerable promise for the prevention of, and planning for, catastrophes.[89] From society's point of view, however, the comparatively efficient economy of information found in markets may be problematic. Some people are always able to obtain, interpret, and deploy information more quickly or fully than others because they are smarter, faster, more responsive, or have better access to key sources. When society views such an advantage not as earned or natural but as manipulated and unfair, it may use law to curb it. To protect overriding nonmarket values such as nondiscrimination, law may also regulate other aspects of information markets, such as the use of genetic data in employment and insurance decisions.

In addition to these distributional concerns, private insurance markets are also vulnerable to three other efficiency-impairing limitations—moral hazard, adverse selection, and political risk—that often compromise the market's ability to get the insurance incentives properly aligned. Moral hazard is the tendency of insured people to act in ways that increase the risk of the insured event. Adverse selection is the tendency of relatively low-risk people to exit an insurance pool as they search for lower premiums in a smaller, low-risk insurance pool. Political risk is the tendency of government to intervene in insurance markets to insulate favored groups from bearing the full cost of the risks that they would otherwise bear through market insurance or self-insurance.

The United States has considerable experience with the inefficiencies caused by federal programs that increase moral hazard and political risk by providing or subsidizing insurance for private losses.[90] In the case of programs insuring savings deposits, pensions, mortgages, and student loans, the financial consequences have sometimes been disastrous; witness the ongoing financial crises unleashed by gross mismanagement of vast guarantee programs like Fannie Mae, Freddie Mac, and Sallie Mae. Much the same is true of the massive subsidies to individuals, businesses, and communities in the wake of natural disasters such as Hurricane Katrina, which create powerful incentives to relocate and rebuild in flood plains and other notoriously vulnerable areas.[91] Drought insurance programs in the western part of the United States have analogous undesirable effects, encouraging overdevelopment in arid regions that in turn requires more insurance and more water projects.[92] As for adverse selection, the refusal of better-off, lower-risk people to continue to pay premiums into a special optional Medicare catastrophic insurance program led to its swift repeal.[93] Perhaps the most straightforward way in which markets can reduce the likelihood or severity of catastrophes is to increase the cost of the activities that tend to cause them. If an activity increases the risk of a catastrophe, we can force the potential actor to "internalize the externality"—here, the increased risk—by taxing or otherwise raising the price of the catastrophe-producing activity. In the case of climate change, proposals to impose a carbon tax or a cap-and-trade emissions system are designed to achieve this goal. By increasing the price of the activity, we encourage actors to find less risky ways to conduct their activities, such as by providing incentives for research and development on hybrid vehicles, ethanol, and other more energy efficient alternatives. This general price-increasing strategy is widely applied in many other catastrophe-prone areas—for example, sanctioning human rights violators to prevent them from creating refugee crises—with varying success in different contexts.

Social Norms

Social norms—the shared beliefs, common practices, and mutual expectations among members of a group—are modes of social ordering in all collectivities, including states, families, friendships, and organizations. The behavior-shaping power of norms, which may draw on both secular and religious values, does not rely significantly on legal sanctions; indeed, legalizing a norm may actually undermine its power.[94] Even in highly legalistic and market-oriented societies, social norms determine and coordinate a great deal of conduct and thought, much of it subconsciously and reflexively. We should not think of norms as a residual category occupying all the social space not already filled by law and markets; they often coexist with and condition law and markets.

Social norms can create and sustain catastrophes. There are many examples of such catastrophes, as with the needle-sharing and multiple-partner practices that have helped to transform isolated cases of AIDS into a vast, global tragedy[95] or with the hopeless, adversarial, anti-education values of many inner-city youths that, by encouraging criminal or irresponsible conduct that inhibits their upward mobility, may create a social catastrophe.[96] American conceptions of the good life, facilitated by poor public policies, contribute to the potential catastrophe of climate change. The Holocaust, according to some commentators, owed less to structural factors than to pervasive anti-Semitic norms.[97]

As noted earlier, the social meanings of catastrophes reflect underlying, widely shared notions about divine will, individual responsibility, luck, morality, the proper role of government, and many other social norms. These norms help explain the tendency of Americans to be less fatalistic about the possibility of bad outcomes than are people in other societies. As Mileti notes, this individualistic culture affects the society's approach to risk mitigation efforts: "Individualism and the sanctity of private property . . . influence the laissez-faire, persuasion-oriented approach that is generally taken to encourage hazard reduction activities."[98] This belief in individual efficacy and responsibility, however, coexists with intense religiosity and supports a remarkably powerful norm of private philanthropy. This outpouring of private wealth by people at all income levels bespeaks a widespread sense of moral community and obligation that, like so much else in American life, is not left to the state to discharge.[99] This philanthropy has been particularly swift and immense in the case of catastrophes like Hurricane Katrina, September 11, the Asian tsunami, and some droughts in Africa.

Interpenetrations

So far, I have discussed science and law as analytically distinct categories and cultures, and in many ways they are, whether as applied to catastrophes or to other phenomena. Equally striking, however—and highly relevant to our inquiry here—is their interpenetration: the ways in which they bleed into each other to form hybrid mechanisms of understanding, action, and (one hopes) accountability.

Science into Law

The law is highly porous to the influence of other disciplines and perspectives. Indeed, some legal analysts believe that it lacks any distinctive or independent substantive content—as opposed to its state-backed coercive force, the procedural and hermeneutic techniques that have grown up around it, and the rule-of-law values that supply whatever moral legitimacy it possesses—that is not provided by other fields, including science. Much of the law's language, doctrines, and procedures are mystifying, seemingly impervious to lay understanding and usage. Legal outcomes—for better and for worse—often have little to do with popular notions of common sense. Legal actors often use this mystification to their advantage, if only to seek the social and professional status that may attach to the possession of esoteric but valuable, worldly knowledge. Over time, however, the law has become steadily more rational and systematic, in the purely techno-cratic sense of these terms, by abandoning many of these mystifications (while occasionally adding new ones). Leading examples are the replace-ment of the common-law writ system with notice pleading, the adoption of more liberal rules of evidence, and the creation of more expert admin-istrative agencies. (At the same time, the law has grown more complex, which is not necessarily inconsistent with its rationalization.[100])

Contributing to this progressive rationalization of law has been the rec-ognition of scientific evidence as compelling authority for the content of legal rules and the resolution of legal disputes. This recognition, however, does not mean that science always speaks with one voice; scientists often disagree on methodologies, interpretations, and much more. Nor is it to say that even when scientists do agree, their claims are always accepted as dispositive of the matter in question. In most controversial areas of law and policy, scientific truth is but one of the contending values in play. This is particularly true where the science is contested, incomplete, or chang-ing. Indeed, much of the current debate over climate change concerns whether, to what extent, and in which respects the relevant science is, in fact, settled—and, if not, whether the prudent course is to delay certain costly decisions until greater consensus is achieved, as Sunstein's option theory suggests (see the discussion of irreversibility earlier in this essay).

Nevertheless, there are clear signs that the law increasingly seeks to exploit scientific expertise so as to claim for itself some of science's epis-temological authority and social prestige. The law does that in so many different ways and in so many different substantive areas that examples are legion. As just noted, proponents for new legal regulation of climate change risks routinely invoke scientific authority, as do the skeptics. Many statutes, especially in the environmental area, routinely require that scien-tific studies be commissioned to inform future policy decisions. The Fed-eral Judicial Center conducts programs and publishes manuals to train judges about how to approach scientific issues arising in various litigation contexts. The law-and-economics movement has been particularly influ-ential in legal education and, to a lesser but significant extent, in legal doctrine. Judicial reliance on social science is conventionally (but mis-takenly) traced to the Supreme Court's 1954 decision in *Brown v. Board of Education of Topeka, Kansas*,[101] which is its most notorious use. In fact, as many have argued, the Court's dubious reliance on Dr. Kenneth Clark's testimony and the underlying studies—albeit in an unquestionably good cause—revealed some of the risks of using shaky social science evidence to support (in that case) broad legal and policy generalizations based on psychological and behavioral facts.[102] Indeed, some would say that social science, by its nature, is inevitably shaky in supporting policy prescriptions, except perhaps in those rare instances—the Income Maintenance Experiments of the 1970s, for example—when adequately controlled experiments can be carefully designed and conducted.

The use of "hard" science in the courtroom is also highly controversial, and for some of the same reasons.[103] Two of the most important developments in this area occurred with the adoption of the Federal Rules of Evidence in 1975 and the Supreme Court's subsequent decision in the *Daubert* case[104] interpreting Rule 702, which provides, "If scientific, technical, or other specialized knowledge will assist the trier of fact to understand the evidence or to determine a fact in issue, a witness qualified as an expert by knowledge, skill, experience, training, or education, may testify thereto." The Court in *Daubert* rejected the traditional *Frye* standard,[105] which had required that a scientific theory, to be admissible, must be generally accepted by the scientific community. Instead, the Court elaborated a four-part test of reliability and relevance, and it instructed the lower courts to act as "gatekeepers" in applying this test to screen such evidence. The implementation of *Daubert* by the federal courts and by the many state courts that have adopted a similar approach has spawned a large literature.[106] "*Daubert* hearings" are now commonly held *in limine* (outside the hearing of the jury) before scientific evidence will be admitted. The important point is that the trial courts now play a pivotal, and often quite intrusive, role in assessing the reliability of scientific evidence.

This role is particularly important, and sometimes even outcome decisive, with respect to arguably catastrophic risks, including mass toxic torts. Whether the injuries for which mass tort litigation seeks relief amount to catastrophes or are instead based on flimsy scientific claims of causality is a matter of fierce debate among lawyers, scientists, and policymakers. Asbestos is the mass tort in which the causal evidence is most powerful; it clearly qualifies as a catastrophe in terms of the number of victims, the seriousness of their conditions, and the effects on the defendants, their insurers, and their communities and the workload of the courts.[107] Other mass torts exhibit some of the features of catastrophe discussed earlier, but the scientific evidence of causal responsibility, and thus of preventability on the defendant's part, tends to be limited or nonexistent compared with that in asbestos; indeed, in some cases, it is weak enough to earn the sobriquet of "junk science."[108]

Science's deep penetration into law, then, is a highly salient feature of contemporary litigation, legal policy, and debate over the regulation of catastrophic risks. That is unquestionably a good thing for law and policy, as long as decision makers are well attuned to the inherent limitations on science's ability to resolve most legal and policy disputes. These limitations—which are often brought to the attention of judges and juries by good trial lawyers skilled in cross-examining expert witnesses—include the epistemological uncertainties surrounding science itself; the imperfections of most scientific methodologies; the difficulty of extrapolating from limited experimental data to diverse human experience; the adversarial, self-interested quality of much expert testimony; and the heavy normative and judgmental (as distinguished from factual) components of most legal and policy decisions. Greater scientific literacy on the part of lawyers, judges, legislators, and bureaucrats would also reduce the distortions created by these limitations.[109]

Whether this penetration is good for science, however, is far less clear. Scientists tend to loathe their encounters with the law, particularly in the courtroom, and they often complain about how law and policymakers dumb down, oversimplify, bowdlerize, corrupt, and otherwise distort the work of scientists. The already bitter disputes over the political uses to which climatologists' research is being put are just a harbinger of future controversies over the prevention and management of catastrophic risks.

Law into Science

Law, as I have written elsewhere, "is everywhere. Like the metaphorical fog in Charles Dickens's Bleak House, it seeps silently into each nook and cranny of our lives, gradually regulating all social behavior and relationships."[110] Science is no more immune to this penetration than any other domain. Indeed, law's claims on science are rising as the public stakes in scientific research—measured both in tax dollars and in the technical, economic, and social value of research and development—grow ever greater. These stakes are at their apogee where catastrophic risks are concerned. These claims take many forms. Universities and other research institutions complain incessantly about the mounting and increasingly complex burdens of public rules, audits, and other impositions by regulators having little or nothing to do (or so the research institutions think) with the merits and rhythms of scientific work. Shifting governmental priorities, embodied in public law, make it more difficult than in the past for scientists to plan their long-term research and obtain the necessary funding, particularly in areas that require immense public investments, such as biomedical research and nuclear physics.

Law, however, increasingly regulates the way in which science is conducted, not only how it is paid for and documented. Two examples—institutional review boards (IRBs) and stem cell research—will underscore the point.

All federally funded research, with very limited exceptions, must be approved by the university-based or other IRB with jurisdiction over that research for conformity with government regulations on the protection of human subjects of research. This requirement was imposed in response to the revelation of shocking mistreatment of black research subjects in the syphilis experiments conducted at the Tuskegee Institute from 1932 to the early 1970s.[111] Over time, the regulations have grown more onerous to administer, and scientific researchers have repeatedly protested about these burdens, contending that the benefits of IRB reviews are minimal relative to the costs.[112]

Surely the most controversial (and, perhaps, unwarranted) intrusion of law into science concerns the restrictions imposed by the administration of George W. Bush and Congress in 2001 on the use of federal funds for stem-cell research beyond the then-existing DNA lines. This area of research raises a host of difficult legal, moral, and policy issues in addition to the very challenging scientific ones.[113] Here, as in other areas in which the market for research and development is shaped by legal controls—regulation of pharmaceutical products by the U.S. Food and Drug Administration is the classic example—normative concerns about the nature of the research compete with competitive, political, and even international ones (most stem-cell research is conducted abroad, with relatively little regulation) in determining its scope and content.

Politics into Law and Science

Where the law intervenes into matters scientific, politics is inevitably an important motive force, not only for personal ambition, symbolism, credit claiming, religious belief, and political mobilization, but also for all the reasons that animate legal intervention. This politicization of law and science is not necessarily regrettable. Law, by reason of its public provenance and especially when it takes the form of general legislative or administrative rules rather than individual adjudications, is inherently political, a highly desirable fact in a democratic society that strives to maintain accountability to the public and—to put the point another way—to keep expertise in its proper place.

Science is valued, indeed revered, as an autonomous sphere of methodical, dedicated, disinterested truth-seeking. Nevertheless, sociologists and historians of science frequently remind us that the world of scientific research is pervaded by politics, understood as the process of competition among diverse interests for influence over resources, norms, and public and those who wield public (and private) power.[115] The wars on cancer, AIDS, and other diseases—like the war on terror and the struggle over the management of climate change—are all intensely political activities in this sense. The same is true of the space program, the green revolution, the campaign for U.S. dominance of the semiconductor field, the human genome project, and many other scientific ventures that must compete aggressively for scarce funds, prestige, sponsorship, and public attention. In truth, Big Science—like Big Pharm, the military-industrial complex, and the Army Corps of Engineers in New Orleans—is deeply involved in politics every step of the way. Sound public law can and should modulate and influence the nature of this involvement—for example, by assuring accountability, regulating potential conflicts of interest, allocating intellectual property rights, and enforcing ethical standards—but politics will inescapably compromise the purity of the scientific ideal and the autonomy of scientific practice. The more catastrophic the risks under debate seem and the higher the perceived stakes in managing them, the more urgent these compromises will inevitably be.

NOTES

Krishanti Vignarajah, Yale Law School class of 2008, provided excellent research assistance.

1. Definition 1 is "the final event of a dramatic piece," and definition 2b is a humorous Shakespearean term referring to the posterior, as in *Henry IV, Part II*: "Away you Scullion. Ile tickle your catastrophe."

2. See, for example, Andrew Delbanco, *The Death of Satan* (New York: Farrar, Straus and Giroux, 1995).

3. See, for example, Nicholas N. Eberstadt, "Doom and Demography," *Wilson Quarterly* (Winter 2006): 26–31; and William R. Easterly, *The White Man's Burden: Why the West's Efforts to Aid the Rest Have Done So Much Ill and So Little Good* (New York: Penguin, 2006).

4. I shall pass by our agonies over our children's prospects for admission to elite pre-kindergarden programs.

5. For an argument that our economic insecurity has increased in recent decades, see Jacob S. Hacker, *The Great Risk Shift: The Assault on American Jobs, Families, Health Care, and Retirement—and How You Can Fight Back* (Oxford and New York: Oxford University Press, 2006). For a contrary view, emphasizing trends in volatility of incomes and job opportunities, see, for example, Kevin A. Hassett, *Shocking Truth about Economy: We're Content,* Bloomberg.com, March 19, 2007, www.bloomberg.com/apps/news?pid=20601 039&sid=aa00pjenPE6s&refer=columnist_hasset (discussing Karlyn Bowman's review of relevant public opinion surveys).

6. See Michele Landis Dauber's chapter in this volume.

7. Richard A. Posner, engaging in a similar process, classifies catastrophes into four classes: natural (e.g., asteroid collision), scientific accidents (e.g., involving particle accelerators), unintentional but man-made (e.g., loss of biodiversity), and deliberate (e.g., cyberterrorism). Richard A. Posner, *Catastrophe* (Oxford and New York: Oxford University Press, 2004), 21–89.

8. Robert Rhee defines catastrophe as "an extraordinary event marked by tragedy or great loss." He uses the term *mega-catastrophes* to describe disasters that are even more devastating to the broader society or the economy. Robert J. Rhee, "Catastrophic Risk and Governance after Hurricane Katrina: A Postscript to Terrorism Risk in a Post-9/11 Economy," *Arizona State Law Journal* 38 (2006): 583. See also Dennis S. Mileti, *Disasters by Design: A Reassessment of Natural Hazards in the United States* (Washington, DC: Joseph Henry Press, 1999).

9. Those who share in the widespread suffering may each be quite isolated socially, as Eric Klinenberg shows in his analysis of heat-wave deaths in Chicago. Social context and organization, then, are important elements of the nature and scale of catastrophes. Eric Klinenberg, *Heat Wave: A Social Autopsy of Disaster in Chicago* (Chicago: University of Chicago Press, 2002).

10. Mileti, *Disasters by Design,* 66. (Mileti notes that "seven of the ten most costly disasters . . . in U.S. history occurred between 1989 and 1994. In fact, since 1989 the nation has frequently entered periods in which losses from catastrophic natural disasters averaged about $1billion per week").

11. See, for example, Niall Ferguson's reinterpretation of World War I, which denies these two conditions. Niall Ferguson, *The Pity of War* (New York: Basic Books, 1999), 460. ("Had Britain stood aside—even for a matter of weeks—continental Europe could therefore have been transformed into something not wholly unlike the European Union we know today—but without the massive contraction in British overseas power entailed by the fighting of two world wars. Perhaps too the complete collapse of Russia into the horrors of civil war and Bolshevism might have been averted.")

12. Kai T. Erikson, *Everything in Its Path: Destruction of Community in the Buffalo Creek Flood* (New York: Simon and Schuster, 1976); Tom Browning, "Lessons from a Killer Flood," *Denver Post,* July 30, 2006, E1; Judy O'Rourke, "Documenting Fatal Disaster," *Daily News of Los Angeles,* February 26, 2007, N3. See also Joan Quigley, *The Day the Earth Caved In: An American Mining Tragedy* (New York: Random House, 2007) (describing the destruction by mine fire of Centralia, Pennsylvania).

13. "Catastrophic risk is fundamentally different from normal risk. It deals with events so rare that experience doesn't help you much to predict them. . . . You don't know what you don't know. The further out into the tail you go—the less probable the event—the greater the uncertainty." Michael Lewis, "In Nature's Casino," *New York Times Magazine,* August 26, 2007, 50.

14. Cornelia Dean, "The Problems in Modeling Nature, with Its Unruly Natural Tendencies," *New York Times*, February 20, 2007, F3 (reviewing Orrin Pilkey and Linda Pilkey-Jarvis, *Useless Arithmetic: Why Environmental Scientists Can't Predict the Future*). On asteroid collisions, see Russell L. Schweickart, "The Sky Is Falling. Really," *New York Times*, March 16, 2007, A23, about NASA's Spaceguard Survey program.

15. Lewis, "*In Nature's Casino*," 51.

16. See, generally, Cass R. Sunstein, "Probability Neglect: Emotions, Worst Cases, and Law," *Yale Law Journal* 112 (2002): 61–108.

17. Mary Douglas and Aaron Wildavsky, *Risk and Culture: An Essay on the Selection of Technical and Environmental Dangers* (Berkeley: University of California Press, 1982); Aaron Wildavsky and Karl Dake, "Theories of Risk Perception: Who Fears What and Why?" *Daedalus* 119, no. 4 (Fall 1990): 41–59.

18. Charles Perrow, *Normal Accidents: Living with High-Risk Technologies* (New York: Basic Books, 1984). This book was written before the 1986 Chernobyl disaster.

19. See, for example, Edward C. Banfield and Laura F. Banfield, *The Moral Basis of a Backward Society* (New York: Free Press, 1958).

20. See Alberto Alesina and Edward L. Glaeser, *Fighting Poverty in the U.S. and Europe: A World of Difference* (Oxford: Oxford University Press, 2004), 60–62.

21. Alesina and Glaeser, *Fighting Poverty*, 61–62.

22. See, for example, Richard H. Thaler and Cass R. Sunstein, *Nudge: Improving Decisions About Health, Welfare, and Happiness* (New Haven, CT: Yale University Press, 2008).

23. Howard Kunreuther, "Disaster Mitigation and Insurance: Learning from Katrina," in *Shelter from the Storm: Repairing the National Emergency Management System after Hurrican Katrina*, ed. William L. Waugh Jr., special issue, *Annals of the American Academy of Political and Social Science* 604, no. 1 (March 2006): 208–27.

24. W. Kip Viscusi, "Do Smokers Underestimate Risks?" *Journal of Political Economy* 98 (1990): 1253–69.

25. Posner, *Catastrophe*.

26. See Brian Toft and Simon Reynolds, *Learning from Disasters* (Stoneham, MA: Butterworth-Heinemann, 1994) (arguing that "organizational learning" can improve the effectiveness of a systems approach response in preventing and responding to disasters); and Tracey King, Note, "Environmental Displacement: Coordinating Efforts to Find Solutions," *Georgia International Environmental Law Review* 18 (2006): 543.

27. See Marvin N. Olasky, *The Politics of Disaster: Katrina, Big Government, and a New Strategy for Future Crisis* (Nashville, TN: West Publishing Group, 2006). ("When Hurricane Fifi wreaked havoc in Honduras in 1974, widespread starvation ensued. Yet when Hurricane Katrina destroyed homes, a robust American economy kept famine from being a fear.")

28. Guido Calabresi, *The Costs of Accidents* (New Haven, CT: Yale University Press, 1970), 198, 224–29.

29. For example, new explanations for earthquakes shifted their "typification" in people's minds. Robert A. Stallings, *Promoting Risk: Constructing the Earthquake Threat* (New York: De Gruyter, 1995), ch. 5.

30. Cass R. Sunstein, "Irreversible and Catastrophic," *Cornell Law Review* 91 (2006): 845. As an example of irreversibility, he cites (p. 842) species destruction, although strictly speaking, even that may become reversible through advances in DNA preservation and cryogenics.

31. Cass R. Sunstein, Symposium, "Preferences and Rational Choice: New Perspectives and Legal Implications: Beyond the Precautionary Principle," *University of Pennsylvania Law Review* 151 (2003): 1003–58.

32. See, for example, Klinenberg's study of heat-wave deaths among many people whose social isolation rendered them, in effect, invisible and thus not part of a crisis, as conventionally understood.

33. There is much disagreement among experts about this issue. Compare William D. Nordhaus and Joseph Boyer, *Warming the World: Economic Models of Global Warming* (Cambridge, MA: MIT Press, 2000), with Sir Nicholas Stern, *The Stern Review: The Economics of Climate Change* (New York: Cambridge University Press, 2007).

34. On 9/11 compensation, see Kenneth R. Feinberg, *What Is Life Worth?* (New York: Public Affairs, 2005). On asteroid collisions, see Schweickart, "The Sky Is Falling. Really."

35. See Peter H. Schuck, *Meditations of a Militant Moderate: Cool Views on Hot Topics* (Lanham, MD: Rowman and Littlefield, 2006), 43–48. See also Charles Ogletree, "Reparations for the Children of Slavery: Litigating the Issues," *University of Memphis Law Review* 33, no. 2 (Winter 2003): 245–64.

36. To implement recommendations of the Commission on Wartime Relocation and Internment of Civilians, 100 Public Law 383; 102 Stat. 903 (1988). See also Restitution for World War II Internment of Japanese-Americans and Aleuts, 50 USCS app. secs. 1989 et seq. (August 10, 1988).

37. For an extensive analysis and critique of these programs, see Peter H. Schuck, *Diversity in America* (Cambridge, MA: Belknap Press of Harvard University Press, 2003), ch. 5. U.S. Supreme Court doctrine has caused these programs to be defended legally on diversity grounds, but they are better understood as remedial and reparative.

38. See, for example, James S. Fishkin, *The Limits of Obligation* (New Haven, CT: Yale University Press, 1982).

39. The outpouring of American support for the victims of the 2004 Asian tsunami is a recent example. See, for example, "New Nonprofit Self-Regulation Principles Emerge," *Nonprofit Business Advisor*, February 1, 2007. (Americans donated $3.16 billion to tsunami relief efforts.) Moreover, the community of concern can grow due to the dispersion of the disaster or its effects, as in the case of the forced migration of Hurricane Katrina victims from New Orleans to Houston and other cities.

40. I thank Leora Bilsky for suggesting this point.

41. Thomas C. Schelling, "The Life You Save May Be Your Own," in *Choice and Consequence* (Cambridge, MA: Harvard University Press, 1984), 113–46.

42. See Quigley, *The Day the Earth Caved In*. See also "Officials Reverse Course and Say the Search for 6 Utah Miners Will Continue," *New York Times*, August 27, 2007, A12.

43. See, for example, James Gow, *Triumph of the Lack of Will: International Diplomacy and the Yugoslav War* (1997), 306 (noting public opinion polls reflecting compassion fatigue); Takashi Oka, "The Ability to Feel," *Christian Science Monitor*, May 10, 1991, 18 (observing that compassion fatigue sets in when problems become too large for society to comprehend or resolve); and Jon Swain, "Voyage of Fear for Boat People," *Sunday Times* (London), June 17, 1990, sec. 1, 26 (describing the global compassion fatigue regarding Vietnamese asylum seekers).

44. See Saul Levmore, "Coalitions and Quakes," *University of Chicago Law School Roundtable* 3 (1996): 1 (asserting that "discrete natural disasters tend to affect limited geographic areas and often, therefore, relatively well organized interest groups").

45. Peter H. Schuck and Richard J. Zeckhauser, *Targeting in Social Programs: Avoiding Bad Bets, Removing Bad Apples* (Washington, DC: Brookings Institution Press, 2006), 44–45.

46. See, for example, Posner, *Catastrophe*, ch. 3.

47. See Levmore, "Coalitions and Quakes," 1.

48. For earthquake examples, see Stallings, *Promoting Risk*, 120–21.

49. See, for example, Olasky, *The Politics of Disaster*, ch. 2.

50. As Michele Landis Dauber has put it, "It is far better when requesting federal funds to be standing hip-deep in water than to be standing in an unemployment line." See her essay in this volume. See also Stallings, *Promoting Risk*, 123–28.

51. See, for example, Martin Gilens, *Why Americans Hate Welfare: Race, Media and the Politics of Antipoverty Policy* (Chicago: University of Chicago Press, 1999).

52. John Hander and Wei Choong, "Disaster Resilience through Local Economic Activity in Phuket," *Australian Journal of Emergency Management* 21, no. 4 (November 2006): 13–14.

53. James Q. Wilson, "The Politics of Regulation," in *The Politics of Regulation*, ed. James Q. Wilson (New York: Basic Books, 1980), 357. See also Peter H. Schuck, "The Politics of Regulation," *Yale Law Journal* 90 (1981): 702 (review of Wilson's book); and Levmore, *Coalitions and Quakes*.

54. Quigley, *The Day the Earth Caved In*.

55. Kathleen J. Tierney and colleagues discuss three traditional theoretical approaches to disasters: the "functionalist" or "systems" perspective, the "vulnerability" perspective, and the "social constructionist" perspective. Kathleen J. Tierney et al., *Facing the Unexpected: Disaster Preparedness and Response in the United States* (Washington, DC: Joseph Henry Press, 2001), ch. 1.

56. See Olasky, *The Politics of Disaster*, 3.

57. Subsequently published as *The Two Cultures and the Scientific Regulation* (Cambridge: Cambridge University Press, 1965). This and the following two sections (on law and politics) draw heavily, often verbatim, from my earlier essay, "Multi-Culturalism Redux: Science, Law, and Politics," *Yale Law and Policy Review* 11 (1993): 1–46, reprinted in Peter H. Schuck, *The Limits of Law: Essays on Democratic Governance* (Boulder, CO: Westview Press, 2000). That essay includes many exceptions, qualifications, refinements, and examples not discussed here. My notes to that essay contain many supporting references not provided here.

58. Peter Huber, *Galileo's Revenge: Junk Science in the Courtroom* (New York: Basic Books, 1991), 222.

59. See, generally, Bruno Latour, *Science in Action: How to Follow Scientists and Engineers through Society* (Cambridge, MA: Harvard University Press, 1987), 29, 140–41; Sheila S. Jasanoff, *The Fifth Branch: Science Advisers as Policymakers* (Cambridge, MA: Harvard University Press, 1994), 12–14; Sheila S. Jasanoff, "What Judges Should Know about the Sociology of Science," *Jurimetrics* 32 (1992): 345, 347, 356–58; and sources cited.

60. See Latour, *Science in Action*, 69. ("When science in action is followed, instruments become the crucial elements, immediately after the technical texts.")

61. See, generally, Randolph N. Jonakait, "The Meaning of *Daubert* and What That Means for Forensic Science," *Cardozo Law Review* 15 (1994): 2103–17; and Pamela D. Harvey, Note and Comment, "Educated Guesses: Health Risk Assessment in Environmental Impact Statements," *American Journal of Law and Medicine* 16 (1990): 399, 410.

62. In an April 7, 2007, e-mail correspondence to me, Grainne De Burca makes the point that "despite its distinctiveness from the scientific enterprise, law nonetheless at times has borrowed the mantle or the language of science and sought to link itself (symbolically, or semantically, at least) with the latter. This has really ceased to be true for a long time in the [United States] (maybe since Langdell) but it still has some attraction in continental Europe where the idea of 'legal science' remains prevalent."

63. Jasanoff, "What Judges Should Know," 345, 353–54.

64. Sunstein, "Probability Neglect."

65. See Olasky, *The Politics of Disaster*.

66. An example is the jockeying for position in post-Katrina Louisiana state politics among those claiming better relationships with Washington. See Adam Nossiter, "Louisiana Opening Offers Chance to Recast a Shaky Relationship with Washington," *New York Times*, March 22, 2007, A17.

67. See Posner, *Catastrophe*, 133.

68. Ibid., 93–112.

69. On the idea of legibility, see James C. Scott, *Seeing Like a State: How Certain Schemes to Improve the Human Condition Have Failed* (New Haven, CT: Yale University Press, 1998).

70. See Kunreuther, "Disaster Mitigation and Insurance."

71. For example, by providing postdisaster housing. See Tierney, *Facing the Unexpected*, ch. 3.

72. For a strong critique of the FBI's counter-terrorism capabilities, see Richard A. Posner, "Time to Rethink the FBI," *Wall Street Journal*, March 19, 2007, A13. See also Louis Freeh, "Former FBI Director Says U.S. Doesn't Need a National Police Force," *Wall Street Journal*, March 31, 2007, A9.

73. Indeed, government financial subsidies for research have come under increasing scrutiny. In combination with increasing budgetary constraints, the private sector is being asked to "fill the gap between government support for research and development and projected research and knowledge needs." Mileti, *Disasters by Design*, 255.

74. Financing research is impeded by the "economics of innovation." See Posner, *Catastrophe*, 123–24.

75. See Mileti, *Disasters by Design*, 149.

76. *Massachusetts v. Environmental Protection Agency*, No. 05-1120, slip op. (April 2, 2007).

77. For example, *In re Katrina Canal Breaches Consolidated Litigation*, Civ. No. 05-4182 "K"(2) (E.D. La., June 29, 2007).

78. See generally, Peter H. Schuck, *Suing Government: Citizen Remedies for Official Wrongs* (New Haven, CT: Yale University Press, 1983).

79. Air Transportation Safety and System Stabilization Act, Public Law No. 107-42, title IV, sec. 405(b)(2), 115 Statutes 230, 237.

80. Daniel A. Farber, *Tort Law in the Era of Climate Change, Katrina, and 9/11: Exploring Liability for Extraordinary Risks*, University of California Berkeley Public Law Research Paper No. 11211125, April 13, 2008.

81. Feinberg, *What Is Life Worth?*

82. See Robert L. Rabin, "The September 11th Victim Compensation Fund: A Circumscribed Response or an Auspicious Model?" *DePaul Law Review* 53 (2003): 769–804.

83. Public Law No. 108-20, 117 Stat. 638.

84. Public Law No. 85-256, 71 Stat. 576.

85. For an account of this sequence of events, see Kunreuther, "Disaster Mitigation and Insurance," 214.

86. Michele Landis Dauber, "The Sympathetic State" (unpublished manuscript, 2008).

87. Mileti, *Disasters by Design*, 148–49.

88. For an analysis of Hurricane Katrina emphasizing how the informational advantages of markets can be used for postdisaster management, see Russell S. Sober and Peter T. Leeson, "The Use of Knowledge in Natural-Disaster Relief Management," *Independent Review* (Spring 2007): 519–32.

89. Schuck and Zeckhauser, *Targeting in Social Programs*, 122.

90. See David A. Moss, *When All Else Fails: Government as the Ultimate Risk Manager* (Cambridge, MA: Harvard University Press, 2002), 311–25.

91. Joseph B. Treaster and Cornelia Dean, "Yet Another Victim of Katrina," *New York Times*, January 6, 2006, C1.

92. Adam F. Scales, "A Nation of Policyholders: Governmental and Market Failure in Flood Insurance," *Mississippi College of Law Review* 26, no. 3 (2007): 17–18.

93. Thomas Rice, Katherine Desmond, and Jon Gabel, The Medicare Catastrophic Coverage Act: A Post-Mortem," *Health Affairs* 9, no. 3 (Fall 1990): 75–87.

94. For examples and references, see Schuck, *The Limits of Law*, 442–43.

95. Maria Isabel Medina argues that racial and class discrimination caused much of the post-Katrina suffering. Maria Isabel Medina, "Confronting the Rights Deficit at Home: Is the Nation Prepared in the Aftermath of Katrina? Confronting the Myth of Efficiency," *California Western Law Review* 43 (2006): 9–20.

96. John U. Ogbu, "Variability in Minority School Performance: A Problem in Search of an Explanation," *Anthropology and Education Quarterly* 18, no. 4 (1987): 312–34; Alejandro Portes and Min Zhou, "The New Second Generation: Segmented Assimilation and Its Variants," *Annals of the American Academy of Political and Social Sciences* 530 (1993): 74–96.

97. See, for example, Daniel J. Goldhagen, *Hitler's Willing Executioners: Ordinary Germans and the Holocaust* (New York: Vintage, 1997).

98. Mileti, *Disasters by Design*, 145.

99. See Arthur C. Brooks, *Who Really Cares: The Surprising Truth about Compassionate Conservatism* (New York: Basic Books, 2006).

100. See, generally, Peter H. Schuck, "Legal Complexity," *Duke Law Journal* 42 (1992): 1–42, reprinted in Schuck, *The Limits of Law*, ch. 1.

101. 347 U.S. 483 (1954).

102. Perhaps because of these risks, its use in subsequent school desegregation cases has been minimal. James E. Ryan, "The Limited Influence of Social Science Evidence in Modern Desegregation Cases," *North Carolina Law Review* 81 (2003): 1659–1702. For the use of social science in law generally, see John Monahan and Laurens Walker, *Social Science and Law: Cases and Materials*, 5th ed. (Westbury, NY: Foundation Press, 2002).

103. See, generally, Sheila S. Jasanoff, *Science at the Bar: Law, Science, and Technology in America* (Cambridge, MA: Harvard University Press, 1995); Marcia Angell, *Science on Trial: The Clash of Medical Evidence and the Law in the Breast Implant Case* (London and New York: W. W. Norton, 1996); and Peter H. Schuck, *Agent Orange on Trial: Mass Toxic Disasters in the Courts* (Cambridge, MA: Belknap Press of Harvard University Press, enlarged ed., 1987).

104. *Daubert v. Merrell Dow Pharmaceuticals, Inc.*, 509 U.S. 579 (1993). A later decision, *Kumho Tire Co. Ltd. v. Carmichael*, 526 U.S. 137 (1999), extended the *Daubert* test of reliability to "engineers and other experts who are not scientists."

105. *Frye v. United States*, 293 F. 1013 (D.C. Cir. 1923).

106. See, for example, David E. Bernstein, "Expert Witnesses, Adversarial Bias, and the (Partial) Failure of the Daubert Revolution," *Iowa Law Review* 93 (2008): 451–90.

107. Stephen J. Carroll, Deborah Hensler, Allan Abrahamse, Jennifer Gross, Michelle White, Scott Ashwood, and Elizabeth Sloss, *Asbestos Litigation Costs and Compensation: An Interim Report* (Santa Monica, CA: RAND Institute for Civil Justice, 2002).

108. See, for example, Angell, *Science on Trial*; Huber, *Galileo's Revenge*; and Kenneth R. Foster, David E. Bernstein, and Peter W. Huber, *Phantom Risk: Scientific Inference and the Law* (Cambridge, MA: MIT Press, 1993).

109. See Posner, *Catastrophe*, 200–208.

110. Schuck, *The Limits of Law*, 419.

111. Susan M. Reverb, ed., *Tuskegee's Truths: Rethinking the Tuskegee Syphilis Study* (Chapel Hill: University of North Carolina Press, 2000).

112. For recent controversy and examples, see, for example, Patricia Cohen, "As Ethics Panels Expand Grip, No Field Is Off Limits," *New York Times*, February 28, 2007, A15. For what it's worth, my own impressions as a member of Yale's IRB for research by the arts and sciences faculty were consistent with these complaints.

113. For a comprehensive review of this subject, see Russell Korobkin and Stephen Munzer, *Stem Cell Century: Law and Policy for a Breakthrough Technology* (New Haven, CT: Yale University Press, 2007).

114. See Korobkin and Munzer, *Stem Cell Century*, 12–27. See also David Guston, *Between Politics and Science: Assuring the Integrity and Productivity of Research* (Cambridge: Cambridge University Press, 2000); and Lawrence O. Gostin, "Global Reach of HIV/AIDS: Science, Politics, Economics, and Research," *Albany Law Journal of Science and Technology* 12 (2003): 747.

2

The Real Third Rail of American Politics

MICHELE LANDIS DAUBER

A Surprising Confidence

In 1962, Frances Perkins, Franklin Roosevelt's secretary of labor, recalled the "Roots of Social Security" for an audience of Social Security Administration staff members. The Committee on Economic Security, which had broad agreement on most issues involved in drafting the Social Security Act, "broke out into a row because the legal problems were so terrible." According to Perkins, the legal committee had deadlocked in the summer of 1934 over the crucial question of the constitutional basis for federal authority over unemployment and old age insurance. Then, as Perkins told the crowd, she paid a social call on Supreme Court Justice Harlan Fiske Stone's wife. Justice Stone himself sat down to tea and asked how Perkins was getting on. She seized the opportunity and laid before him the problem that was occupying the committee:

> Well, you know, we are having big troubles, Mr. Justice, because we don't know in this draft of the Economic Security Act, which we are working on— we are not quite sure, you know, what will be a wise method of establishing this law. It is a very difficult constitutional problem you know. We are guided by this, that, and the other case. [Justice Stone] looked around to see if anyone was listening. Then he put his hand up like this, confidentially, and he said, "The taxing power, my dear, the taxing' power. You can do anything under the taxing power."[1]

Perkins returned to work from her encounter with Justice Stone and firmly, although somewhat mysteriously, informed the committee that Social Security and unemployment compensation should be justified as an exercise of congressional power under the taxing and spending clause of the Constitution.[2] According to Perkins and her chief legal advisor, Tom Eliot, the entire act was structured around Stone's admonishment.[3]

Today, if Perkins's tale is remembered at all it is as a confession of an overly cozy, if not flat-out improper, relation between the Supreme Court and the Roosevelt administration that in the end saved the infant welfare state from the Four Horsemen, the bloc of conservative justices who seemed set on blocking the New Deal. We can glean a more interesting insight, though, if we look past the tantalizing image of the whispering Justice Stone and listen to his advice: What was this power under which the federal government could "do anything," and why was he so confident, in the summer of 1934, that the Supreme Court would ratify a scheme for which its advocates strained to find a constitutional basis?

Justice Stone's assurances of broad federal power should strike us as odd, coming as they did three years before 1937's "switch in time" forestalled Roosevelt's court-packing plan.[4] It is axiomatic in contemporary legal historiography that before 1937, federal intervention in the economy was proscribed by a narrow interpretation of congressional power under the Constitution, especially during the late nineteenth and early twentieth centuries. In particular, it is commonly believed that prior to the New Deal, the development of a U.S. welfare state had been stunted by a strict "Madisonian" view of the power of Congress—under the very clause cited by Stone—to appropriate funds only in the service of a specific enumerated power rather than in the "general welfare."[5] In this view, apart from a few specifically defined categories such as Civil War pensions,[6] welfare spending was outside the scope of federal authority and fell to states, local governments, and charities. Even worse, the taxing power had been the focus of particular anxiety during the *Lochner* era and had been treated by conservative commentators to a legendarily narrow interpretation in the form of the "public purpose doctrine."[7] To us, then, it may well appear that Justice Stone was pointing Perkins toward not a safe haven but a locked door.

Four years before Perkins's conversation with Justice Stone, during the summer of 1930, drought crept across the rural American South. Millions of families in an area spanning twenty-six states faced the coming winter literally barefoot and starving to death. In the bituminous coal fields of West Virginia and Kentucky, thousands of miners struck against the greedy brutality of the mine operators and were turned out of their homes with no means of survival. As fall wore on, the urban centers of the North fared little better, entering their second winter of bread lines and soaring unemployment. That winter, the Senate agonized from December to February over whether the federal government would dispense funds to ameliorate the suffering.

Those favoring relief were led by the insurgent Wisconsin Republican Robert La Follette Jr., who filled hundreds of pages in the *Congressional Record* with letters that meticulously documented the plight of the needy. In speech after speech, he asked relief opponents to "explain, if he can, what difference it makes to a citizen of the United States if he is homeless, without food or clothing in the dead of winter, whether it is the result of flood, or whether it is due to an economic catastrophe over which he had no control? I see no distinction."[8]

President Herbert Hoover and the regular Republican leadership insisted that only state, local, and private funds could lawfully be expended to relieve both the drought and the Great Depression. Despite Hoover's efforts to force the Red Cross to dispense private relief, the agency resisted, arguing that unemployment and drought were both outside its mandate because neither was a "natural" disaster.[9] According to the agency's Central Committee, the drought was caused by bad weather and bad credit, and unemployment was a purely "economic" problem. Only during true natural disasters could "victims of circumstance" be distinguished from those who were "willfully and maliciously" needy.[10] The winter dragged on as Congress, Hoover, and the Red Cross stalemated over aid.

Hoover's inaction is consistent with the standard modern scholarly account of this period. The traditional story is that there was no federal relief or redistribution at all before the New Deal because of the twin evils of laissez-faire economic theory and laissez-faire constitutionalism. Revisionist histories of the period have chipped away at this account in several respects. Most prominently, Theda Skocpol has argued that pensions for Civil War veterans constituted a kind of proto-welfare state for the general population, and the extension of pensions from veterans to the general elderly population failed to occur because of elite claims that the pension program was plagued with corruption.[11] Other scholarship[12] has focused on the development of various state-level benefits and on the growth of the federal bureaucracy as a prerequisite to the later emergence of the New Deal state,[13] but no accounts have hinted at anything like widespread direct federal relief before the New Deal. This lack of precedent makes the New Deal seem even more wondrous an innovation, springing as it did from the apparently barren soil of the weak, laissez-faire federal state.[14]

In the standard account, and even in revisionist variants like Skocpol's, the Great Depression was the motive force for the New Deal, acting as a deus ex machina breaking, through its sheer size and scope, the hold of weak and contradictory precedents on policy formation.[15] Hoover's stand against drought and unemployment relief was the last gasp of the Old Order[16] before Roosevelt's New Deal swept both it and a recalcitrant Supreme Court away and restructured federal spending in a "constitutional moment"[17] ratifying, in Carl Degler's view, a "third American revolution."[18] The sheer scale of the Depression and the desperate need it engendered created a legal and political tidal wave that overwhelmed the obstacles that had previously prevented the development of a modern welfare state on the federal level. The attempts to find precursors to the New Deal have only served to confirm its singular quality.

Hoover eventually acknowledged as much. Speaking in St. Louis in 1935, he complained bitterly that despite his efforts to "relieve distress which flows from national calamity," history had rewritten him as a heartless scrooge: "All this was forgotten on March 3, 1933. We may accept that the date of Creation was moved to March 4," the date of Roosevelt's inauguration.[19] Hoover appears to us now as a kind of tragic figure, like the last scientist to hold to the phlogiston theory of combustion before the modern oxygen theory swept it away.

It is therefore curious that neither La Follette nor Stone demanded a rethinking of U.S. institutions as a necessary prerequisite to federal aid to the unemployed. La Follette's speeches on the Senate floor during the winter of 1930 urged not a break with tradition but adherence to it:

> This cry of dole is preposterous . . . we have been told by those speaking for the administration that to appropriate money to relieve distress and suffering in the drought-stricken States would be to violate a great American principle. If that be true, Mr. President, we began violating that great American principle in 1827, when the policy of appropriating funds from the Federal Treasury for relief purposes was inaugurated . . . in order to assist relieving conditions created by a fire at Alexandria. . . . On the contrary, to refuse to meet this situation by a Federal appropriation is a violation of traditional American policy and is counter to the spirit of generosity which has always actuated the Government of the United States under similar conditions.[20]

If relieving those caught in the Dust Bowl required a fundamental revamping of American government, not just a New Deal but a new constitutional order, why was La Follette talking about tradition and pointing as precedent to events that occurred more than a century before? And why was he pointing to a fire in Alexandria, Virginia, rather than to pensions for Civil War veterans or poor relief? This essay condenses research from my larger book project, titled *The Sympathetic State*, in an effort to answer that question.

Origins

Stone and La Follette both based their expansive understanding of the possibilities of federal intervention in the economy on the long history of federal disaster relief, a history with which they and their contemporaries were completely familiar, although it has since become obscure. The history of disaster relief was appealing on a number of grounds: by the 1930s, it represented a century and a half of direct aid by the national government to a wide swath of the population without a single reversal by the Supreme Court; it was governed by a strong concern with equity and precedent; and it provided a clear narrative of relief of blameless loss into which the federal response to the economic depression of the 1930s could be fit.

Despite La Follette's claim during the 1930 relief debate, federal disaster relief did not begin with the Alexandria fire of 1827. Direct payments from the federal treasury to relieve "sufferers" actually began nearly forty years earlier, in 1790.[21] These payments began as a series of private bills for the relief of individuals and gave way by 1822 to general relief bills benefiting a defined class of claimants. By the time of the Alexandria fire, Congress had already granted twenty-seven separate claims for relief, encompassing thousands of claimants and millions of dollars, for relief following events such as the Whiskey Rebellion, the slave insurrection on St. Domingo (Haiti), and various fires, floods, and storms. Beginning in 1794, with the relief of distress caused by the Whiskey Rebellion, these funds were most often administered through centralized federal relief bureaucracies appointed by the executive branch that evaluated applications and distributed benefits according to statutory eligibility criteria.

These early appropriations quickly hardened into a set of legislative precedents that were repeatedly invoked both for and against proposed relief measures. In this respect, Congress often acted less like a legislature than a court, with members arguing that the government was either constrained or compelled by its prior decisions. Concerns among members of Congress about the equitable application of these precedents contributed to the construction of narratives that distinguished among events and petitioners—certain events were compensated while others were ignored. Successful appeals told of events in a particular narrative form: sudden, unforeseeable loss for which the claimant was morally blameless. By 1827, disaster relief was already established as a nascent federal entitlement program that was seen as entirely constitutionally permissible.[22]

Although there were some early conflicts over the constitutionality of relief, the permissibility of federal relief for acts of "Providence" was only rarely and half-heartedly revisited by Congress after the Alexandria fire.[23] By the mid-nineteenth century, dozens of relief appropriations following such events as grasshopper plagues, Mississippi River floods, and the Civil and Indian wars were so uncontroversial that they were most often made by unanimous joint resolution. At that point, members of Congress turned their attention from whether they *could* provide relief to whether they *should*. Over the course of the next century, relief appropriations for events such as the Alexandria fire, the Whiskey Rebellion, the St. Domingo revolution, the Caracas earthquake, and hundreds of other grants served as precedents invoked in contested claims for relief.

Often precedents were cited by opposing sides of the same claim. Massachusetts Federalist Benjamin Goodhue complained about a request for relief due to a fire in 1794: "A fire happened lately in Boston, which destroyed perhaps ten or twenty thousand pounds worth of commodities that had paid duties. What kind of business would it be if all these persons were to come forward and make a demand of compensation. . . . Claims of this kind would never have any end." Other congressmen recalled that the House had granted more than $10,000 in precisely this sort of relief six months prior and argued that the claimants "should have the same justice with other petitioners to that House."[24] It was agreed that the petition could be "treated as others of that nature had been."[25]

Most strikingly, long lists of precedents were often marshaled to support requests for relief; the first statements uttered on the floor of the House in favor of relieving the Savannah fire recited a list of precedents. South Carolinian William Laughton Smith, chairman of the House Ways and Means Committee, asserted that these prior instances of national aid, including relief following the Whiskey Rebellion, *controlled* the decision, leaving Congress no room to refuse.[26] Similarly, lists of precedents were cited several times during the 1836 debate over relief for white settlers following the Seminole War.[27] Representatives cited the Caracas earthquake, an earthquake at New Madrid, Missouri in 1812, and other "repeated acts of this Government in charity for the visitations of Providence."[28] The massive outlays for the War of 1812 were cited with particular force by anti-Jacksonian James Harper of Pennsylvania: "If a precedent was wanted, if would be found in a vote given yesterday, to pay a man for a barn which was burnt in Virginia, by the enemy, twenty years ago; and could the House hesitate to vote for the relief of these women and children?"[29]

By the time of the 1827 Alexandria fire, it was clear that many members in Congress felt bound by earlier grants. As the above examples indicate, this was true across both party and sectional lines. The experience of forty years of relief measures, including huge outlays for the War of 1812, led advocates of the Alexandria relief bill to charge that Congress was bound by its earlier actions to grant relief on grounds of equity.

This legislative preoccupation with reasoning from cases and adhering to precedents critically shaped the terms of the American contest over relief, as La Follette recognized in calling on the Alexandria fire to justify drought relief a century later. As Congress came to consider itself obligated to entertain—and pay—federal claims for the relief of similar circumstances, the categories defining that similarity became the site of intense contest. The need to fit new claims within a set of precedents required successful appeals to describe events in a particular narrative form: sudden, unforeseeable events for which the petitioner was blameless and that caused losses implicating the federal government. Conversely, opponents attempted to distinguish claims along the same dimensions, arguing that the claim should be denied because the petitioner was responsible for his own plight. Ultimately, whether or not an event was a "calamity" deserving of federal intervention turned on the ability of the claimants to argue that they, like those who previously received aid, were innocent victims of fate rather than irresponsible protagonists in their own misery.

For example, one of the earliest relief debates, for losses arising out of the Whiskey Rebellion, centered on this question. Because nearly everyone in western Pennsylvania vehemently hated the federal government and its excise tax, thousands rioted, and many members of Congress resisted granting any relief on the principal that it would be impossible to find anyone who was innocent of wrongdoing.[30] Even if it were possible to identify those who "exerted themselves in defence of the Government,"[31] it was difficult to see how they might be distinguished from others who had been denied relief following similar losses, such as Georgia settlers decimated in struggles with Creek Indians. Supporters of the Pennsylvanians responded by asserting a difference in the relative moral fault of the actors for their own losses. They argued that the Georgia settlers had assumed the risk of loss by "'plac[ing] themselves in a place of danger knowingly.' The Creeks were an open enemy, but the insurgents an unexpected one."[32] Although relief was ultimately granted, it followed a month of bitter argument about principles of fairness to others who had been rebuffed or ignored by Congress. Eventually, Congress made an open-ended appropriation for the president to disperse funds on an "emergency basis."[33]

The pace of disaster relief declined somewhat in the twenty years immediately preceding the Civil War.[34] According to some commentators,[35] the fall-off in national spending during this period was due to fears within the dominant Democratic Party that any extension of federal power no matter how benign would incite secessionist sentiments and split the party.[36] This fear briefly overcame both the logrolling logic of federal appropriations—after all, trading votes was premised on the political order persisting long enough to collect favors in return—and the moral logic of blameless victimization. That reticence lasted until 1865, when the massive Freedmen's Bureau relief effort threw the door to federal aid wide open again.

Even with the complications introduced by the Civil War and its aftermath, the practice surrounding disaster relief grants in the late nineteenth and early twentieth centuries was strikingly similar to that of the first half of the nineteenth century: concerned with precedent, couched in a language of moral blame and obligation, and largely uninhibited by constitutional objections. The power of this practice was such that even new questions, such as the entitlement of African Americans to relief funds, were assimilated into the moral logic of fate and fault. Indeed, the most significant change was not the political or moral bases of relief, but a dramatic increase in both the frequency of appropriation and the amount granted in particular cases.

Between 1860 and 1930, there were more than ninety separate relief measures for various fires, floods, droughts, and famines,[37] compared with approximately half as many similar grants from 1790 to 1860.[38] Some of them were quite large, such as the millions expended by the Freedmen's Bureau for southern relief following the Civil War and the similar sums for victims of repeated Mississippi River floods.[39] Others were relatively small, such as $10,000 for emergency food and transportation following a flood of the Rio Grande River in 1897.[40] During the same period, only a handful of proposals were rejected by Congress, and only two were vetoed by the executive: President Andrew Johnson vetoed the first Freedmen's Bureau extension bill in February 1866[41] (a subsequent effort passed a few months later over his veto),[42] and an appropriation for Texas drought relief was vetoed by President Grover Cleveland in 1887.[43] This tradition of federal aid was well known to the public, and there was extensive press coverage of congressional debates[44] as well as numerous editorials in favor of the practice, such as an 1897 demand by the *New York Daily Tribune* for "the prompt benefaction of the Federal Government" following a Mississippi River flood.[45]

Helping Ourselves

Deference to precedent and the early crystallization of the basic structure of the disaster narrative did not preclude innovation in what counted as a "disaster." Instead, it defined the hurdles that a claimant had to overcome to be compensated as others had been in the past. In particular, a successful disaster story had to identify an entity or event that was wholly outside the control of the would-be victim yet that was causally linked to an outcome intimately affecting his or her material condition. The plot structure of the disaster narrative is fixed, but the set of plausible occupants for the roles of "disaster" and "victim" have expanded and contracted over the last two centuries. Not surprisingly, politicians advocating various types of federal transfer payments sought to represent them as responses to "disasters" using this template. Notable examples include the Freedmen's Bureau in the immediate aftermath of the Civil War through such varied measures as unemployment relief during the depression of 1893 and the effort to secure federal aid to education in the 1880s.

As I have shown elsewhere, this expansion occurred during precisely the period now most closely associated with the dominance of laissez-faire ideology and the decided lack of any federal welfare state.[46] Significantly, constitutional objections to disaster relief spending were infrequently raised in Congress and typically were brushed aside as irrelevant to the imperative to respond to blameless suffering. Beginning in the 1890s with the Sugar Bounty cases, the long history of congressional appropriation for disaster relief was repeatedly cited in Supreme Court briefs and opinions and in policy debates as conclusive evidence that Congress had virtually unlimited power not only to spend in the service of the general welfare, but also to define what the "general welfare" consisted of. The idea that the appropriation power of Congress was unconstrained by the enumerated powers was by the 1920s widely accepted as settled doctrine, taught in law schools and political science departments and cited as support for policies as diverse as the tariff and workers' compensation. The few opponents of an unfettered congressional spending power, notably southern advocates of state's rights, were increasingly marginalized in discussions about national power.[47]

This history of federal disaster relief was tremendously appealing to La Follette and later to proponents of the New Deal because it allowed them to call on the long series of unchallenged federal payments as precedent for their own plans for relief. These advocates called on this history to make an argument that was a central element in the political mobilization of the New Deal: that the Great Depression was a disaster that deserved, even mandated, federal relief, just as the federal government had relieved earlier disasters. La Follette therefore devoted his time on the floor of the Senate to reading hundreds of letters from public officials and business owners from across the country detailing local conditions and establishing that the economic downturn was both severe and national in scope. The Democrats' indictment of Hoover was thus not that he was too bound by tradition to respond to the economic disaster before him, but that he refused to take up the tools that were already at hand.

La Follette's effort reflected the fact that the most significant obstacle to using disaster relief as an authorizing precedent for the New Deal was fitting the Depression into the disaster relief narrative: that is, representing the Depression as an event, like a tornado or hurricane, to which its victims loss could be ascribed and for which they were blameless. This work is perhaps the hardest for us to recover, situated as we are decades after its successful completion. For us, the Depression is a singular event, a disaster with a capital "D" that held the entire country in its grip for an entire decade. But when La Follette first stood up to argue for drought relief, and again when Roosevelt introduced legislation to relieve unemployment, the Depression had to be conjured out of disparate local circumstances, fashioned from statistics, reports, and images rather than encountered fully formed. Proponents of the New Deal undertook this task, in media as diverse as political speeches, pictures by photographers such as Dorothea Lange, films by Pare Lorenz, and novels by John Steinbeck. Once the Depression solidified in the popular imagination as a single event, it could be redeployed in many arenas, including Congress and the Supreme Court, as a national disaster for which, Stanley Reed told the Court in 1936, it could be "safely assumed" that federal relief was constitutional.[48]

As Reed's argument suggests, Roosevelt administration lawyers drew on the precedent of disaster relief in a similar, although more focused, way to assert that the history of deference to legislative judgments on spending should extend to cover such programs as old age insurance, unemployment compensation, and agricultural price supports. Rather than arguing that the Depression demanded that the Constitution change to accommodate changed circumstances, the New Deal's lawyers insisted that the Supreme Court need not overrule any existing precedent to sustain Roosevelt's legislative agenda for relief and social security. For example, it is now widely understood that the Constitution was an impediment to the adoption of a national scheme for unemployment and other forms of social provision during the New Deal, but this view was absent at the time. Instead, all the lawyers involved in producing the Social Security Act believed that the spending power, based on the precedent of disaster relief, was broad enough in 1934 to permit the government to operate a national system of unemployment insurance. Indeed, the federal-state programs that were pursued for political reasons were viewed by the legal experts at the time as far more constitutionally vulnerable.[49]

New Deal lawyers defending administration initiatives in fields like agriculture, public power, slum clearance, and social welfare thought that representing the Depression as a "disaster" also offered them a legal fallback in case the Court decided to assert the right to review congressional spending in the service of the general welfare. Even if the Court did have the right to review Congress's decisions in this area, the long history of disaster relief provided ample precedent, the administration argued, for wide latitude in relieving calamity. Relief of the Depression was solidly in line with earlier measures relieving victims of fires, floods, and hurricanes, measures that were presumably immune from constitutional question by virtue of their frequency and longevity.[50]

Roosevelt's relief captain, Harry Hopkins, brought these strands together in a radio speech in early 1937, just as the Supreme Court was considering the legitimacy of the Social Security Act. The Mississippi River had overflowed its banks in January, and more than a million people were then homeless and living in tent cities throughout the South. The 1937 flood of the Mississippi and Ohio rivers, the worst natural disaster in U.S. history, left a swath of destruction throughout the South unparalleled since the Civil War. Thousands died, and more than half a million people were left homeless and stranded in disease-plagued tent cities.[51] The *New York Times* designated it a "super flood," far worse than anything the country had ever seen.[52] Levees were dynamited across the Midwest in a desperate attempt to save towns and cities, such as Cairo, Illinois, from inundation.[53]

As government photographers such as Walker Evans and documentary filmmaker Pare Lorentz fanned out from Illinois to Arkansas to film the destruction (as well as the government's benevolent response), Hopkins took to the airwaves to argue that "we should consider Government spending in the light of this country's history, to see whether or not it is something new and revolutionary and frightful, or whether it is entirely traditional and has been going on for a long time." As examples of "traditional" spending, Hopkins mentioned "direct subsidies" to the sugar industry, and then said: "And as for the spending of Federal money to relieve the distress of individuals, there are more than 100 acts or resolutions of Congress dating back to 1803, which provide special subsidies or concessions to help groups of citizens recover from disaster or other circumstances beyond their own control. These policies were not mere official generosity. They were intended to promote the general welfare in accordance with the Constitution."[54]

Efforts by New Deal proponents to stress continuity over change are at odds with our understanding of the New Deal as a heroic break with a benighted past in which the federal government was hobbled by an activist Supreme Court and an institutional structure increasingly inconsistent with modern reality. But that is winners' history, following a script that began to be written from the safe harbor of the 1940s, in the main by participants in the administration such as Perkins and Arthur Schlesinger. Contemporary proponents of the New Deal did not have the luxury of arguing that their proposals required a wholesale rethinking of the U.S. political and constitutional order. In the 1930s, it was only Roosevelt's opponents, such as John W. Davis and James M. Beck, who charged that New Deal social programs had no constitutional precedent. The Roosevelt administration faced the practical, and uncertain, task of passing legislation and then defending it against legal challenge. For this purpose, portraying New Deal legislation as unprecedented, revolutionary, or requiring a tacit constitutional amendment for it to survive would have been foolhardy at best. It was a far better tactic to represent the New Deal as entirely continuous with the past and opponents like Beck's American Liberty League as out of touch with traditional American values rather than as defenders of them.

As La Follette's speech on the Senate floor shows, however, representing the Depression as a disaster and New Deal relief programs as merely relief for its blameless victims was more than simply a way to defend federal aid as permissible under the law. It was an attempt to locate relief payments in a moral context that would render them necessary as a required response to victims' circumstances. In casting the entire nation as a victim whose plight demanded a response, proponents of the New Deal were acting as practical sociologists of the moral order, translating the enormous complexity of national conditions in the 1930s into terms that would impel support for the administration's programs.

The Disaster Relief Welfare State

If disaster relief, and what I have called the "disaster narrative" of blameless loss, is so central to the U.S. welfare state, why have scholars missed its importance? After all, during the Roosevelt administration officials from the president down gave countless speeches comparing economic conditions to earthquakes and hurricanes, politicians and lawyers cited instances of disaster relief from the previous 150 years, and the government's lawyers wrote numerous legal briefs reciting the history of disaster relief in defending New Deal spending measures. Could it be that disaster relief played a rhetorical role in securing passage of legislation and surviving constitutional challenges in the 1930s, but not a practical role in shaping the welfare state that resulted?

The key issue for addressing this question is the logic of welfare provision: how do prospective recipients establish a claim on resources, and what determines the strength of that claim? Scholars have long noted that in the U.S. context, unlike in European welfare states, need is not sufficient to determine welfare eligibility. U.S. relief efforts have historically sorted the poor by their relative moral worth,[55] but scholars have not fully understood the source and significance of this distinction between the "deserving" and the "undeserving" poor. Generally, the undeserving are thought to be disqualified because they are able-bodied.[56] More recently, moral distinctions among the needy have been attributed to gender and race disparities.[57]

However, disaster victims have escaped any serious scrutiny as the able-bodied recipients of large, long-standing federal transfer payments. They have consequently been ignored by this moral and theoretical framework, omitted even when the definition of welfare is expanded to include all "programs that provide cash to citizens" such as college loans, home mortgage tax deductions, or Medicare.[58] One of the few exceptions to this inattention is notable for its brevity: "federal aid was . . . given in cases of disasters such as floods and drought but not for the disaster of unemployment."[59] Disaster relief has been less a subject of serious inquiry than an ironic trope in the plot development of "real" redistribution.

This distinction between disaster relief and other state benefits may seem to be solidly grounded in reality. Surely floods and drought are fundamentally different from old age or unemployment, making discussion of welfare as disaster relief at best metaphorical. Floods and drought are acts of nature, whereas unemployment has human origins. When New

Dealers and their predecessors cited disaster relief precedents as support for measures like the Freedmen's Bureau, universal public education, and old age pensions, they must have been indulging in hyperbole or just arguing by analogy.

Unfortunately for this argument, the boundary between natural and man-made events has proven in practice to be of only secondary importance to decisions about whether to provide disaster relief. As discussed above, even the first disaster relief measures included both natural and man-made disasters, including relief for victims of the Whiskey Rebellion in western Pennsylvania and for various Indian attacks on white settlers. In establishing claims for disaster relief, nature is less a gatekeeper than a particularly useful ally in making the case that a loss was beyond the victim's control to prevent. Historically, however, there have been many such allies, ranging from war to unemployment to old age, although all have been mobilized in the same way—to show how they constitute a force larger than and outside the control of their victims. Hence the effort devoted by proponents of the New Deal to representing the "Depression" as a national calamity overwhelming the ability of Americans to provide for themselves.

Roosevelt himself happily ignored the boundary between nature and other sources of misfortune, as when he declared in 1936 in the midst of a severe western drought that "we no longer believe that human beings hit by flood, drought, unemployment or any other national disaster" should be left to the care of private charity or state and local governments. Often he compared the flood or hurricane to the depression, telling the crowd to "take a lesson" about the role of the federal government in helping those in need through no fault of their own.[60] For Roosevelt, "natural" disasters became occasions for arguing that the federal government should be just as generous and responsive to victims of the Depression as to more traditional disasters. Addressing an audience in Gainesville, Georgia, in March 1938, the president called attention to the tornado that demolished the town two years before: "Gainesville suffered a great disaster. So did the Nation in those eight years of false prosperity followed by four years of collapse." He reminded the conservative southern Democrats that they had received more than $1 million in federal disaster relief and urged their continued support for aid to the unemployed because "the application of this principle to national problems would amply solve our national needs."[61]

The apotheosis of Roosevelt's enlisting of natural disasters as a political ally in his fight for the New Deal came in his famous speech on his

Supreme Court-packing plan, delivered on Victory Day, March 4, 1937. The speech came near the high-water mark of the 1937 Mississippi River flood and as the courts contemplated the fate of the Social Security Act. In the singular devastation of the 1937 flood, Roosevelt saw a singular opportunity to rally support for federal power. He railed against the Court's striking down the New Deal's programs by arguing that the Court had left the nation defenseless against disaster, saying: "The Ohio River and the dust bowl are not conversant with the habits of the Interstate Commerce Clause. But we shall never be safe in our lives, in our property, . . . unless we have somehow made the Interstate Commerce Clause conversant with the habits of the Ohio River and the dust bowl. . . . Here too we cannot afford, either individually or as a party to postpone or run away from a fight on the advice of defeatist lawyers. Let them try that advice on sweating men piling sandbags on the levees at Cairo!" He portrayed the Supreme Court as tying the hands of the federal government in dealing with a whole range of disasters, including "floods and droughts and agricultural surpluses, strikes and industrial confusion and disorder." Roosevelt's call to action against the Court was, tellingly, an appeal to the force of nature: "Here are Spring floods threatening to roll again down our river valleys, NOW! Here is the dust bowl beginning to blow again, NOW! . . . I say we must act NOW."[62]

Renderings of the Depression by Roosevelt, La Follette, and others likened it to hurricanes, floods, fires, tornados, droughts, storms, wars, tidal waves, plagues of locusts, and other disasters. Harry Hopkins gave the nation's Works Progress Administration (WPA) workers the moniker "shock troops of disaster" and conspicuously dispatched them to the scene of every flood, fire, hurricane, and storm during this period. Fifty thousand WPA workers were assigned to relieve the 1937 flood alone.[63] Hopkins's radio address reciting the early history of disaster relief discussed above reminded listeners of the century-long "tradition" of U.S. relief to "help groups of citizens recover from disaster or other circumstances beyond their own control."[64] Assistant Attorney General Robert Jackson, who argued the government's case for the Social Security Act in the Supreme Court, that spring echoed Roosevelt's Victory Day accusation that the Court, if not checked, would eventually stop the government from providing disaster relief. Jackson told a Carnegie Hall audience on March 24 that only the national government could respond to the needs of the people in a country "increasingly stricken with flood, drought, and dust storms. The elements will wait for no [constitutional] amendment."[65]

The mobilization by Roosevelt and others in his inner circle of the 1937 flood and other natural disasters helped make the case for the unemployed, who, in turn, became "these innocent victims of this economic disaster."[66] In Roosevelt's speech accepting the Democratic presidential nomination in 1936, he characterized the Democratic Party platform, and, in particular, its social security plank, as one that "sets forth that government in a modern civilization has certain inescapable obligations to its citizens, among which are protection of the family and the home, the establishment of a democracy of opportunity and aid to those overtaken by disaster."[67] His description was then quoted in the Democratic Party's campaign literature and disseminated to campaign workers all over the country, who were instructed to use it when responding to Republican arguments against Social Security.

As Roosevelt's mobilization of the precedent of disaster relief to support aid to the unemployed shows, the distinction between natural and "man-made" itself has been more a site for contest than a clear-cut standard. As discussed above, the Red Cross refused to provide relief for the 1930 drought because it saw the unemployment and financial distress that resulted as a consequence of poor planting practices and reckless use of credit rather than a paucity of rain. Claims for relief of floods and hurricanes have long been subject to criticism that their victims could have foreseen and prevented the damage by avoiding building in areas that had repeatedly suffered similar events. Not only is it possible to have a man-made "disaster," it is possible to move a "natural" disaster outside the realm of disaster entirely. Given this fluidity, in examining the history of disaster relief and the welfare state, we will do better to observe these contests over the meaning and content of the concept of disaster than to enroll ourselves as partisans on one side or the other of the question of what constitutes a true "disaster."

Money is the driver of these contests: there is a direct relationship in the U.S. context between the ability to represent a loss as blameless and the amount of relief that can be claimed. It is far better when requesting federal funds to be standing hip-deep in water than to be standing in an unemployment line. That is not because there are two different logics for resolving claims on public resources, one for disaster victims and one for the needy. Rather, there is one logic that sorts claimants into more or less generous relief systems depending on their ability to demonstrate that their deprivation is not their own fault.

Living in the Disaster Relief State

Sometimes circumstances conspire to enable the same people to move from one state of moral blameworthiness to another, making the moral economy of disaster and relief vividly clear. The destruction by Hurricane Katrina of New Orleans in August 2005 provided an abundance of such jarring moments as reporters and politicians competed with one another to express outrage over the treatment of the same poor black residents of New Orleans who, up until the day before the storm, had been the targets of popular and sustained cuts in welfare and public housing programs. The Bush administration faced a firestorm of criticism over its failure to provide adequate help for storm victims, which it tried to counter by distributing thousands of debit cards loaded with $2,000 in cash and promising to speed other financial help to anyone who needed it. In ordinary times, network television news anchors would not have been standing outside of public housing projects in New Orleans castigating the government for a failure of generosity. What changed with Hurricane Katrina was not the people themselves, but their ability to portray themselves as the victims of circumstances beyond their control.

In the wake of Katrina, commentators wondered whether the hurricane and its aftermath would cure Americans of their acceptance of racial inequality because it was the poverty of blacks in New Orleans that left them so vulnerable to the hurricane. They lived in the least valuable, lowest lying areas of the city, and many of them lacked the ability to flee in the face of the oncoming storm. Katrina, though, showed nearly the opposite: that a disaster can temporarily enable even a disadvantaged group to successfully claim large-scale resources while leaving undisturbed their inability to receive help for their chronic condition. The same logic that put $2,000 government-issued debit cards into the hands of poor black residents of New Orleans propelled the success of welfare reform: although they were not responsible for the hurricane, surely they were responsible for their own poverty if they failed to become self-supporting after five years on welfare.

George W. Bush's mistake was the same one that Herbert Hoover made seventy-five years earlier. The New Deal called Hoover to account for failing to recognize that farmers with barren fields and workers without jobs could be successfully portrayed as victims of circumstances not their own fault and hence people with powerful claims on the federal treasury. The same state that can be hard-hearted even in the face of great need can be sympathetic in cases of blameless loss, and for exactly the same reasons.

Opting for the wrong choice between these options, as Hoover and Bush did, can result in considerable political peril for failing to see the "obvious" imperative, whether it be to dispense or to withhold.

Bush and his lieutenants seem to have been caught flat-footed by the transformation of the poor black residents of New Orleans, who are usually safely ignored, into disaster victims for whom a generous response was a moral imperative. Bush compounded his initial mistake by turning on the aid spigot only fitfully, perhaps trusting that blacks in New Orleans would at some point have to resume their spot at the bottom of the American moral and racial hierarchy. Unfortunately for this strategy, the route back to the bottom for poor disaster victims runs through generous disaster relief because only compensation can quickly restore the judgment that the poor are responsible for their own deprivation.

Unlike Hoover in 1930, Bush could not argue in response to his critics that Hurricane Katrina was the sort of disaster that was outside the scope of federal powers or responsibility and instead should be left to private agencies. Of course, Hoover discovered that he could not make this argument very persuasively either, and he suffered the fate of becoming a political poster child for stinginess and aloofness. In this, Hoover was, in fact, no "Hoover" himself as his relief activities during and after World War I, in the Mississippi River flood of 1927, and even his program of tax increases, farm price supports, and increased government spending in response to the economic downturn of 1929–1930 demonstrate. That "Hoover" became a political millstone to hang around the neck of the Republican Party for generations is testimony that disasters are the real third rail of U.S. politics: dangerous in the extreme, but also a source of great power for those who can tap into them.

NOTES

1. Frances Perkins, "Roots of Social Security" (address delivered at Social Security Administration headquarters, Baltimore, October 23, 1962).

2. Perkins claimed that she never told Eliot or any of the other lawyers on the committee how she—a non-lawyer—came to this conclusion: "As far as they knew, I went out into the wilderness and had a vision." See Perkins, "Roots of Social Security." In another version of the story in Perkins's 1946 memoir, she admits that she told Roosevelt but swore him to silence "as to the source of my sudden superior legal knowledge." Frances Perkins, *The Roosevelt I Knew* (New York: Random House, 1946), 286.

3. Perkins, "Roots of Social Security"; Thomas Hopkinson Eliot, "Legal Background of the Social Security Act" (address delivered at a general staff meeting at Social Security

Administration Headquarters, Baltimore, February 3, 1961). ("Suffice it to say that with very little discussion at the Technical Board level, practically none at the Advisory Council Level, the research staff brought in the basis of what we have today, a contributory old-age insurance system based on the taxing and spending power, a la Justice Stone.")

4. The phrase has been attributed to Thomas Reed Powell, and the "switch" refers to the Court's decision in *West Coast Hotel v. Parrish*, 300 U.S. 379 (1937).

5. U.S. Constitution, art. I, sec. 8, cl. 1. ("The Congress shall have power to law and collect taxes, duties, imposts, and excises to pay the debts and provide for the common defense and general welfare of the United States; but all duties, imposts, and excises shall be uniform throughout the United States.")

6. Theda Skocpol, *Protecting Soldiers and Mothers* (Cambridge, MA: Belknap Press of Harvard University Press, 1992).

7. This doctrine, popularized by Thomas Cooley's authoritative *Treatise on the Law of Constitutional Limitations Which Rest upon the Legislative Power of the States of the American Union*, 6th ed. (Boston: Little, Brown, 1890), and *Treatise on the Law of Taxation, Including the Law of Local Assessments*, 2d ed. (Chicago: Callaghan and Company, 1886), argued that there was an implicit constitutional limit on the power of state and municipal governments to impose taxes such that all expenditures of such funds must be for a "public purpose." A number of state supreme courts relied on the doctrine in striking down various state tax assessments during the late nineteenth century. Examples include *Lowell v. Boston*, 111 Mass. 454 (1873), and *State v. Osawkee Township*, 14 Kan. 418 (1875). The Supreme Court initially found that the power of state and local governments to tax is limited by "implied reservations of individual rights, without which the social compact could not exist, and which are respected by all governments entitled to the name." *Loan Ass'n v. Topeka*, 87 U.S. 655, 663 (1874). Thus, "there can be no lawful tax which is not laid for a *public purpose*." at 664. The doctrine reached its apex toward the end of the nineteenth century when the Court recognized the public purpose doctrine as a requirement of substantive due process under the Fourteenth Amendment. *Fallbrook Irrigation District v. Bradley*, 164 U.S. 112, 159 (1896). The Court never applied this doctrine against Congress despite repeated requests that it do so; at least one lower court did, however. See, for instance, *United States ex rel. Miles Planting and Mfg. Co. v. Carlisle*, 5 App. D.C 138 (C.A.D.C. 1895) (relying on *Loan Ass'n v. Topeka* and *Lowell v. Boston* in holding that the sugar bounty provisions of the McKinley Tariff Act are unconstitutional because Congress may expend the tax revenues only for a "public purpose").

8. *Congressional Record*, 1930, 74, pt. 1:703.

9. Nan Elizabeth Woodruff, *As Rare as Rain: Federal Relief in the Great Southern Drought of 1930–31* (Urbana: University of Illinois Press, 1985), 40; Foster Rhea Dulles, *The American Red Cross, A History* (1950; Westport, CT: Greenwood Press, 1971), 258.

10. Dulles, *The American Red Cross*, 277–78.

11. Skocpol, *Protecting Soldiers and Mothers*. In contrast with Civil War pensions, disaster relief was untainted by political party associations, was generally supported by both parties and by both the executive and the legislative branches, and had been provided to every area of the country and every class and to both black recipients and white recipients rather than merely to the favored North or to blacks in the South. The pattern of party domination of distribution for supporters and voters that Skocpol documents for Civil War pensions was not replicated in the case of disaster relief even though it was a quintessentially "distributive" program. Richard L. McCormick, "Party Period and Public Policy: An Exploratory Hypothesis," *Journal of American History* 66 (1979): 279; Theodore J. Lowi, "American Business, Public Policy, and Political Theory," *World Politics* 16 (1964): 677. Moreover, perhaps owing to its temporary emergency nature, disaster relief failed to spark fears of a large, standing bureaucracy based on spoils. Thus, disaster relief

was a national distributive program that provided an alternative precedent for expansion of the subsequent national welfare state. Indeed, to the extent that Progressives fretted about the evils of Civil War pensions, disaster relief likely looked all the more attractive as an authorizing precedent for an expanded system of public social provision.

12. Harry Scheiber, "Government and Economy: Studies of the 'Commonwealth' Policy in Nineteenth Century America," *Journal of Interdisciplinary History* 3 (1972): 135–51; Oscar Handlin and Mary Handlin, *Commonwealth: A Study of the Role of Government in the American Economy 1774–1861* (Cambridge, MA: Harvard University Press, 1947).

13. Stephen Skowronek, *Building a New American State: The Expansion of National Administrative Capacities 1877–1920* (Cambridge: Cambridge University Press, 1982).

14. The account that Congress was not permitted by the Constitution to engage in national welfare spending before 1937 was perhaps a product of the vision of the New Deal lawyer-hero promoted by participants-cum-historians such as Rexford Tugwell, Arthur Schlesinger, and, to a somewhat lesser extent, William Leuchtenberg. Rexford Tugwell, *The Democratic Roosevelt* (Garden City, NJ: Doubleday, 1957); Schlesinger, *The Coming of the New Deal* (Boston: Houghton Mifflin, 1959); and William Leuchtenberg, *Franklin D. Roosevelt and the New Deal* (New York: Harper and Row, 1963). These authors have emphasized both the legal acumen and political skills of the New Dealers in forcing the Court to back down. A narrative account of the long-established and undisputed power of Congress to spend however it pleased to advance the general welfare (and the Court's century and a half of acquiescence in that practice) would, after all, produce a far less dramatic narrative of liberal triumph. Meanwhile, conservative opponents of the Roosevelt administration were not interested in highlighting the legitimacy of the New Deal in the light of history and precedent. It is reasonable to conclude that although this history of the spending power was clearly well known and important prior to 1937, there was no one remaining after 1937 who saw much benefit in recalling it, and it faded into obscurity.

15. Skocpol, *Protecting Soldiers and Mothers*, 526.

16. Arthur Schlesinger, *Crisis of the Old Order: 1919–1933*, vol. 1, *The Age of Roosevelt* (New York: Mariner Books, 2003).

17. Bruce A. Ackerman, *We the People*, vol. 1, *Foundations* (Cambridge, MA: Belknap Press of Harvard University Press, 1993) [[AU: Pls check; 1993 correct? Lib of Cong gives 1991 for vol. 1.]], 40; Cass R. Sunstein, "Congress, Constitutional Moments, and the Cost-Benefit State," *Stanford Law Review* 48 (1995): 253–55.

18. Carl N. Degler, *Out of Our Past* (New York: Harper Perennial, 1983).

19. Herbert Hoover, "Speech in St. Louis," November 2, 1928, in *The Two Faces of Liberalism*, ed. Gordon Lloyd (Boston: M and M Scrivener Press, 2006), 385.

20. *Congressional Record*, 1931, 74, pt. 4:4437.

21. There were two such appropriations that year. See An Act for the Relief of Thomas Jenkins & Company, ch. 20, 6 Stat. 2 (1790); and An Act for the Relief of John Stewart and John Davidson, ch. 37, 6 Stat. 3 (1790).

22. Michelle Landis, "Let Me Next Time Be 'Tried By Fire': Disaster Relief and the Origins of the American Welfare State, 1789–1874," *Northwestern University Law Review* 92 (1998): 975–78, 999–1004.

23. There was no mention of the Constitution in the debate over relieving the Whiskey Rebellion, the War of 1812, the Venezuelan earthquake of 1812, or twenty-six other relief measures passed between 1790 and 1827 (Landis, "Let Me Next Time Be 'Tried by Fire,'" 999–1004). The Constitution was raised as an argument against relief in debate following a fire in Savannah, Georgia, in 1796, the Alexandria fire, and for the white refugees fleeing the St. Domingo slave revolution.

24. 4 *Annals of Congress* 988 (statement of Rep. Parker).

25. 4 *Annals of Congress* 988.

26. 4 *Annals of Congress* 1724 (1796).

27. 12 *Congressional Debates* 2445 (1836).

28. 12 *Congressional Debates* 2445 (1836).

29. 12 *Congressional Debates* 2447 (1836).

30. Thomas Slaughter, *The Whiskey Rebellion: Frontier Epilogue to the American Revolution* (New York: Oxford University Press, 1988).

31. 3 *Annals of Congress* 985 (statement of Rep. Sedgwick).

32. 3 *Annals of Congress* 993 (1794) (statement of Rep. Dexter).

33. 3 *Annals of Congress* 995 (1794); 9 *American State Papers* (Claims) no. 114 (1800).

34. During this period, the Congress approved such things as aid to the Irish famine victims, Resolution of March 3, 1847 (9 Stat. 207, no. 10) (*Congressional Globe*, 29th Congress, 2d sess., 1847, 16, pt. 1:505); and $200,000 in direct relief to victims of the Sioux Indian depredations in Minnesota. Act of February 16, 1863 (12 Stat. 652, ch. 37) (*Congressional Globe*, 37th Congress, 3d sess., 1863, 34, pt. 1:179, 192, 440–45, 509–18).

35. Sidney Fine, *Laissez-Faire and the General Welfare State* (Ann Arbor: University of Michigan Press, 1956), 21; Edward Corwin, "The Spending Power of Congress—Apropos the Maternity Act," *Harvard Law Review* 36 (1923): 548; Charles Warren, *Congress as Santa Claus: Or, National Donations and the General Welfare Clause of the Constitution* (Charlottesville, VA: Michie & Co., 1932), 142.

36. Corwin argues that the narrow interpretation of the taxing power was dominant only during the period 1845–1860 "when state's rights principles were dominant with all sections and parties" ("The Spending Power of Congress," 579). Warren similarly notes that though relief was granted for the Irish potato famine in 1847, President Franklin Pierce vetoed the Dorothea Dix bill providing federal aid for indigent insane asylums in 1854, and President James Buchanan vetoed the Homestead Act in 1860. Warren, *Congress as Santa Claus*, 110–12.

37. *Congressional Record*, 71st Congress, 1st sess., 1931, 74, pt. 1:3241–43; Senate Committee on Manufactures, *Federal Aid for Unemployment Relief: Hearings on S. 5125*, 73d Congress, 1st sess., February 2–3, 1933; Brief for the United States at app. C. 61–62, *United States v. Butler*, 297 U.S. 1 (1936) (no. 401); Brief for Respondent Harold I. Ickes as Federal Emergency Administrator of Public Works at 164 and 80n, app. D, 68–69, *Duke Power Co. v. Greenwood County*, 299 U.S. 259 (1936) (no. 32).

38. Landis, "Let Me Next Time Be 'Tried By Fire.'"

39. Examples of appropriations for Mississippi River flood relief include the following Acts of Congress: Act of April 23, 1874 (18 Stat. 34, ch. 125) (indefinite amount); Act of May 13, 1874 (18 Stat. 45, ch. 170) ($190,000); Joint Resolution of February 25, 1882 (22 Stat. 378, no. 6) ($100,000); Joint Resolution of March 10, 1882 (22 Stat. 378, no. 8) (indefinite amount); Joint Resolution of March 11, 1882 (22 Stat. 378, no. 9) (same); Joint Resolution of March 21, 1882 (22 Stat. 379, no. 12) ($150,000); Joint Resolution of April 1, 1882 (22 Stat. 379, no. 16) ($100,000); Act of April 11, 1882 (22 Stat. 44, ch. 77) ($20,000); Act of March 27, 1884 (26 Stat. 269) ($125,000); Act of March 31, 1890 (26 Stat. 33, ch. 58) ($25,000); Joint Resolution of April 21, 1890 (26 Stat. 671, no. 16) ($150,000); Joint Resolution of April 7, 1897 (30 Stat. 219, no. 9) ($200,000); Joint Resolution of May 9, 1912 (37 Stat. 663, no. 19) ($1,239,179.65); Act of August 26, 1912 (37 Stat. 601) ($4,500); Act of March 4, 1913 (37 Stat. 919); Act of October 22, 1913 (38 Stat. 215–16) ($785,388.79); Joint Resolution of February 15, 1916 (39 Stat. 11, ch. 28) (indefinite amount); Joint Resolution of August 3, 1916 (39 Stat. 434, ch. 267) ($540,000); Act of March 23, 1928 (45 Stat. 359) ($1,500,000 for emergency work relief on levees); and Act of February 28, 1929 (45 Stat. 1381) ($3,654,000) (emergency flood relief and restoration of roads and bridges).

40. Joint Resolution of June 9, 1897 (30 Stat. 221, no. 14).

41. *Congressional Globe*, 39th Congress, 1st sess., 1866, 37, pt. 1:916.

42. *Congressional Globe*, 39th Congress, 1st sess., 1866, 37, pt. 5:3913 (House), 3842 (Senate).

43. *Congressional Record*, 49th Congress, 2d sess., 1887, 18, pt. 2:1875.

44. See, for example, "Congress Affords Relief: Joint Resolution Passed Appropriating $200,000 for Mississippi and Red River Flood Sufferers," *New York Times*, April 8, 1897, 3; "Congress to the Rescue: Appeal from the President in Behalf of the Flood Sufferers," *New York Daily Tribune*, April 8, 1897, 1; "Relief for El Paso Sufferers," *New York Daily Tribune*, June 1, 1897, 5; and "Aid for the Mississippi Valley Sufferers," *New York Times*, March 16, 1882, 1.

45. "Relief for the Flood Stricken," *New York Daily Tribune*, April 8, 1897, 5.

46. Michele Landis Dauber, *The Sympathetic State* (Chicago: University of Chicago Press, forthcoming); Michele Landis Dauber, "The Sympathetic State," *Law and History Review* 23 (2005): 387–442; Michele Landis, "Let Me Next Time Be 'Tried by Fire': Disaster Relief and the Origins of the American Welfare State, 1789–1874," *Northwestern Law Review* 92 (1998): 967–1034.

47. Dauber, *The Sympathetic State*, ch. 3.

48. Solicitor General's Notes for Oral Argument, 1936–October Term, p. B-C-2, Stanley Reed Papers, Solicitor General Series, Box 13, University of Kentucky Libraries, Lexington.

49. Dauber, *The Sympathetic State*, ch.5.

50. Ibid., ch. 6.

51. Leonard Requa, "The Ohio-Mississippi River Flood Disaster of 1937," *American Sociological Review* 5 (1940): 994; President's Proclamation, *New York Times*, January 24, 1937, 1; "400,000 Homeless," *New York Times*, January 25, 1937, 1.

52. "A Relentless Tide," *New York Times*, January 26, 1937, 1.

53. "Cairo Fights River," *New York Times*, January 27, 1937, 1.

54. Radio Address, 1937, Harry L. Hopkins Papers, Box 12, Speeches and Articles, Franklin and Eleanor Roosevelt Library, Hyde Park, NY.

55. Herbert Gans, *The War against the Poor: The Underclass and Anti-Poverty Policy* (New York: Basic Books, 1996); Joel Handler and Yeheskel Hasenfeld, *Moral Construction of Poverty: Welfare Reform in America* (New York: Sage, 1991); Michael Katz, *The Undeserving Poor: From the War on Poverty to the War on Welfare* (New York: Pantheon, 1990); Linda Gordon, *Pitied but Not Entitled: Single Mothers and the History of America Welfare* (Cambridge, MA: Harvard University Press, 1998).

56. Katz, The *Undeserving Poor.*

57. Gordon, *Pitied but Not Entitled*; Nancy Fraser and Linda Gordon, "A Genealogy of 'Dependency': Tracing a Keyword of the U.S. Welfare State," *Signs* 19 (1994): 309; Martha Fineman, *The Neutered Mother: The Sexual Family and Other Twentieth Century Tragedies* (New York: Routledge, 1995); Jill Quadagno, *Color of Welfare: How Racism Undermined the War on Poverty* (New York: Oxford University Press, 1996).

58. Gordon, *Pitied but Not Entitled.*

59. Francis Piven and Richard Coward, *Regulating the Poor: The Functions of Public Welfare* (New York: Vintage, 1993), 42.

60. Dauber, *The Sympathetic State*, ch. 4.

61. Franklin D. Roosevelt, "The United States Is Rising and Rebuilding Along Stronger Lines," March 23, 1938, ngeorgia.com/voices/fdr_gainesville2.html. Roosevelt had visited Gainesville in the weeks after the disaster in 1936. He now returned two years later on a campaign visit, during which he endorsed Senator Walter George's opponent in the Democratic primary because George had opposed some of Roosevelt's measures

in the Senate, including the Social Security Act. The speech, known now as the "Brother's Keeper" address, criticized the leaders, including George, of a southern "feudal" economy that resulted in wages for the region that Roosevelt said were "way too low." Because of the controversy, the speech (including the president's equation of the hurricane with the depression) was reprinted on the front pages of hundreds of papers around the country.

62. Franklin D. Roosevelt, "Victory Day Speech," March 4, 1937, newdeal.feri.org/court/fdr.htm.

63. "WPA Expands Aid for Flooded Zone," *New York Times*, February 13, 1937, 28.

64. Radio Address, Harry L. Hopkins, early 1937, Harry L. Hopkins Papers, Box 12, Speeches and Articles, Franklin D. Roosevelt Library, Hyde Park, NY.

65. Speech, Robert Jackson, March 24, 1937, Carnegie Hall, New York, NY. Papers of Robert H. Jackson, Library of Congress.

66. *Congressional Record*, 1930, 74, pt. 1:707.

67. "Don't Go Back and Backward with Republicans," Democratic Party Campaign Literature, 1936.

3

New Orleans Everywhere
Bureaucratic Accountability and Housing Policy after Katrina

SUSAN M. STERETT

There will be a little bit of New Orleans everywhere when our refugees move into your communities. Here are some of the changes: . . . You will no longer experience any faith in your government—if you still have any. Our refugees will teach you how to be self-reliant, depend on your community, and live without any faith in the government.   —ANDREI CODRESCU, 2006

States and Disaster

Housing assistance for those displaced from New Orleans after Hurricane Katrina began immediately after the hurricane and continued for those who have qualified through March 2009, although the numbers have decreased over the years. Some lost assistance because they had found jobs and housing where they had moved. Others moved back to New Orleans. Still others lost assistance for reasons they could not understand or because they could not document where they had been living.

Extended housing assistance presents a puzzle in the U.S. social welfare state. Why offer extended assistance to displaced people, many poor and imagined to be almost exclusively African American? It would seem unlikely that the central state would institute a generous policy to those who had been long neglected and most isolated, and yet in the context of substantial cuts to assistance to the poor over the years, extended housing payments seem generous. Where public assistance has been imagined to go primarily to African Americans, it has been most stigmatized.[1] Little about U.S. politics would suggest extended payments.

The aftermath of Katrina rapidly came to represent governmental failure. As people waited on rooftops for rescue the week after the storm, the world recognized long-term neglect of the urban poor.[2] The extent of displacement and the slowness of rebuilding in New Orleans means that the practices of assistance *outside* New Orleans are significant in understanding the state's management of Katrina.[3]

Setting the puzzle as one of extended assistance to stigmatized people assumes that the state settles principles and acts upon them. People are or are not deserving of assistance when injured through no fault of their own. The American state, however, does not settle issues once in a way that is then implemented throughout governance. First, the American state is *disaggregated*. Caseworkers, courts, and executive agencies make decisions that are not tightly linked either with one another or with a decision set in principle from a statute. The state in the United States has never been one of a unitary sovereign, and as the state has taken on tasks of managing the population, networks and nodes of exercising power have come ever closer to describing governance.[4] Governance draws people into surveillance by the state when it offers benefits, for one must document that one qualifies, and one's life must become one that fits within state categories. The puzzle is best understood by analyzing the conjunction of decisions by multiple authorities, including negotiations through lawsuits, rather than holding that the state did or did not assess people as deserving victims after disaster. Decisions are emergent in the ties between judges, advocates, clients, shared homes, and the hurricane that blew them all together and apart.[5]

The very puzzle would seem limited to Hurricane Katrina only. The damage was extraordinary, as was the chaotic policymaking embedded in a mass displacement that no one experienced in the field of disaster relief in the United States had ever dealt with before. What could such a series of cascading events tell us about race, or disaster, or hurricanes, or housing as it rippled through networks of governance? First, events such as disasters reconfigure connections between organizations that are often otherwise not visible.[6] The disaster allows us to trace housing, race, social welfare, and advocacy through mud, roads, telephones, the Internet, and the court cases that advocates brought. Second, coastlines in the United States, vulnerable to violent storms, include billions of dollars in development; property values on the coasts have increased dramatically since World War II. In a state in which social welfare spending appears in fits and starts, often in response to events, relief to displaced people is likely to increase rather than decrease. In September 2008, the damage that Hurricane Ike brought to Galveston, Texas, evoked displacement again. Expectations of extended displacement color human rights conversations about climate change.[7] Katrina invites consideration of disaster policy as poverty policy and displacement as a way of thinking through governance.

States acting in the aftermath of disaster act as what theorist Adi Ophir has called a catastrophic state, acting through a proliferation of orders and decisions rather than systems of norms and rules. He distinguishes the catastrophic state from the providential state, which cares for citizens in ordinary times.[8] In developing this conception, Ophir extends and revises Giorgio Agamben's concept of the state of exception, in which the state acts through "not law" or individual decisions rather than norms, often still brought within the juridical order.[9] Agamben wrote after September 11. That disaster evokes analyses of suspensions of civil liberties and the centralization of power in the executive in the name of protection more than Katrina does. The Bush administration had made reorganization of response to catastrophe a hallmark of its governance after September 11. The "all-hazards" approach that disaster experts advocate tracks the reorganization of the state in which the Federal Emergency Management Agency (FEMA) was housed in the Department of Homeland Security, responsible for managing attacks on the United States and extreme weather events. Critics of the immediate response to Katrina by FEMA explained that much of emergency management effort had gone into preparation for terrorist attacks rather than planning for extreme weather events.[10] Extreme weather events and their aftermath can provide support for centralization, control, and suspension of rules just as political attacks can, particularly when the management of both is a hallmark of capability of the state.[11]

In the late modern era states claim to provide security, and we ascribe damage to failures in the state rather than to misfortune.[12] In disaster, "the administrative state must be both omniscient and omnipresent" in support of its claims to total control.[13] States also act for relief after disaster in the name of protection, raising questions about how the disaster does or does not suspend rules in the administration of what we might think of as the social rights of citizenship. A catastrophe stretches the capacity of law to act in lawlike ways.[14]

In extending Agamben's formulation, Ophir argues that states have a generally recognized "universalistic duty" to act in "very particular circumstances, when the state can anticipate the eruption of a catastrophe."[15] Rather than wholly focusing on the state as responsible for creating and defining the exception, Ophir explains the force of catastrophe as taking a state by surprise and itself "initiating and establishing the exception."[16] Although the force of exception stretches the capacities of states we expect the state to be in control and to offer relief. Rather than extending benefits out of concern for victims, state actors can extend benefits because it begins to meet expectations that the state is capable, particularly important after both September 11 and Katrina.

Expectations that the state must be capable worked their way through a chaotic, disaggregated state. Benefits were the result of the suspension of decisions by FEMA, the effort to domesticate orders to pre-existing rules by negotiation and lawsuits from housing advocates, and political pressure on the central state by affected cities. The national state paid housing assistance to displaced victims of Katrina for longer than housing assistance has ever been offered before in the United States to victims of disaster. Officials with a long history of working disasters could not remember FEMA paying more than two months' rent before, whatever the governing statute allows. Why would that be? United States social welfare policy often pays the deserving poor more generously; perhaps victims of disaster were deserving. However, no unitary state decided that victims were or were not deserving. Rather, state officials claiming competence and the capacity for control want to bring exceptions into the juridical order, particularly when much of the apparatus for that order was already in place.

The ordinary organization of interest groups, lawyers, and courts persisted after Katrina, allowing the administration of relief to be brought within the administrative state's due process. The due process to which lawyers asked courts to hold the central state was continually violated, but the expectation that it should be available made it possible to bring suits and negotiate with the administration. State officials have more choices in governing if they can keep both a rule and its exceptions,[17] and courts are unlikely to make large-scale orders to government agencies to spend money on public assistance.[18] As a result, although advocates for low income people worked hard on housing cases, FEMA granted extensions in housing assistance without court orders, while also threatening cut-offs that frightened and demoralized clients. The orders courts made were limited to some procedural grounds, overturned on appeal, and functioned to inform upper-level administrators that their policies were not being pursued on the ground.

Writing in a civil-law tradition that imagines a unitary sovereign, Agamben argues that the state of exception is defined by law that formally remains in effect, but separated from individual decisions.[19] He also argues that a characteristic of a state of exception is a blurring of legislative and executive powers.[20] Blurring of powers has been subject to constitutionalist critique in the United States ever since the New Deal, but the critique works from assumptions of the possibility of separation that has never captured the American state. Agamben describes states with complete suspension of constitutions and constitutionalist procedures, which did not happen after Katrina, but suspension of expected procedures and accountability through administration did.

The usefulness of thinking through exceptional governance in disaster would also be extended by conceptualizing the "catastrophic state" not as something that does or does not exist, but on a continuum. As Kim Lane Scheppele has argued in finding a set of "symptoms" concerning emergency, "emergencies are as emergencies do."[21] Symptoms include centralization in the executive,[22] and that centralization could concern both the constitutionalist procedures required and the substance of relief administered. Even when some part of the rules of state operation are suspended, if state actors have not wholly abolished every element that supported the practices of the state—interest organizations, lawyers, doctrine stating decision-making procedures—suspension could be brought within ordinary governance. In the modern administrative state, those ordinary practices are unlikely to look like a set of generalizable norms applied through a unitary actor, but they are also unlikely to have the characteristic of proliferating disorder that decision making by a catastrophic state can. After Katrina, the state both enacted and denied the capability for total control and continued ordinary administrative procedures. It allowed general rules to continue while suspending them in the instance, or it extended relief in a wholly discretionary way, both of which disaster relief had done before. It signaled that disaster relief could fit within the ordinary structure of the social welfare state by adopting administrative due process from other arenas, without court orders requiring it.[23] Signaling the juridification of chaotic decision making could signal competence and accountability, but state organizations could follow procedures without actually distributing benefits to people or without extending the mission to rebuild New Orleans or the competence of clients.

Disaster Relief and the American Social Welfare State

The expectation that the state will meet the demands of disaster could have a particular American variant. Ophir writes of states in general and the expectation that they will provide relief. Michele Landis Dauber in her essay in this volume argues that an historical trajectory in the United States created a state with obligations of care much less limited during disaster than in ordinary circumstances. Dauber locates public policy sympathy for victims of disaster in a vigorous public propaganda campaign that centered on the aftermath of the 1937 Mississippi and Ohio river flood. Governing elites were searching for ways to create a welfare state, with general support and care offered for all. U.S. governance at all levels had been reluctant to enact general social rights of citizenship, and disaster provided a way into more general care. Dauber argues that the central state used the flood to elide the distinction between the problems that resulted from the disaster with longer-term problems of poverty, noting that the collapse of the two allowed the creation of a welfare state based in sympathy for disaster victims. Effectiveness of the public campaign depended on its occurrence during the Great Depression, for the 1927 Mississippi River flood wreaked more damage and resulted in the mass displacement of over 700,000 African American citizens, yet it did little to precipitate relief.[24]

The ease with which the 1937 debate slipped between alleviating long-term poverty and misery after disaster highlights the problem of understanding when we might demarcate the end of disaster. The end of disaster would imply the end of disaster relief. Dauber argues that the impossibility of marking the end of disaster relief is part of the point of not distinguishing between long-term poverty and disaster victimization: disaster relief would, indeed, have no end, and the catastrophic state would become the welfare state. The two states Ophir distinguishes could simply become one another. Although he notes that they are indeed continuous,[25] as a matter of practical politics states usually distinguish disaster as an event limited in time and space that disrupts daily life.[26] That definition can quickly collapse into the long lead-in and long aftermath of disaster.[27] Dauber traces the collapse of disaster relief policy into general welfare policy as a particular element of policy in the United States. Ophir would argue that we see a more general secular trend toward a duty of care the state must enact to demonstrate its control; the United States would only be a special case.[28]

The expectation that states care might be tactically limited or expanded.

When state officials wish to extend social welfare spending, they might blur distinctions, as Dauber argues. However, money and time are seldom limitless, so state officials search out ways to limit what counts as disaster. When the catastrophic state becomes a version of the welfare state, people raise questions about why one group of recipients gets more assistance than another. Because demarcating when a disaster ends is difficult, organizations find strategies for limiting engagement. Humanitarian intervention in disaster focuses on immediate response, providing people with food, basic sanitation, and medical care; state aid blurs with humanitarian aid offered by nongovernmental organizations. Even outside the state, those who focus on relief could be framing problems they might need to address for a very long time. Peter Redfield has argued that the humanitarian organization Médecins Sans Frontières (MSF) engages in a politics of refusal of engagement with the state and on short-term relief that will minimally sustain life.[29] MSF intends to show what is possible, raising questions about why states do not do all they can. By setting up their own relief centers, MSF can choose the extent of engagement; as Redfield quotes one representative, were they to step into local hospitals, they would not get out for years.[30]

Structuring limits into relief requires thoughtful effort, and both observers and recipients of assistance can perceive any withdrawal of support as abandonment. If the problems that become evident after disaster are partially the problems of a state lack of will or capacity to care for citizens, however, it becomes a question why the state should offer special care to those injured in disaster rather than to all who face housing problems, medical problems, and the aftermath of trauma. The longer problems persist, the less they seem to be the result of disaster rather than accumulated disadvantage and neglect.

States and nongovernmental organizations may limit disaster but they leave behind what Redfield and Rackley call, in their essay in this volume, "unexploded ordnance." The aftermath of disaster can have long-term consequences not only because disaster reveals and exacerbates already existing problems, but because disaster creates problems not readily resolved by short-term relief. We might not only think of the psychological problems of post-traumatic stress disorder or orphaned children, both of which are central to Redfield and Rackley's discussion, but also of long-term displacement.

After Katrina, no one could make a priori choices about how to mark the end of disaster. As disaster blurred into long term poverty, no one official could set the reasons for relief and why and whether those most immediately devastated by the hurricane but poor before it deserved more assistance than those who had been poor for other reasons. Displacement made the contrast most evident.

No one could set limits to disaster or explain what to do about "unexploded ordnance" in part because no one person or group made decisions. Although writing from very different perspectives, both Ophir and Dauber write as though the state is a unitary actor. Once a state acts in principle on a universalistic duty and expectation that it will care, or once it decides that disaster victims deserve relief, bureaucrats implement policies. That stance offers analytical clarity. The inability to locate sovereign power in the United States in one institution of the state, however, makes it possible to continually revise what disaster relief is and when it ends through multiple agencies of the state. Positing a state as unitary implies a tight coupling between state agencies: what one arm of the state enacts, other agencies of the state do. Where we see a proliferation of legal orders, it is because all arms of the state have abandoned the practice of governing through law. The American state has not acted in that tightly linked fashion. Instead, state agencies are loosely coupled, allowing a legislature, for example, to make a law that is then suspended or reinterpreted by an executive agency and in turn reapplied by case-level decision makers and sometimes courts. Thus, a rule can stand while a state agency works out a resolution in a situation that would seem to contradict the rule. A disaggregated state allows a claim to total control while ascribing failures of control and relief to others, sometimes to individuals and sometimes to particular units in the state, and sometimes to the force of disaster.

Resolving to allow a rule to stand while making an exception allows an organization to get its work done Rules might have wrongly mapped the situations to which they would apply.[31] Getting the decisions made is particularly challenging when the mandate from a legislature is to spend money to help people and yet agencies face political pressures to limit spending and police fraud.[32] Attending to *how* state structures signal compliance with central-state rules while also getting the work before them done provides a link in understanding mechanisms for implementing the proliferation of orders and non-rules that disasters bring about. Enacting policies and limiting follow-through allow states to signal sympathy for victims of disaster while also protecting budgets, limiting the definition of the extent of disaster to something temporary. When a state does extend payments, it may be as much a result of the challenge of getting decisions done in an environment in which interest groups require accountability as a clear extension of sympathy or even recognition of a duty of care. After Katrina, state officials made rules work by coaching people on how to prepare cases that then fit within the evidentiary requirements of the rules; such coaching allows acknowledgement of the rules while also allowing the work of the agency to get done. That was only possible when neither caseworkers nor FEMA civil servants were overwhelmed by numbers of cases; that is, it was difficult to provide casework in Houston. FEMA extended payments after Katrina, but it did so while negotiating in the shadow of the law.[33]

Only a method of tracing the process of policy would allow us to see the settlements concerning who does and does not deserve assistance and why.[34] Such an approach allows a complex and context-specific explanation of housing policy after Katrina. The dispersal of decision making through courts, bureaucracies, and voluntary agencies as well as the stop-and-start extension of assistance allowed state actors to avoid deciding in principle how much one deserved. As Paul Pierson has argued in thinking through how to analyze public policy, "outcomes emerge from activities in multiple sites,"[35] many of which are far from the glare of public attention.

Orders and Legal Disorder: Housing Assistance for Displaced People after Katrina

On August 29, 2005, Hurricane Katrina struck the Gulf Coast, and more than one million people evacuated.[36] Only in 2007 did the population of New Orleans grow, and even so it remained less than half the size it had been in 2000; Katrina had accelerated population decline.[37] The city is likely to remain smaller, whiter, and wealthier than it was for many years to come. Rental and public housing have not all been rebuilt. Governor Kathleen Blanco's Road Home program distributed money very slowly, contributing to the difficulties people from damaged areas have returning.[38] Bill Quigley, a longtime New Orleans attorney and law professor at Loyola University, argued that the aftermath of Katrina allowed the local government to take advantage of the opportunity to have fewer poor people in the city.[39]

The agency responsible for managing disaster, FEMA, had become housed in the Department of Homeland Security, itself reorganized after September 11, on the justification that reorganization was absolutely crucial to keep the citizenry safe. Safe from what is the question left unanswered; the Department of Homeland Security has emphasized threats from terrorism rather than weather-related disasters and the mass evacuation and relief they can require.

Private Insurance and Public Assistance

The immediate visible aftermath of disaster is the responsibility of state and local governments working with FEMA. Private insurance is the primary assistance to people after a disaster in the United States as people look for compensation for goods and housing they lost.[40] People with good credit can get low-interest loans from the Small Business Administration (SBA). Those without private insurance and who do not qualify for SBA loans can rely on relief from the federal government. Private insurance has been the primary model of social welfare provision in the United States. The less stigmatized social spending programs such as Social Security have long been framed as only insurance rather than assistance.[41] Relief that is not insurance against a risk we all share and payments that people have not seemed to earn by contributing look unearned and charitable and are stigmatized in the United States. The disasters once envisioned as the most likely to befall people were industrial accidents, and early-twentieth-century programs attempted to provide public insurance for the problems that befell people after those accidents. In more recent years, the risks people face are more likely to be a result of major medical expenses, declines in retirement accounts, and divorce, although public imagination focuses on terrorism, viruses, and crime.[42] The former risks do not have systematic public insurance and justifications backing them.

Because people were uninsured and unable to move back to the Gulf Coast, many thousands engaged government housing assistance, made in stop-and-start lurches between the national administration and the courts. The Bush administration did not choose to house people who had been in private housing by expanding Section 8 housing vouchers through the Housing and Urban Development Department (HUD); those vouchers are available to low-income people generally. HUD had been under attack. Advocates for low-income housing attacked the Secretary as corrupt (and he resigned while under investigation).[43] The administration saw HUD as wasteful. Those who had Section 8 vouchers in Louisiana were able to transfer them to places where they relocated. The Section 8 program had undergone cutbacks, and waiting lists are long. Expanding to accommodate new Katrina evacuees might have raised even more questions about why one route into poverty received assistance when others did not. By keeping housing assistance for evacuees separate from other forms of assistance, the administration could keep to a commitment that assistance was temporary. By the end of January 2007, 132,579 households were still receiving assistance, whether direct (via trailer) or financial. By that date, those receiving financial assistance were only about one-third of the total numbers receiving housing assistance. They were concentrated in Texas, Louisiana, Arkansas, and Tennessee.[44]

The poet and New Orleans resident Andrei Codrescu imagined the displacement of community rather than its demolition. He believed that Americans in other parts of the country would learn from New Orleans citizens how to rely on community. Relying on community is necessary when one is accustomed to a corrupt government that closely follows bureaucratic turf lines. Relying on community is more possible when one has long lived with the same neighbors, as many in New Orleans did[45]. Dispersal after Katrina spread New Orleans residents across sprawling metropolitan areas around the country, often with no transportation within a city, making it difficult to reconstruct community. People whom many in the United States seemed to see as foreigners[46] became locals. Finding help in new places was easier for people who had friends there, and job skills in demand, and cars; many people had a difficult time resettling. Reliance on the state for housing assistance became necessary, for those who could get it.

The Stafford Act instructs the federal government to spend money to assist people after a disaster.[47] Although there is a general structure of relief from the Stafford Act, FEMA interpreted it in unique ways after Katrina. This discussion will therefore weave together the statute with what FEMA did under the statute after Katrina and how FEMA reacted to court cases.

The Stafford Act provides for emergency assistance after a disaster under Section 403.[48] It will pay for housing in addition to other emergency needs. There is no cap on assistance under this program.[49] After Katrina, it was the assistance that made the national press: FEMA paid for housing in hotels, motels, and on cruise ships. FEMA also paid rental assistance directly to cities or to agencies that could administer housing programs for cities. In guidance to state and local governments issued on September 9, 2005, FEMA said that the states would be reimbursed for a "period of up to 12 months."[50] In addition, FEMA had cut checks to assist with rent very quickly for those who had evacuated after Katrina. The checks were for $2,358, the national average of three months' fair market rent.

Weeks later, FEMA sent letters explaining that the money must go toward rent and recipients must save receipts. Those checks would count toward the capped benefits provided under Section 408of the Stafford Act, which provides for individual assistance.[51] Under that section, no one could receive more than $26,200 in benefits, in total, for replacement of housing and goods. To qualify, one must document the loss of a home. It later became clear that some who evacuated New Orleans after Katrina were homeless before the storm and because they had not lost a home due to the disaster could not qualify for individual assistance. HUD provided some disaster housing vouchers for people who had been homeless, eventually called the Disaster Voucher Program.[52]

Individual assistance does not allow duplication of benefits; receiving private insurance payments for living expenses, for example, while a home is repaired precludes receiving governmental assistance for housing expenses. Homeowners who hold mortgages in the conventional housing market are likely to have insurance not least because mortgage holders require it.[53] Renters are not required to have insurance and therefore are less likely to have it. In addition, insurance is more expensive per dollar of coverage for lower-income people; the insurance industry justifies the disparity in terms of greater risk of loss. The greater expense for lower-income people is a further disincentive to purchasing insurance. In New Orleans, which had the highest rate of African American home ownership in the United States, many people had inherited their homes. Some may not have held homeowners' insurance because it is expensive and no mortgage holder was there to require it. Individual-level housing assistance distributed after emergency assistance was complete would go to renters and lower-income homeowners.[54]

Katrina required that FEMA decide many more cases than it had previously. FEMA hired more than 30,000 new case-level decision makers, and new people often had no experience of such work. The Government Accountability Office cited the large number of new decision makers when later explaining extensive fraud.[55] The computer system did not work well, FEMA did not process decisions quickly, new inspectors made questionable decisions concerning the damage to houses in New Orleans, and no one had carefully tracked who was where.

Those who applied for individual assistance had to document where they lived and that their homes had been damaged. In requiring documentation, states require signaling compliance with rules rather than recognizing the substantive status they claim to recognize. That is, being able to *show* an address mattered more than mapping how people understood how they lived: some shared with a friend, and others sometimes slept in the childhood home a relative still owned. Both could be difficult to document. Official knowledge has become depersonalized knowledge, and legal rules often make it difficult to allow personal narratives to document a life. Reliance on professional knowledge can wholly miss whether a status matches the truth people know about their lives.

The late administrative state often makes policy choices through documentation, outside the glare of public discussion. States use paperwork tactically to choose to incorporate or exclude people from the civil, political, and social rights of citizenship.[56] To place choices concerning recognition at case-level proof does not confront the more programmatic decisions not to grant relief or status to people. In analyzing the documentation of evidence to support claims for asylum, Didier Fassin and Estelle D'Halluin have argued that in France medical certificates documenting the traces of torture have become to seem necessary.[57] The state's and then clients' demands for medical certificates shift the grounds for recognition of refugees: the Geneva Convention requires a well-founded fear of persecution, and that fear need not be based on past torture. Furthermore, torturers have become good at not leaving marks on bodies; requiring professional medical knowledge limits the numbers of refugees recognized. Problems of documentation partly constituted by failures in the state plagued people applying for relief after Katrina, and the demand for documentation shaped applications for assistance, jobs, and leases for displaced people. The official knowledge that would show who one was, allowing one to re-establish a life outside of New Orleans, required documents not available from the state after Katrina if one had not evacuated with them. Those documents included drivers' licenses, birth certificates, and leases. As a result, FEMA officials urged people to submit any letters they may have received at an address or a utility bill. Paperwork meant for one purpose could serve another, broadening what would count as an official document for the purposes of this disaster, all to signal that FEMA was trying to ensure that people complied with rules. Without the documents people lost assistance, allowing case-by-case attrition to supplement programmatic decisions about when to end assistance.

The dispersal of hundreds of thousands of people after Katrina did not allow for community organizations to voice demands to the state; accountability to people was grounded in rule and administration rather than voice. The administration of policy for the poor, which offers payments rather than incorporating what people articulate what they might need, does not facilitate voice. Even voting after Katrina was difficult to organize for all who were displaced because people had to apply for absentee ballots if they still considered themselves residents of New Orleans. Accountability through administration is, first, a hallmark of the post-1970s due process administrative state in the United States. Second, accountability through administration substitutes paper for voice in a way that John Stuart Mill first offered as a strategy for justifying the administration of empire in the nineteenth century.[58] States could be held accountable via paper when they were administering a colony, imagined as a territory rather than a people. Administering assistance to people within the United States also envisions a distance between rulers and ruled that is central to a bureaucratic state, but neither a territory nor an imaginary unified people is the subject of administration. People from New Orleans had not been delineated administratively as a people before. Because payment went to people far from home, they were not in one limited territory within the United States. Rental assistance was administered to the *idea* of a territory—that of New Orleans—and indeed the *idea* of a people.

When Is the Emergency Over? Contesting Limits on Assistance

Ordinary expectations of rule-bounded decision making provided leverage for advocates for the displaced. FEMA had issued many checks very rapidly; it then needed to determine eligibility, so there were many opportunities for mistakes. The program was ripe for litigation concerning statutory and constitutional rights, something not readily said about other social welfare programs anymore. As one attorney said, the field was wide open and it was possible to discuss the relevance of the 1970s rights revolution due process cases in a way that had not been possible for years.[59] Several class action lawsuits provided leverage for negotiating delay in cutting people off from rental assistance or gaining some attention to those who needed accessible trailers. These cases were handled by consortia of legal services attorneys, class action firms, and housing advocacy organizations, including Oakland's Public Interest Law Project and the Association of Community Organizations for Reform Now (ACORN). Preliminary injunctions did not make extensive orders against FEMA, but the accompanying negotiations by attorneys and advocates for low-income housing did make some gains. The lawsuits also made visible to the courts survival strategies and mismatches between those strategies and government policy.

Almost immediately, the housing policies ended up in court. The first large case was *McWaters v. FEMA*; the complaint was filed November 10, 2005, in federal district court in Louisiana.[60] The firm Schulte, Roth in New York took on the work for plaintiffs that a large law firm could handle. It had recently hired Danny Greenberg to run its pro bono program; he had been a New York legal services attorney and advocate for housing for low-income people. The case went before Judge Stanwood Duval, a Clinton appointee and a lifelong citizen of Louisiana. The complaint challenged FEMA's slowness in determining eligibility for individual assistance, the lack of notice about its policies, and its decision to require people to document how they had spent the $2,358 issued soon after the storm. People may not have received the letters telling them it must be spent on rent and that they must save receipts, and many received letters after they had spent the money. The complaint concerning FEMA's lack of notice of its policies was a classic welfare state due process claim. The case also challenged applications of FEMA's much-disliked "shared household rule," under which FEMA only pays rental assistance to one member of a household.

Under that rule, if people shared a household before a disaster, they must share one after disaster. The statute signals both sympathy and fiscal prudence concerning individuals getting state payments: one can gain assistance but cannot get duplicate benefits. Nor can people use disaster to reorganize a household, escaping family one wanted to escape anyway. Although policy entrepreneurs frame disaster as opportunity in the United States, opening spaces for new policies that might have otherwise been unpopular or difficult to enact,[61] FEMA rules hold that individuals receiving help cannot use disaster assistance to reorganize their lives.

The provision is sometimes reinterpreted or its application is challenged after disaster because it does not accommodate some living arrangements. Households may be divided after disaster, a particular problem after Katrina. Requiring that only one person in a household receive assistance when parents and adult children were scattered from "Texas to Baltimore"[62] worsens at least one member's living from what he or she had before. In addition, sharing addresses need not mean sharing expenses, and sharing of expenses and income might well be reluctant, informal, and occasional. Whether sharing is nonexistent or occasional, or whether people lived far apart after the hurricane when they had lived together before, state payments to one person in a house would be unlikely to be shared with others.[63] The instantiation of the rule requires its suspension if sympathy is to be enacted, yet signaling fiscal prudence and publicly imagining households as sharing resources requires that the rule not be abolished.[64] After Katrina, signaling compliance with rules became particularly important because FEMA received extensive press concerning its ready distribution of money to all who asked for it;[65] vivid stories concerning payments to prisoners who claimed they had lost the homes in which they were currently residing put pressure on FEMA to recoup wrongly made payments, whether or not it made financial sense. To require that people follow the rules also required that the rules be workable. Because they were not, exceptions to rules that remained on the books accompanied by case-level coaching on how to work them could prop up defense of the distribution of money as a rule-bound process.

An institutional resolution that allows both norm and exception to exist requires discretionary, temporary revisions of rules. In a disaster-specific guidance it issued in September 2005,[66] FEMA recognized that people who shared a home before the disaster may not have been able to afterwards and that roommates did not constitute a household. That guidance, however, did not always make it to case-level decision makers. People could be denied on the basis of the rule or could be pursued for fraud later.

FEMA conceded points before Judge Duval could decide them. Conceding before a court order could be made could save the court the embarrassment of making a potentially ineffective order to FEMA to spend money. It could also save FEMA the embarrassment of the possibility of such an order. FEMA conceded the challenge to the slowness of its decision making as a due process problem by speeding up and denying up to 70 percent of applications for individual assistance. FEMA explained to the court that it had waived the shared household rule in September 2005, before *McWaters* was filed.[67] FEMA also agreed to allow people to "self-certify" that they had spent the $2,358 check they had received on rent or necessities and made a form for self-certification available on the Internet. Claimants would not need to produce receipts. Documentation signaled compliance and responsible government spending. Self-certification did not actually give evidence of anything other than a willingness to sign a form. Self-certification signaled compliance with the law without substantively requiring it, yet signing the document did more than allow state officials to assure auditors that the state was spending money responsibly. Self-certification still allowed FEMA to try to recoup money later and pursue accusations of fraud; one was self-certifying that the money had gone to rent, not to large-screen televisions, as volunteers worried some of the money had.

FEMA had planned to end its hotel and motel payment program in December 2005; the litigation delayed that as attorneys negotiated with FEMA. One attorney involved explained that the negotiating strategy was no different from that in suits involving businesses; the attorneys could "box in" FEMA by getting it to acknowledge that it had to comply with requirements concerning giving notice and by asking how it might do so in a short time. Meanwhile, they could play the case in the newspapers, an arena that seemed as important as the court. Those who fled Katrina still gained public sympathy, and the response of governments at all levels still provoked outrage. Political reasons suggested delay in cutting off housing as well. December is a cold month in many of the places to which people from New Orleans had evacuated, and it represents generosity and charity.

On December 12, 2005, Judge Duval issued a temporary restraining order that prohibited FEMA's ending the temporary housing program before early January. As he noted in his December 12 order, the decision concerned people who "had the very real fear of being without shelter for Christmas."[68] The president's popularity rating was low, the war in Iraq was not going well, and a public reminder of the national embarrassment of Katrina was unlikely to improve those ratings. Cutting off housing assistance in December was not a good political sell for the administration, and the program did not stop. The court's order overlapped with an interest in maintaining the mission of the organization as one that protected citizens in disaster. FEMA responded to the court in January that it would extend the program beyond early January to February for those still in hotels.

When the final order came out in June 2006, FEMA had done much of what the plaintiffs had asked for, including agreeing to provide two weeks' notice before cutting off someone's uncapped emergency housing assistance. FEMA had lost its claim that it should be exempt from lawsuits based on sovereign immunity, and the court did find that there was a due process property interest in housing. FEMA had not violated due process, however. The final injunction was limited. The case had helped delay FEMA from evicting people from hotels while also not setting a precedent requiring due process for recipients of assistance or binding FEMA to following its own interpretation of its rules.

FEMA had agreed to provide notice to thousands of people before terminating them from emergency assistance and to more rapidly determine whether they were eligible for individual assistance. Promising some sort of process made it make sense for FEMA to extend the emergency assistance program, which it did. First it extended to the end of March 2006, then until the end of May. Cities had committed to leases with landlords; should FEMA cut off emergency assistance, the cities would be left responsible. Extending emergency assistance meant extending assistance for which there was no cap, so to advocates it was a victory. By March 2006, FEMA sent out letters to evacuees letting them know whether they would be eligible for individual assistance, the program for which people had to apply and which they exhausted once they had received $26,200. FEMA notified people that they would no longer have their leases paid after the end of March. In late March 2006, FEMA issued a disaster-specific guidance explaining that it would be moving people to individual assistance or, if they did not qualify, off assistance altogether. If states or localities had signed a lease for longer, they would have to end the lease for those either who were in places that were too expensive or who were ineligible for individual assistance. These dates were less than the "up to one year" that FEMA had told states and localities it would support leases.[69] FEMA planed to end payments for emergency relief by the end of May 2006.[70] The confusing, mind-numbing detail of changes in deadlines and disaster-specific guidances was inaccessible to clients. They only sometimes knew that FEMA was going to stop paying rent, and then it was not, and why.

When filing the next class action complaint in May 2006, lawyers first meant to stop FEMA from limiting assistance, to protect the city of Houston as well as displaced people. The very suspensions and rapid decision making FEMA justified by the extent of the disaster provided the grounds for challenge in the existing framework of administrative due process. The case came out of Houston, which had received the largest number of evacuees outside the Gulf States; FEMA still had more than 80,000 evacuees registered in Houston almost a year after Hurricane Katrina. The city faced many more homeless people if the federal government stopped paying rental assistance. Mayor Bill White, a Democrat, had every reason to support the lawsuit as part of ongoing negotiations with FEMA,[71] and he did, as did members of Congress from Texas. Evacuees without jobs and without federal housing support would become the responsibility of the city that had born the brunt of receiving displaced evacuees. Not least was a complaint that the program would end and that there were no further plans for housing people.[72]

The complaint claimed that decisions were also arbitrary because FE-MA's determination of documentable damage for the purposes of individual assistance did not map onto the damage to their homes people suffered. FEMA initially went by addresses and satellite photographs to assess whether a home was in a damaged area. In response, the city of Houston sent inspectors to New Orleans, and contested 70 percent of FEMA's claims that housing was not damaged; it placed that report in evidence in *Watson v. FEMA*.[73] People could also be denied assistance due to insufficient damage to their home. A home might indeed have not been horribly damaged, but a landlord could have rented it out for a higher rent after the disaster, so the previous renter had no home to return to in New Orleans. Once again, FEMA issued a disaster-specific guidance allowing that a home might be unavailable because it had been rented at a new, higher rent and that an evacuee might thereby be eligible for individual assistance.

FEMA granted extensions of uncapped emergency assistance to cities, and it responded to *Watson* by saying that it had granted extensions to any city that asked. Those extensions only applied to cities in Texas, however. The case had drawn Judge David Hittner, whom the lawyers for the plaintiffs did not believe was the most favorable judge. As a result they had limited what they asked for. When the judge issued his preliminary injunction in July, he only ruled on the relatively narrow question of whether FEMA had to include utilities in its fair market rent. The judge ruled it must pay utilities,[74] and that decision was rapidly disseminated to advocates via an e-mail list. In September, Judge Hittner was overruled on appeal even on the narrow utilities issue.[75] What stood from *Watson* was FEMA's discretionary decision to extend housing payments for people in cities in Texas. Advocates agreed that they could gain little from the Fifth Circuit Court, which included Texas as well as Louisiana.

Decision making by FEMA still did not fit with the public legal order's statements of administrative due process in other fields. Denials of individual assistance, supported in letters by computer codes, provided the grounds for the next lawsuit, filed in August 2006. Codes referenced a document that had been made available immediately after the hurricane, months earlier. ACORN was the plaintiff in a lawsuit filed by Public Citizen in the District of Columbia District Court, a court long accustomed to supervising administrative agencies.[76] The ACORN office was in Houston, not in the nation's capital. ACORN argued that notifying people via these letters that they were losing assistance violated due process. Judge

Richard Leon, an appointee of President George W. Bush, was assigned to the case.

On November 29, 2006, Judge Leon granted a preliminary injunction against FEMA, calling its decision procedures "Kafkaesque" in a widely quoted part of his opinion.[77] He ordered that FEMA explain to each person it had cut off from housing assistance why it had done so and to pay back rent for two months. When FEMA protested that it did not have the staff to explain decisions to everyone, he snapped back (and he was also widely quoted for this statement): "I'm not looking for a doctoral dissertation. I'm looking for a couple of paragraphs in plain English."[78] Although Judge Leon's order gained widespread attention in the elite national press and required spending money by reinstating people who had been denied, it was stayed three weeks later by the Circuit Court. That follow-up did not merit an editorial in the *New York Times*, as Judge Leon's decision had. The plaintiffs gained some favorable press coverage and possibly an extension of benefits, but not a court order. As in the other cases, no order stood, yet housing payments continued. Public Citizen stopped pursuing the suit and claimed victory because FEMA reinstated people and extended housing benefits despite the stay.[79]

By December 2006, FEMA payments of housing benefits under emergency assistance for those displaced from Hurricane Katrina had been extended from the end of December 2005 to March 2006 to May 2006, and August 2006 in Texas. In late November, the program was extended again, and yet again in January 2007 for those who had not been denied or approved for individual assistance. Judges noted that the continued erratic extensions were only likely to make the lives of evacuees more difficult and uncertain. Caseworkers speculated that people had become so used to extensions granted two weeks before they thought they would lose all benefits that it became difficult for them to take any deadline seriously and actually act on it. (It is also difficult for people suffering from post-traumatic stress to act on their own behalf, and many of the displaced suffered from post-traumatic stress.[80]) One official sighed that it would have been better to treat evacuees as refugees, which she explained would have given them guaranteed benefits for six months and nothing after that. The extensions made it difficult to delimit disaster, as having a statute separating disaster relief from other forms of social assistance implies it must be. The work that voluntary organizations such as MSF do to define some assistance as the emergency relief needed to sustain life and other assistance as something else had a parallel in federal housing assistance. Policies were disaggregated across sectors, from administrative agencies to courts, with advocates able to press in each.

As each policy gave way to the next—from emergency assistance as it extended, then to individual assistance, then to recoupment—FEMA's computer system, decision makers, and the opportunities presented by the due process social welfare cases from forty years before allowed advocates to bring procedural challenges. A consortium of lawyers next filed another suit in April 2007 in Louisiana contesting the incomprehensible reasons for denial of assistance under individual assistance, the lack of notice when ending assistance, the recoupment efforts, and FEMA's continued application of the shared household rule. They lost on appeal.[81]

No court ever made a direct order to extend payments. Indeed, the negotiated settlements and the vacated court orders meant that multiple practices and principles could co-exist. Disaster relief could be wholly discretionary and outside due process requirements, yet subject to administrative due process for *this* disaster. Administrative due process could signal to professional communities that FEMA was doing its job according to the public legal order, yet it could deny claimants or keep them on a program that was discretionary. Disaster decision making could be brought within the administrative juridical order, but not in a way that changed anything FEMA did for future disasters.

Households, Housemates, and Home in Disaster Assistance

The shared household rule continued to reappear in cases, in appeals, and in recoupment. It illuminates the difficulty of documenting and supervising what counts as a household and, sometimes, what might count as fraud. Problems in delineating fraud joined with the difficulty in recovering from very poor people and the expense of recoupment highlight that the policy concerning shared households is at least as much about demonstrating policing as in actually saving money. The stories told in cases, appeals, and petitions to FEMA from other disasters tell stories about responsibility and survival in New Orleans before the flood. Consider how lawsuits and stories by volunteers represented people who shared households and how FEMA denied payments to those who shared. Because FEMA had suspended the shared household rule, lawyers gained for the claimants they found who had been denied under it. Home was what one could document more than where one lived. Those two places could be different, so home remained contested, with accusations of fraud and risks of homelessness on the line.

The statute and its implementation by FEMA contain models of what housing is, what households are, and what constitutes fraud. What counted as a household was contested in lawsuits. Households are people who live together regularly and predictably, sharing expenses and benefits with no more than common mutual concern enforcing that sharing. When households of people move, they move together. Their home is a place they hold exclusive of other people not part of the household; people do not come and go as they choose or as they need a bed. The home that people have is documentable through leases, utility bills, rent receipts, and other detritus of life in a single-family home or an apartment with a lease. Disaster can reveal longer-term problems of poverty, where households are more ambiguous than that model of exclusivity and shared expenses implies. Once again, demarcating what is the result of disaster and what is not reveals the effort that goes into limiting disaster relief.

Defining a home as a place held exclusive of others is particularly narrow.[82] That definition does little to accommodate the very poor or those who rely on family for assistance. It does not include shared housing that is shared because it is convenient and cheap, where people may partially share resources. Nor does it include the housing of the very poor in cities, such as single-room occupancy hotels. Christopher Jencks[83] has argued that loss of private housing through loss of single-room occupancy hotels accounts for a portion of the rise in homelessness; only recently have cities begun to commit to building more palatable versions of this inexpensive housing.

Exclusivity and documentation do not even wholly match everyone's home ownership. New Orleans had a high rate of African American home ownership. Houses could have been handed down within a family over the years, with a rough understanding of rights to the property divided among many family members. Those understandings may not have been registered or may have been subject to liens from local lenders, again not completely registered. The problem was not peculiar to the stability of the people who had long lived in New Orleans. Even after the Loma Prieta earthquake in California in 1989, low-income housing advocates explained that people could have lifetime occupancy rights to a house. Without documentation of those rights predating the earthquake, the disaster relief agencies treated the housing loss as nonexistent.[84]

FEMA reinterpreted the shared household rule to accommodate dispersal, extended families, and shared homes in September 2005, yet complaints about the rule's continued application abounded. One might never have received a utility bill nor have had a lease. The shared household rule was suspended, but people had to find a way to document their lives. In exchange for payments, state clients and citizens are drawn into state-mapped categories, applying categories concerning how one lived backwards in time to a life that might have been lived more ambiguously.[85]

For example, in Colorado, volunteers and state workers who worked on intake of evacuees remembered people who had all given the same address in New Orleans, an address that was only a small apartment and was unlikely to have housed all the people who claimed it at once. As workers gathered from stories, people had shared the rent on an inexpensive apartment that they used occasionally for bathing or sleeping, whether in shifts or on nights they were not sleeping on the streets. Others tried to live under the radar of the state in Louisiana: one man who had resettled in Colorado had lived with his girlfriend, whose last name he did not know and with whom he had not evacuated. He was not on her lease or any other documentation; neither he nor she wanted him to be held responsible as a stepparent for her children. Were people who lived in such ambiguous circumstances entitled to benefits as people who had lost a home? Or did they not have a home to lose but needed to get a disaster voucher? Although disaster vouchers entitled one to public housing and disaster victims are often placed at the top of the waiting list for housing, placing people there is a matter of local choice. That choice need not have extended to victims of a disaster in another part of the country.

A person is designated the head of household and eligible for benefits when she or he files a claim; people from the same household who file later will be denied because the head of the household had already received the money. It is administratively convenient to organize groups of people into households, with one point of contact for officials, yet paying one householder and assuming that he or she will share resources presumes a commonality of interests that may not exist. People sometimes live together because it is easier than anything else: we house adult children because they need the help and perhaps they can help around the house or with an ill family member. We house mentally ill family members or close friends who work off and on because we can't see an alternative. The people living together may barely tolerate each other, or only tolerate each other for short periods; a federal check to one may provide a way to leave, and asking to share it may be just too much. In addition, it may be that people sharing space actually did form a shared household, but it could be impossible to keep people together after a disaster.

In sum, three kinds of problems were clear in treating a group of people as a household with one head. First, people might have shared living quarters without having shared expenses regularly. Second, people might have shared expenses and been one household before the disaster, and ordinary legal procedure would mean that they were a household afterwards as well. They might, however, have been separated because one person chose not to evacuate and another did, or because they fled to different places whether through forcible evacuation, spreading the burden among different friends and family or responding to different job opportunities. Finally, families that were not households before a disaster could gather together afterward.

The attorneys in *McWaters* collected stories before filing their complaint. Some illustrated the difficulties with demarcating households. One plaintiff, Mr. Billy Smith, is described in the complaint: "He rented a room in a building where six other men also lived and shared a phone number. On September 2, 2005, Mr. Smith applied with FEMA for Temporary Housing Assistance. The FEMA worker told him that his application would be frozen because someone else had applied for benefits with the same [phone] number."[86] Individuals have family homes that not only allow one to exclude others who are not part of the family; single-family homes each must have a separate phone.

McWaters also included Davis as a plaintiff. He lived with his mother, and his brother "was living with them on and off, but when they evacuated they lost touch." Even months later, Davis did not know where his brother was. Davis was turned down for assistance because his brother had applied. According to the shared household rule, families do not separate after disaster, or, if they do, they must bear the cost of doing so. If that rule makes anything other than fiscal sense, it depends on believing that families cannot separate after disaster because families consist of adults who care for dependents and the dependents who require that care. The rule depends on there not being choice for any members of the household, whether in evacuating or deciding where to live. Alternatively, it requires that household members not exercise those choices separately. It requires helplessness, which is recognizable from other means-tested programs and indeed the homelessness litigation. The deserving homeless are those who have exercised no choice.[87] The rule also depends on there being housing for family members who do evacuate together and a process of evacuation that is more orderly and shorter term than what happened after Katrina.

FEMA explained in *McWaters* that although it had sent out a memo reinterpreting the shared household rule for Katrina, the automated computer system kicked out an applicant if someone else had filed from the same address. The plaintiffs argued that it was useless to have a policy if no one knew of it; FEMA issued a press release waiving the rule again at the end of November 2005.

Months later, in May 2006, *Watson* was filed. That complaint also listed people who had been denied benefits based on FEMA's shared household rule. The examples reveal how we tell stories in court about responsibility.

Mr. and Mrs. Hughes lived together in a rental house. Mr. Hughes was disabled. As a result, Mrs. Hughes's son, Mr. Taylor, occasionally lived with his mother. He cosigned on her lease. After they evacuated, Mr. Taylor moved back to Louisiana to work on the oil rigs. Mrs. Hughes was denied assistance from FEMA because she had shared her home with her son. FEMA told her that she needed to prove that she was the head of household.

The Mitchell family consisted of Mr. Mitchell and his three children. They had lived with his mother in New Orleans. He had worked in New Orleans. When he evacuated with his children before the storm hit, she did not. She was forcibly evacuated after the storm to Tennessee, and she filed for assistance from FEMA. Mr. Mitchell and his children were in Houston, far from his mother, and FEMA denied his claim because his mother had already claimed funds.

The stories told in the courts are of innocence and a lack of choice: families share resources and caretaking, and through no fault of their own were split after the hurricane. We don't know other ways to tell the stories the court saw: whether Mrs. Hughes supported her son's collecting benefits or whether they saw themselves as competing for money. There are other stories told by advocates: married couples who split, each collected funds, and accused the other of fraud; men who did not want to live with their adult daughters; boyfriends who absconded with funds after having been declared the head of household. Being deserving requires telling stories of lack of choice, or having made responsible choices, and family members do not cheat each other.

While the upper reaches of FEMA reinterpreted the shared household rule, case-level decision makers applied it in some cases; how many is impossible to know. It is also impossible to know how many times FEMA inappropriately ignored the rule where people did share a home and expenses both before and after Katrina. The latter would be caught by the audits FEMA began to do as it tried to recoup funds after December

2006. The cases in which it had applied the rule inappropriately would be caught only if someone appealed, placing the burden on the citizen rather than the agency.

Revising the shared household rule was a crusade for advocates who had dealt with FEMA in previous disasters, including the Loma Prieta earthquake in California and Hurricane Andrew in Florida. The Public Interest Law Project (PILP) based in Oakland, which participated in post-Katrina litigation, had written petitions to FEMA long before Katrina. Stephen Ronfeldt from PILP had become involved in disaster work because of Loma Prieta. In a petition submitted a year and a half after the earthquake, the advocates explained: "If two families were sharing an apartment, and the families did not relocate to the same unit after the earthquake, then IFGP [the California program under the federal Stafford Act] would only provide for the personal property needs of one of the families. . . . Even if the two families had two complete sets of furniture in one household, IFGP would only give one family an award."[88] Nothing marking a household tells us how to distinguish fraud, identified by multiple applications using one address or phone number, from the strategies that make it possible to live on low wages and public assistance. If FEMA wanted to try to recoup money, preventing recoupment could require advocacy for each person.

By December of 2006, FEMA had begun recoupment procedures against people it had determined were not eligible for assistance. The public stories of fraud had concerned blatant fraud, including prisoners who had claimed money. FEMA looked collectively stupid and incapable of administering a program, bringing it even further into scrutiny both in the press and from the Government Accountability Office (GAO). Those who claimed housing assistance looked like scammers; GAO reports, in turn, provided material for news stories that was easy to use. None of it did anything to increase the sympathy for those claiming housing assistance.[89] Legal aid attorneys saw recoupment as part of FEMA's response to continued criticism for its ready distribution of assistance and its inability to check identities. The public stories concerned prisoners, nonexistent addresses, and checks spent on champagne or football tickets.[90] The stories legal aid attorneys had included continued application of the shared household rule, where FEMA just didn't understand the "unusual living circumstances" of people in Louisiana. In addition, giving people expedited checks without checking documentation first allowed for many mistakes. FEMA could make errors of both under- and overinclusiveness, enraging both those who saw public money wasted and those who believed they deserved payment but would have to pay it back. The publicly told story of clear fraud stood for the less publicly acknowledged one of ambiguity concerning who had a home, who shared one, and how one documented where one lived. The appeal process against recoupment also provided a way of spreading the word that FEMA had waived its shared household rule, which some legal aid attorneys did not believe all FEMA case-level decision makers knew. Policymaking is diffused and dispersed, much of it well beyond public discussion, and restrictions can appear as much in rule application as in new legislation.

Conclusion

Governance after Katrina brought a proliferation of exceptions to rules and expansion of the state via decision making rather than via norm expansion. The extension of housing payments was incoherent, difficult to follow, and unpredictable. We could then conclude that this is how an administrative state treats poor people, particularly those who are imagined to be exclusively African American. This critique emerged immediately after the storm. Both elements—the generosity and the Kafkaesque impossibility of policy—were embedded in the multiple agencies of the state.

The advocates for low-income housing and the federal courts allowed the administration of relief after disaster to be brought into the administrative due process order. It was never done as a matter of principle, though; the concessions FEMA made allowed it to claim legitimacy under existing norms before the professional legal community and in the face of extensive criticism, whereas the courts never actually set a precedent requiring any procedure or abandoning. Concessions, orders, and disaster-specific guidances allowed multiple norms to persist alongside one another: the state offered housing relief, but it policed fraud and protected budgets. The rules still stood: FEMA could continue to maintain that no law required it provide any due process to claimants, and the shared household rule remained to be deployed or not in later disasters. In relief, little was resolved as a matter of principle. The courts provided some cover for the bureaucracy, widely attacked as incompetent and overwhelmed by more cases than it had ever designed its system to handle, bringing the exception to the state. The judges made very limited orders; victories came from delay and concessions FEMA made in the course of litigation.

Despite disaster being "not your fault," individual assistance in the United States is means-tested relief embedded in a system that rests on private insurance, and the orders from courts are consistent with how means-tested programs have been treated in court.[91] The courts were reluctant to order FEMA to spend money, and the orders that judges did make were overturned on appeal. Although the Katrina disaster provided opportunity to advocates for low-income people, they were advocates within courts unlikely to order vast expansions of funding. Furthermore, the ongoing contest between FEMA, the courts, and advocates concerning what constitutes a household worthy of relief reveals one more place that the legibility state benefits require mismatches the ambiguity of how people live; broad definitions of documentation when cases were appealed made the reality fit the rules.

McWaters, Watson, and *ACORN* resulted in settlement agreements or concessions that FEMA made, not from any orders from appellate courts. Clients gained time with housing assistance while judges rebuked FEMA. Even the concessions—the application of the shared household rule or not requiring certification concerning how money was spent—still came back when FEMA returned to consider fraudulent payments. To answer concerns about fraud, people had to document their lives in a way that FEMA had sometimes already waived. Although the courts were reluctant to make extensive orders against FEMA, those who might have been homeless without assistance after Katrina were able to get into court and gain due process hearings when those homeless outside disaster relief would not have. Litigation and concessions in a climate of skepticism about public assistance and contempt for FEMA extended relief without requiring any institution to address in principle what people deserve after disaster and why, or what a disaster is and when it ends. Though the numbers of claimants dwindled over time, unemployment remained high, so it is unlikely people did not need assistance. The Bush administration extended the program into the next administration, and the Obama administration decided to continue rental assistance for the 31,000 people still claiming it in February of 2009.[92] The catastrophic state blurred into the welfare state, with a disaster defined as ending and renewing again and again.

NOTES

This research was supported by NSF SGER grant #0555117, the University of Denver's Public Good fund, and its Rosenberry fund. I am grateful to Jennifer Reich and to Austin Sarat and the participants in the Amherst Conference on Catastrophe in Science and Law for comments on earlier drafts as well as to reviewers for this book manuscript. I am also grateful to those who spoke to me about their work and to the publicly accessible conference calls sponsored by the National Low Income Housing Coalition.

Epigraph: Andrei Codrescu, "After the Deluge: Letter to America," in *New Orleans, Mon Amour* (Chapel Hill, NC: Algonquin Books of Chapel Hill, 2006), 271–72.

1. Jill Quadagno, *The Color of Welfare: How Racism Undermined the War on Poverty* (New York: Oxford University Press, 1996).

2. Spike Lee, *When the Levees Broke* (New York: HBO Home Video, 2006), DVD.

3. Shaila Dawan, "Hurricane Assistance Is Extended for Some," *New York Times,* July 24, 2007, A20.

4. Edward Rubin, *Beyond Sovereignty* (Princeton, NJ: Princeton University Press, 2005); James Scott, *Seeing Like a State: How Certain Plans to Improve the Human Condition Have Failed* (New Haven, CT: Yale University Press, 1998).

5. Bruno Latour, *Reassembling the Social: An Introduction to Actor-Network Theory* (New York: Oxford University Press, 2005).

6. Latour, *Reassembling the Social,* 81.

7. Walter Kalin, "A Human Rights Perspective for Major Natural Disasters," Brookings Institution, www.brookings.edu/speeches/2008/0114_disasters_kalin.

8. Adi Ophir, "The Two-State Solution: Providence and Catastrophe," *Journal of Homeland Security and Emergency Management* (Berkeley Electronic Press) 4, no. 1 (2007): 1–44.

9. Giorgio Agamben, *State of Exception,* trans. Kevin Attell (Chicago: University of Chicago Press, 2005), 35.

10. Donald F. Kettl, *System under Stress: Homeland Security and American Politics* (Washington, DC: CQ Press, 2007).

11. Naomi Klein, *The Shock Doctrine: The Rise of Disaster Capitalism* (New York: Picador, 2008).

12. Ophir, "The Two-State Solution," 3.

13. Ophir, "The Two-State Solution," 19; Lawrence Friedman, Total Justice (New York: Russell Sage Foundation, 1994).

14. Lawrence Douglas, Austin Sarat, and Martha Merrill Umphrey, "At the Limits of the Law," in The Limits of Law, ed. Austin Sarat, Lawrence Douglas, and Martha Merrill Umphrey (Palo Alto, CA: Stanford University Press, 2005), 17.

15. Ophir, "The Two-State Solution," 10.

16. Ophir, "The Two-State Solution," 18.

17. Agamben, *State of Exception,* 31.

18. Ran Hirschl, *Towards Juristocracy: The Origins and Consequences of the New Constitutionalism* (Cambridge, MA: Harvard University Press, 2004); R. Shep Melnick, *Between the Lines* (Washington, DC: Brookings Institution, 1994).

19. Agamben, *State of Exception,* 37.

20. Ibid., 13–18.

21. Kim Lane Scheppele, "The Anatomy of a State of Emergency" (manuscript in possession of the author, 2007), 32.

22. Ibid., 34.

23. On legal structures as building blocks of organizational myths of rationality, see Lauren B. Edelman and Mark Suchman, "The Legal Environment of Organizations,"

Annual Review of Sociology 23, no. 1 (1997): 479–516; and Lauren B. Edelman, Christopher Uggen, and Howard Erlanger, "The Endogeneity of Legal Regulation: Grievance Procedures as Rational Myth," *American Journal of Sociology* 105, no. 2 (1999): 406–55. The latter work discusses legal structures as adopted by business organizations rather than arms of the state. Signaling compliance could be even more important for arms of the state not wholly brought within the public legal order, however.

24. John M. Barry, Rising Tide: *The Great Mississippi Flood of 1927 and How It Changed America* (New York: Simon and Schuster, 1995).

25. Ophir, "The Two-State Solution," 6.

26. Gary A. Kreps, "Disaster as Systemic Event and Social Catalyst: A Clarification of Subject Matter," *International Journal of Mass Emergencies and Disasters* 13, no. 3 (1995): 255–84.

27. E. L. Quarantelli, "What Is a Disaster?" *International Journal of Mass Emergencies and Disasters* 13, no. 3 (1995): 221–30.

28. Ophir, "The Two-State Solution," 18.

29. Peter Redfield, "Doctors, Borders and Life in Crisis," *Cultural Anthropology* 20, no. 3 (2005): 328–61.

30. Ibid., 38.

31. John W. Meyer and Brian Rowan, "Institutionalized Organizations: Formal Structure as Myth and Ceremony," in *The New Institutionalism in Organizational Analysis*, ed. Walter W. Powell and Paul J. DiMaggio (Chicago: University of Chicago Press, 1991), 43; Scott, *Seeing Like a State*.

32. On paying benefits while also effectively policing fraud, see Peter H. Schuck and Richard J. Zeckhauser, *Targeting in Social Programs: Avoiding Bad Bets, Removing Bad Apples* (Washington, DC: Brookings Institution Press, 2006).

33. Tracing a process of policymaking centering on a substantive problem with multiple actors deciding requires relying on a wide range of data. I have read all publicly available documents concerning the case law, including briefs and court orders and FEMA announcements. In the fall of 2005, the National Low Income Housing Coalition sponsored national conference calls concerning FEMA policy and strategy to deal with it, and some conversations centered on lawsuits. I listened to the conference calls and to training concerning FEMA's claims for recoupment of benefits, offered in December 2006. I also interviewed some of the attorneys involved in the lawsuits. I have also attended meetings where caseworkers assigned to FEMA claimants discussed how to make the rules work for clients, and I have interviewed caseworkers and some longtime FEMA disaster relief specialists.

34. Paul Pierson, "The Costs of Marginalization: Qualitative Methods in the Study of American Politics," *Comparative Political Studies* 40, no. 2 (2007): 154–57.

35. Ibid., 157.

36. Michael Chertoff, "Statement by Homeland Security Secretary Michael Chertoff before the United States House Select Committee on Hurricane Katrina" (Washington, DC: Department of Homeland Security, 2005).

37. United States Census Bureau, "New Orleans Population Continues Katrina Recovery; Houston Leads in Numerical Growth," 2008, www.census.gov/Press-Release/www/releases/archives/population/012242.html.

38. William Frey and Andrew Singer, "Katrina and Rita Impacts on Gulf Coast Populations: First Census Findings" (Washington, DC: Brookings Institution Metropolitan Policy Program, 2006), www.brookings.edu/reports/2006/06demographics_frey.aspx?more=; Louisiana Recovery Authority, 2006 Louisiana Health and Population Survey Expanded Preliminary Results (2006), popest.org/popestla2006/files/PopEst_

Orleans_SurveyReport.pdf; John Logan, "The Impact of Katrina: Race and Class in Storm-Damaged Neighborhoods," www.s4.brown.edu/Katrina/index.html; Adam Nossiter, "New Orleans of Future May Stay Half Its Old Size," *New York Times*, January 21, 2007, A1.

39. Bill Quigley, "Half New Orleans Poor Permanently Displaced: Failure or Success?" *Facing South*, March 3, 2008, southernstudies.org/2008/03/half-new-orleans-poor-permanently.html; Klein, *The Shock Doctrine*.

40. Tom Baker and Karen McElrath, "Whose Safety Net? Home Insurance and Inequality," *Law and Social Inquiry* 21, no. 2 (1996): 229–62.

41. Susan Sterett, *Public Pensions: Gender and Civic Service, 1850s–1937* (Ithaca, NY: Cornell University Press, 2003).

42. Jacob S. Hacker, *The Great Risk Shift: The New Economic Insecurity and the Decline of the American Dream* (New York: Oxford University Press, 2008); Jonathan Simon, "Wake of the Flood: Crime, Disaster, and the American Risk Imaginary after Katrina," in *Issues in Legal Scholarship: Catastrophic Risks: Prevention, Compensation, and Recovery* (Berkeley Electronic Press, 2007), www.bepress.com/ils/iss10/art4/.

43. Dan Eggen and Carol D. Leonnig, "Jackson Resigns as HUD Secretary," *Washington Post*, April 1, 2008, A1.

44. FEMA, "Katrina and Rita (DR-1603-DR-1607) Direct and Financial Housing Assistance Breakdown as of 01/26/07" (2007), www.fema.gov.

45. See, e.g., George Lipsitz, "Learning from New Orleans: The Social Warrant of Hostile Privatism and Competitive Consumer Citizenship," *Cultural Anthropology* 21, no. 3 (2006): 451–68.

46. Andrei Codrescu, "New Orleans or Baghdad?" in *New Orleans, Mon Amour* (Chapel Hill, NC: Algonquin Books of Chapel Hill, 2006), 269–70; Henry Jenkins, "'People from That Part of the World': The Politics of Dislocations," *Cultural Anthropology* 21, no. 3 (2006): 469–86.

47. Stafford Act 42 U.S.C. secs. 5121 et seq.

48. Ibid.

49. Ibid.

50. Sheila Crowley, "Where Is Home? Housing for Low-Income People after the 2005 Hurricanes," in *There Is No Such Thing as a Natural Disaster*, ed. Chester Hartman and Gregory D. Squires (New York: Routledge, 2006); *Watson v. FEMA*, Civil Action No. H-06-1709, order, complaint, briefs, decision on appeal (No. 06-20651), www.femaanswers.org.

51. Stafford Act. 42 U.S.C. sec. 5174.

52. Crowley, "Where Is Home?"

53. Baker and McElrath, "Whose Safety Net?"

54. For an excellent overview of insurance as the primary mode of relief and the requirement that homeowners carry insurance, see Baker and McElrath, "Whose Safety Net?"

55. Government Accountability Office, "Unprecedented Challenges Exposed the Individuals and Households Program to Fraud and Abuse; Actions Needed to Reduce Such Problems in Future," GAO-06-1013 (Washington, DC: GAO, September 2006).

56. Annelise Riles, ed., *Documents: Artifacts of Modern Knowledge* (Ann Arbor: University of Michigan Press, 2006); Kamal Sadiq, "When States Prefer Non-Citizens over Citizens: Conflict over Illegal Immigration into Malaysia," *International Studies Quarterly* 49 (2005): 101–22; Barbara Yngvesson and Susan Bibler Coutin, "Backed by Papers: Undoing Persons, Histories, and Return," *American Ethnologist* 33, no. 2 (2006): 177–90.

57. Didier Fassin and Estelle D'Halluin, "The Truth from the Body: Medical Certificates as Ultimate Evidence for Asylum Seekers," *American Anthropologist* 107, no. 4 (2005): 597–608.

58. Kim Fortun in this collection also explains deployments of law that enable people to be active citizens rather than passive subjects. After Katrina, Wiki technology and e-mail lists that allowed advocates to post and to find information about changes in policy enabled advocates and caseworkers. See www.femaanswers.org. Clients may have found this website more difficult to use.

59. See, for example, *Goldberg v. Kelly*, 1970. For a discussion of these cases in court, see Susan Lawrence, *Poor People in Court* (Princeton, NJ: Princeton University Press, 1990).

60. *McWaters v. FEMA*, 2005, Civil Action No. 05-5488, order, complaint, briefs, www.femaanswers.org.

61. Klein, *The Shock Doctrine*; Kevin Rozario, *The Culture of Calamity: Disaster and the Making of Modern America* (Chicago: University of Chicago Press, 2007).

62. Bruce Springsteen, "How Can a Poor Man Stand Such Times and Live?" YouTube, www.youtube.com/watch?v=jYsSVNl8xmE.

63. I explore contests over the shared household rule in greater detail below.

64. On instantiation and norms as allowing the emergence of "not law" in exception, see Agamben, *State of Exception*, 32–35.

65. Eric Lipton, "Study Finds Huge Fraud in the Wake of Hurricanes," *New York Times*, June 14, 2006, A1.

66. FEMA, "Extended Families Living Together May Be Eligible for FEMA Disaster Assistance," September 19, 2005. www.fema.gov / news / newsrelease_print.fema?id= 20868.

67. Ibid.

68. *McWaters v. FEMA*, Order. Spike Lee's film *When the Levees Broke* vividly pointed out the possibility of people losing housing assistance just before Christmas (Act 3).

69. *Watson v. FEMA*, Order, 4.

70. Judge Duval also presided over the class action suit concerning the inaccessibility of FEMA trailers for those with federally defined disabilities; that case reached a settlement in September 2006 (*Brou v. FEMA* Class Action Complaint, www.femaanswers. org). *Brou* concerned direct housing rather than rental assistance, so it was not for people displaced far from Louisiana.

71. Bruce Nichols, "Houston Mayor a Governor?" *Dallas Morning News*, December 4, 2005; Cheryl Smith, "Stalling FEMA," *Austin Chronicle*, May 26, 2006, www.austinchronicle.com/gyrobase/Issue/story?oid=oid%3A368478; Mike Snyder, "Cut-Off Families Sue FEMA," *Houston Chronicle*, May 27, 2006, www.chron.com/disp/story.mpl/ special/05/katrina/3874016.html.

72. *Watson v. FEMA*.

73. Ibid.; "Houston Inspectors Differ with FEMA," *Houston Chronicle*, April 15, 2006, A1.

74. *Watson v. FEMA*.

75. Ibid.

76. R. Shep Melnick, "Courts and Agencies" (2003), www.bc.edu/schools/cas/polisci/ facstaff/melnick.html.

77. "Kafka and Katrina," *New York Times*, December 2, 2006, 14.

78. "Judge Chastises FEMA as Botching Katrina Housing Program," *New York Times*, December 14, 2006, 35.

79. "Public Citizen Dismisses FEMA Lawsuit after Securing Relief for Victims of Hur-

ricanes Katrina and Rita," *Public Citizen* (January 31, 2007), www.citizen.org/pressroom/release.cfm?ID=2372.

80. Martha E. Wadsworth, Cate D. Santiago, and Lindsey Einhorn, "Coping with Displacement from Hurricane Katrina: Predictors of One-Year Post Traumatic Stress and Depression Symptom Trajectories," *Anxiety, Stress, and Coping* 22, no. 4 (2009): 413–32.

81. *Ridgely v. FEMA*, Civil Action No. 07-2146, www.femaanwers.org.

82. Leonard Feldman, *Citizens without Shelter* (Chicago: University of Chicago Press, 2004), 110–18.

83. Christopher Jencks, *The Homeless* (Chicago: University of Chicago Press, 1995).

84. State of California Office of Emergency Services and State of California Individual and Family Grant Program, "Petition to Federal Emergency Management Agency, The Continuing Disaster: Disaster Relief Agencies Fail Low Income Earthquake Victims" (1991), www.pilp.org.

85. Scott, *Seeing Like a State.*

86. *McWaters v. FEMA*, Order, 12.

87. Feldman, *Citizens without Shelter.*

88. State of California Office of Emergency Services and State of California Individual and Family Grant Program, "Petition to Federal Emergency Management Agency," 9–10.

89. Government Accountability Office, "Improper and Potentially Fraudulent Individual Assistant Payments Estimated to Be Between $600 Million and $1.4 Billion," GAO-06-844T (Washington, DC: GAO, June 2006); Government Accountability Office, "Unprecedented Challenges"; Government Accountability Office, "Continued Findings of Fraud, Waste, and Abuse," GAO-07-252T (Washington, DC: GAO, December 2006); Lipton, "Study Finds Huge Fraud in the Wake of Hurricanes."

90. Lipton, "Study Finds Huge Fraud in the Wake of Hurricanes."

91. Melnick, *Between the Lines*, 280–83.

92. "Some Sense, at Last, about Katrina," *New York Times*, February 12, 2009. A34.

4

Emergency Management and the Courts in the Wake of Hurricane Katrina

Thomas A. Birkland

This essay describes emergency management issues facing the courts, with a particular emphasis on the generally poor response to Hurricane Katrina by the courts in New Orleans (Orleans Parish), Louisiana. A broader purpose is to examine this failure through the lens provided by more than fifty years of research on human behavior in natural disasters. Particularly since the attacks of September 11, 2001, and continuing to the aftermath of Hurricane Katrina, a considerable body of literature on disasters has been developed and published by nonexperts. Much of their findings and advice are naïve, ungrounded in theory or evidence beyond one or two cases and disconnected from the research that preceded it. Hurricane Katrina has also caused many very talented natural and social scientists to study the broad range of disaster issues, from the reasons the floodwalls along the canals failed, to understanding the physical and mental health aspects of disasters, to understanding the sociopolitical, economic, and institutional reasons for the failure of New Orleans, the state of Louisiana, and the U.S. government to respond effectively to this disaster. It therefore worthwhile to approach the question of the collapse of the New Orleans courts from this "hazards research" perspective. Failure to do so will result in the continued propagation of myths and false-hoods about disasters in general and Katrina in particular.

A key reason for the destruction wrought by Hurricane Katrina is the failure to mitigate the effects of the storm: the levees were not properly de-signed and constructed to withstand the storm surge Katrina generated,[1] and the city and state had limited capacity, as matters of law, politics, or leadership, to take preventative steps before Katrina to minimize the ef-fects of such a disaster. The federal government had largely abandoned its efforts to improve hazard mitigation and response in favor of a near single-minded focus on "domestic terrorism" or "homeland security," thereby reducing the federal government's effectiveness in natural disasters to pre-1992 levels; in 1992, Hurricane Andrew was the debacle that induced the federal government to put professionals, not political appointees, in charge of sound disaster management and policy advice. Thus, a running theme is that the failures of the New Orleans courts to effectively prepare for and respond to Hurricane Katrina are reflective of the broader lack of capacity and commitment in the region: capacity to effectively plan for a storm and the commitment to actually practice and then carry out the plans. The outcome of Katrina also reflects the federal government's return of the Federal Emergency Management Agency (FEMA) to a civil defense organization, away from the organization it became during the 1990s, when it focused on disaster mitigation and effective relief aid.

An Overview of Disaster Research

The study of natural hazards and disasters, and the interrelation between natural disasters and national security disasters as fields for study, dates to well before World War II. Of particular interest to social science are two major questions: how do people and groups behave in the face of an impending or actual disaster, and how do communities increase or decrease their vulnerability to natural hazards?[2] Within these broad questions have come many questions, including what kind of policy tools governments can adopt to mitigate hazards,[3] what sort of relief schemes should be developed to compensate people for their losses after disasters,[4] how do people alter their physical environment to increase or decrease disaster vulnerability, and what measures can be taken to reduce vulnerability[5]?

Many of these key questions stem from pioneering work in sociology and geography, the two major disciplinary wellsprings of disaster research. The sociological strand can be dated to 1920, with the publication of Samuel Henry Prince's[6] research on the community response to the 1917 explosion of an ammunition ship, the *Mont Blanc*, which destroyed nearly the entire north end of Halifax, Nova Scotia. Prince found that the initial psychological shock and the physical damage of the event was mitigated by the emergent organization of community effort to take care of the injured, fight fires, assess damage, and plan recovery. Sociological case studies of natural disasters become more important during and after World War II. Much of this research was driven by interest in the results of the Strategic Bombing Surveys and the implications of that research: residents of bombed cities were remarkably resilient, despite heavy bombing of those cities. These findings were considered in nuclear war planning.

Sociological research gained momentum in the early 1960s, when E. L. (Henry) Quarantelli and Russell Dynes founded the Disaster Research Center (DRC) at the Ohio State University. The DRC played a major role in the studies of the effect of the Good Friday earthquake in Alaska in March 1964. This earthquake devastated south central Alaska, killing 114 people as a result of the earthquake and its tsunami. This earthquake led to a series of reports sponsored by the National Academy of Sciences on the physical, engineering, and social aspects of the disaster[7] in which the DRC played a prominent role not only in the research itself, but in the training of some of the most senior and respected students of disasters.

Gilbert H. White was key figure in geography during this period. His influence on disaster studies started with his doctoral dissertation "Human Adjustment to Floods,"[8] a then-heterodox argument that people should work *with* nature to reduce social vulnerability to floods while ensuring that flood-dependent ecological systems could thrive. White's argument is now orthodox among most floodplain managers and among river ecologists, but not all his ideas have been translated into policy.[9]

Other disciplines have become more involved in disaster studies. Economists study aspects of public policy such as disaster relief and hazard mitigation to determine whether and to what extent policies encourage or discourage development in hazard areas, and whether and to what extent insurance influences individual risk decisions.[10] Economists also seek to understand the actual economic damage done by disasters. Planners seek to understand how to shape the development of communities in a way that balances economic development, quality of life, and hazard mitigation.[11] Social psychologists seek to understand what drives individuals to make decisions about where to build homes and businesses; of particular importance is their work on how people make decisions about whether and how to evacuate in the wake of an impending disaster.[12]

Public administration, public policy, and political science are also represented in academic studies of the politics of disasters and disaster policymaking.[13] Law professors, on the other hand, are not deeply engaged in the broader study of disaster. Disasters will trigger commentary in the legal press about various legal duties or powers of government or about criminal justice and civil causes of action after disasters. Particular concerns that arise in law and in public policy immediately after disasters include the possibility of increasing crime, looting, civil disorder, and price gouging, and, on the civil side, bankruptcies, insurance disputes, and business disputes, particularly when overtaxed or fraudulent contractors fail to provide proper services to consumers.

One area of social science and legal scholarship that has gained some attention is the functioning of the criminal and civil justice systems in general in the wake of a natural disaster. In many ways, the management of the judicial system is not greatly different than the continued management of what in the jargon is known as "mission critical" functions of other government and private-sector organizations. Effective plans, drills and training, system of communication, visible leadership, and continuity of business planning are important aspects of crisis and disaster planning for any public-sector organization, regardless of the branch of government.

These arguments are made consistently in the small but growing literature on emergency planning in the courts[14] as well as other prescriptive literature for communities and institutions. Case studies of successes and failures in planning for, responding to, recovering from, and mitigating disasters abound. In addition, at least two reports and one firsthand account conclude that such efforts paid dividends in the New York State courts' ability to rebound fairly quickly from the September 11 terrorist attacks, which considerably disrupted judicial activity, in both the courtroom and in managers' offices, for days and weeks after the attack.[15] This accumulated experience—including the management of courts after the 1989 Loma Prieta earthquake, the 1997 Red River floods, and the 1995 bombing of the Alfred P. Murrah Federal Building in Oklahoma City—was shared at the September 11 summit in September 2002, a remarkable gathering of some of the most serious, experienced, and committed court managers and judges in the nation.[16]

Despite this accumulation of knowledge, and the well-known hurricane hazard in New Orleans, the courts in New Orleans were unprepared for Hurricane Katrina. They were closed for months, and, on top of pre-existing backlogs, major case backlogs accumulated in both the criminal and civil courts. The failure, in particular, of the criminal justice system as a whole—the police, the jail, and the criminal courts—led to actual or probable miscarriages of justice. The federal courts, by contrast, were better prepared, having, it appears, learned important lessons from the

September 11 attacks and the attack on the Murrah Federal Building in
Oklahoma City in 1995.

It may be too late to ask the question, how did this happen? with respect to the New Orleans courts. Instead, it is instructive to consider what
happened as well as whether and to what extent the New Orleans courts
followed what have come to be known as best practices in judicial management in Katrina. Even though the analysis here contains implicit and
explicit comparisons between the Katrina and September 11 cases, a direct
comparison between the World Trade Center (WTC) attack and Hurricane
Katrina may not be entirely apt, however. The September 11 attacks on
New York can be said to have been a *disaster*, whereas Hurricane Katrina
is a *catastrophe* from which the affected areas have yet to recover. The differences between a disaster and a catastrophe include the spatial extent of
the disaster and the resources that a state or local government can bring
to bear in relief and recovery.[17] Thus, the WTC attacks were shocking and
horrifying, but they directly affected a relatively small area, and the city
and state of New York were able to effectively respond with their own
resources. The federal government's role in the response was limited and
did not attract much immediate controversy.[18] By contract, Hurricane Katrina struck a city with long-standing problems, including a marginally
functional city government; an understaffed, underfunded, and often corrupt police department; substantial crime problems; and an inefficient
court system that had not, even in one of the most hurricane-prone areas
in the nation, prepared an effective emergency plan. All this occurs in a
city that was demonstrably not resilient—that is, was not able to quickly
"bounce back"—after a storm that flooded 80 percent of the city and that
rendered other nearby communities and the state unable to provide aid.
Overall, the history of corruption, inefficient government, and the "laissez
les bon temps roulez" attitude for which the city is best known has made
New Orleans one of the most poorly managed cities in the nation even
before Katrina. Although the state of Louisiana, according to the Government Performance Project at Syracuse University, is reasonably well managed, the state's attention to infrastructure—the very system that must
be robust during a storm—has not been sufficient. "Louisiana's attitude
toward keeping up its physical assets over the years can best be described
as determinedly negligent."[19] This was before Hurricane Katrina; the situation is likely worse since then as a resource strapped state must address
significant and rapidly growing needs.

Lessons and Prescriptions between September 11 and Katrina

September 11 and events that predate that disaster have led to a considerable amount of advice for court managers. A review of several representative documents[20] finds remarkable commonalities.

Leadership

As the National Center for State Courts notes, "The court's leaders set the tone for effective emergency management."[21] As Oren Root notes, "The type of leadership structure in place at the time of a crisis can influence the performance of an organization during a period when its regular mode of operation is disrupted."[22] Following September 11, the United States Fifth Circuit held an emergency planning workshop at the request of Chief Judge Carolyn Dineen King to consider the threats to and the safety of those who work and frequent the circuit's courthouses. The Fifth Circuit was the first of thirteen federal courts of appeals to take this step to gauge its emergency preparedness,[23] which paid considerable benefits after Hurricane Katrina.

Predisaster leadership in emergency planning and management is not evident in Louisiana. The state Supreme Court had been "encouraging" such disaster planning for the lower courts after Katrina. To its credit, the Fifth Circuit court had already begun doing continuity of operations planning and was able to use some of the knowledge gained in the not-yet-completed effort to manage the Katrina crisis. In addition, the court has learned "lessons" from Katrina that have translated into concrete actions, such as having back-up computers at the ready and having easily accessible information about the court's personnel.[24] But the Supreme Court was further ahead in this planning, and the trial courts, in particular, lagged far behind the Supreme Court in its preparedness, as Katrina laid bare. Of course, hurricanes are the major hazard confronting Louisiana, and one cannot say that they are completely unexpected, particularly considering they strike within a reasonably well-defined hurricane "season." This fact makes the lack of planning at the local level particularly troubling.

Louisiana's trial courts and its appellate courts did seek to recover through the hard work and improvisation skills of its managers and staff. The clerks of court and their staffs took major leadership roles in a wide range of activities, from working with the information technology staff to ensure that critical computers were recovered from buildings, to ensuring that payroll systems were in place, to finding court personnel and assessing their safety and ability to come to work. The Supreme Court of Louisiana does not have direct managerial control over the district courts and the parish courts, however, and could only recommend emergency plans; it could not compel the courts to plan. Leadership and improvisation were further hampered by the catastrophic nature of the hurricane, which made communication among and between courts very difficult. Unlike the process after September 11, the Louisiana Supreme Court issued blanket orders extending deadlines, and considering the damage both to bench and bar, these orders are probably sensible. The New York courts, by contrast, would only issue continuances on a case-by-case basis, while simultaneously assisting the 1,300 attorneys whose offices were in the WTC and its environs to reconstruct their files. Of course, the New York courts were not as badly damaged in as large an area as were the Louisiana courts, so the New York courts faced fewer challenges in restoration of its own records and other functions.

Priorities

A key aspect of leadership is setting priorities. Given limited resources, the courts and their managers cannot possibly plan for every possible threat. The courts must prioritize their emergency management needs based on the most likely and the most injurious events that could influence the administration of justice. Many emergency management experts emphasize the "all-hazards" approach to planning for, mitigating, preparing for, and recovering from any human, natural, or terrorist disaster. Proponents of all-hazards planning suggest that planning for one kind of natural disaster builds capacity and capability to address a range of natural disasters as well as terrorism. Most local organizations, such as cities or court systems, also pay special attention to the most likely disaster that could befall a court (a hurricane or a hurricane-induced flood, in New Orleans's case). At the federal level, September 11 shifted a disproportionate amount of attention to terrorism compared with other more likely local hazards.[25] This lopsided attention to terrorism to the exclusion of other hazards was amply demonstrated by the fumbling responses to Hurricane Katrina at both the federal and state levels. Ultimately, court leaders need to find an efficient way to address the most likely hazards without leaving them vulnerable to a less likely but still foreseeable disaster.

Plans

Plans are often criticized as being static or rote exercises, but the process of planning is as important, if not more so, than the actual planning document itself. Thus, many of the guidance documents for emergency planning are small: New York's is twenty pages, with seventy pages of practical, fill-in-the-blanks forms that people can use to customize their plans. Wisconsin's guidance document is nearly as short, but outlines the considerations that courts should address during planning. In addition, organizations such as the Institute for Building and Home Safety and FEMA publish similar templates and guidance for emergency planning that is well suited to any kind of organization, although courts must modify these more generic documents to meet their needs. Of particular importance to the courts is the safeguarding of records and evidence, information flows to stakeholders such as parties before the court and the public (including jurors), and the fair treatment of prisoners and detainees. Each court must, before a disaster, understand and communicate its own priorities. The New Orleans courts generally failed in this task; the criminal justice system, in particular, almost completely collapsed in New Orleans from both a throughput perspective and, perhaps much more important, from the perspective of procedural fairness, as discussed below.

Communications

Court managers must also be prepared to communicate key information to court employees, the public and to those having business with the courts. Each stakeholder group requires a *different* communications strategy. Most members of the public, for example, do not have an ongoing relationship with the courts and therefore must be reached through the mass media. The court's chief information officer or equivalent should be prepared to provide the mass media with information about court closings, alternative locations, changes in hours, and the like. The importance of this information should be stressed to media representatives, who may not have a good sense of why it is that the courts need to communicate with the public.

Communication with stakeholder groups with an established relationship with the court can readily be maintained. Staff can be reached through a phone-tree system, for example. Attorneys, for example, can be notified of issues relating to practice through the courts and in conjunction with the local bar association. Attorneys, in turn, will notify litigants of changes in their cases' status and schedule. The specialized media serving the bar are particularly important channels for disseminating information on the courts' status, changes in court procedures, and other information that helped the bar understand the courts' efforts to remain in business.

All these communications strategies presume that some communications media and modes remain in place, which was not true in New Orleans after Katrina. Because of the significant damage to the legal community in Louisiana, a communications system was also necessary to communicate with members of the bar. The federal courts, under a special master, established a communications system under a court order issued by Judge Richard Haik of the Western District of Louisiana. This communications center provided a point of contact for the displaced members of the federal bar and provided assistance with, among other things, file reconstruction and reestablishing contact with other displaced counsel. The Louisiana Bar Association opened a business center for displaced lawyers, which provided work space, access to the Internet, meeting rooms, and online legal research tools. This business center was important in helping members of the bar reestablish contact with one another.

Witnesses must also be informed as to the status of the courts. In Louisiana, the Orleans Parish Criminal Court established a toll-free call-in line for grand and petit jurors, attorneys, and witnesses, and another line for defendants, specialty court clients, and those owing fees and fines.

Continuity of Operations

Continuity of operations is an important aspect of management in all levels of government,[26] including the judiciary[27] and the private sector. It is particularly relevant to large firms in sectors such as finance, which learned years ago that a continuity of operations plan (COOP) is important when disaster threatens to slow or halt business. This interest in and implementation of business continuity planning and operations in the private sector is uneven, however, as firms confront the same resistance, uncertainties, and resource constraints as in the public sector.[28] The emergency plan elements outlined above are important parts of COOPs because the COOP creates the conditions for an orderly response to and recovery from a disaster. New York's Office of Court Administration requires that New York City courts file their COOP with the Deputy Chief Administrative Judge for the New York City courts and the Chief of Public Safety.

Although some courts may deem alternative work sites needlessly redundant, experience has shown that natural hazards, in particular, can affect broad areas, so a long distance between the regular and alternative work sites is often the best assurance that the alternative site will be functional. The North Dakota courts learned the importance of having an alternative courthouse after the Red River floods in 1997.[29] Most alternative sites in the Katrina case were based on ad hoc improvisation after the storm and were not preplanned. Preplanning would have ensured that all stakeholders knew where the court would move when the emergency plan was activated and would have promoted justice and efficiency.

Hurricane Katrina as Another Failure of Imagination

It is well known by now that the most familiar aspects of the current national security state—more stringent aviation security as managed by the Transportation Security Administration, the various activities of the Department of Homeland Security (DHS), and even more stringent documentation requirements for Americans traveling to and from Canada and Mexico—largely stem from the September 11 attacks. Of course, one of the major outcomes of the September 11 attacks was the creation of that department. The creation of something like DHS was first proposed by the Hart-Rudman commission (the familiar name for the U.S. Commission on National Security/21st Century) well before President George W. Bush took office. Although the creation of the DHS was supposed to bring under one roof most, if not all, crisis and disaster management expertise and authority in the United States, the department, from its official establishment in 2003 through the present day, has been primarily focused on its antiterrorism mission. This activity is based on an assumption—one that is very badly mistaken, it is clear now—that the major threat to U.S. national security and well-being is September 11–style terrorism. The capacity and morale of FEMA had already begun to decay under Bush, and its demise as an effective emergency support agency was swiftly hastened by the inexpert leadership of two political appointees, first Joe Allbaugh and then Michael Brown. Meanwhile, after September 11, the agency was largely buried in the civil defense function of the DHS. The first secretary of DHS was Tom Ridge, a former governor of Pennsylvania with no obvious emergency management experience. When he retired, Bush sought to appoint former New York Police Department Commissioner Bernard Kerik, but Kerik's personal scandals led Bush to appoint Michael Chertoff, a respected former federal judge and prosecutor, albeit one with little or no emergency management or national security experience.

The September 11 commission described the failure of the nation to adequately detect and prepare for those attacks as a "failure of imagination." Perhaps because of a desire to never again be caught by surprise, the DHS (and other agencies) have focused on outlandish terrorism scenarios while nearly ignoring much more likely natural disasters. The federal response to Hurricane Katrina was therefore undermined. Federal efforts to develop plans for "all hazards" were generally assembled by law enforcement and former military experts, with few if any experts on natural hazards (or modern terrorism) represented in this planning. Indeed, many appointed and career DHS officials disdained FEMA's career staff and substituted their own beliefs and opinions—usually derived from inappropriate analogues to military or law enforcement examples—for those of experienced FEMA staffers. Those beliefs, as earnestly felt as they were, were largely wrong. Much post–September 11 disaster policy has been made based on, or made reinforcing, a set of tenets or beliefs about how individuals and community institutions behave that are often not borne out in the extensive research literature.

A widely held belief is that people "panic" in disasters so that "first responders" must intervene to induce socially functional behavior. More than four decades of disaster research suggest that people do not panic, however; rather, they tend to be reasonably calm, rational, and even prosocial, helping others whose ability to help themselves is limited by injury, frailty, poverty, or other circumstances.[30]

Related to the panic myth is the myth of the helpless victim or would-be victim.[31] Dangerous policies flow from the belief that citizens cannot help themselves. Officials often withhold information based on a belief that victims or would-be victims would misunderstand or misuse risk data, either in real time or over the longer run.[32] Indeed, the considerable secrecy that characterizes post–September 11 homeland security policy is predicated on this very belief: that citizens are helpless and cannot be trusted with risk information.[33] This policy exists notwithstanding years of social science research that suggests that, when presented with sound information, citizens can make informed risk decisions.

In a world of panic and helplessness, the breakdown of social norms cannot but inevitably follow. Officials have thereby accepted the idea that, in the face of a disaster, people and communities move from a functional community to a devastated community in which society becomes a free-for-all, and to entirely new systems of government, of community, and of the rule of law and accompanying order after the disaster. Fortunately, this myth is false. As Kathleen Tierney notes, "As [Cold-War era] studies on public responses in disasters continued, it became increasingly evident to researchers that endangered publics and disaster victims respond and adapt well during and following disasters."[34]

Scientific facts have never prevented the news media from creating their own compelling, if false, story frames in disaster reporting, and these frames are avidly taken up and repeated by government officials. Put simply, the news media *expect* to find helpless citizens, panic, looting, assaults, and other antisocial behaviors. For example, New Orleans Police Chief Eddie Compass tearfully related in a press conference the deteriorating conditions at the Superdome, claiming that babies were being raped, among other atrocities. These tales were false. As Sarah Kauffman notes, newspapers were filled with lurid headlines about violent and property crime.[35] When prosocial behavior is described in news stories—stories of people helping rescue others or of people creating ad hoc aid systems to rescue, feed, clothe, shelter, and otherwise support people in their communities—the news media treat these instances as *exceptions* rather than as the norm. Of course, exceptional behaviors, along with dramatic stories, are key news hooks. The problem, in this case, is that these behaviors are typical of what is found in the immediate postdisaster period. Even later conflicts over whether and how to rebuild are normal conflicts over peoples' sense of what their communities should be like after the disaster; they are not deviations from normal human behavior or from "politics" as understood by political scientists. The danger of these myths, however, is that many elected and appointed officials believe the myth and believe that crime is reduced when the National Guard is sent to "prevent looting" and disorder where it probably would not happen in any case.[36] The result of poor sociology (the belief in civil disorder) results in bad public policy (the deployment of guard units for police duty rather than for recovery work).

Thus, the mirror image of the helpless, panicky, and kleptomanical disaster victim is the heroic "first responder." The September 11 attacks mythologized the first responders' heroic role particularly because, on that day, more than fifty police officers and three hundred firefighters were killed (perhaps needlessly[37]) when the towers collapsed on them and the people they sought to rescue. In popular lore, the first responders are the rescuers, and those at the scene wait helplessly. In fact, the real *first* responders are the people on the scene: the "victims" of the disaster. There is often a range of "victimization" in a disaster, from the fatally wounded to the unwounded or those with only minor injuries.

Even so, as Tierney notes, the DHS has been very generous in its efforts to mythologize both the stalwart first responder and the cowering, ineffectual disaster victim:

> Research conducted under the auspices of agencies such as the DHS Science and Technology Directorate almost completely lacks social science content, concentrating instead on such topics as sensors, equipment, and protective gear for what the agency refers to as "first responders." Social science research has consistently shown that community residents are the true first responders in both disasters and terrorist attacks, but homeland security initiatives ignore the vital role the public plays in disaster response. Instead, as we saw so vividly in Hurricane Katrina, the government's stance is that the public in disaster-ravaged communities mainly represents a problem to be managed—by force, if necessary—and a danger to uniformed responders.[38]

Social scientists must directly confront the ill-informed policies emanating from Washington, particularly when these policies are often crafted by people who themselves have little or no disaster management experience and are unaware of, unfamiliar with, or explicitly disdainful of social science. Managers of all sorts of institutions would also do well to learn from social scientists rather than from the instant experts that have burgeoned since September 11. As discussed below, this disdain for science and for proper preparation led, directly or indirectly, to the failures of key institutions in New Orleans and in Louisiana.

What Happened in Hurricane Katrina

Hurricane Katrina did more than $100 billion in damage and killed more than 1,800 people, making it one of the costliest and most destructive natural disasters in the history of the United States. As noted earlier, Hurricane Katrina was therefore not merely a disaster; it was a catastrophe, the effects of which are still greatly felt more than a year after the storm struck the coast. The primary damage from Hurricane Katrina in New Orleans was due to a strong storm surge—one typically associated with the strongest, or category 5, storms[39]—that came when the hurricane made landfall along the Mississippi-Louisiana border on August 29, 2005. Although it was a strong category 3 storm, one that might do substantial but not catastrophic damage, Hurricane Katrina resulted in a storm surge of up to thirty feet which led, ultimately, to key levee failures in New Orleans and the resulting flooding to more than 80 percent of the city of New Orleans. Some neighborhoods experienced twenty feet of water.

Louisiana's court system as well as the Federal Court of Appeals for the Fifth Circuit were profoundly affected. New Orleans was home to 7,500 attorneys, about one-third of the state's bar. The offices of the Louisiana State Bar Association and the New Orleans Bar Association were flooded. The building housing the Louisiana Supreme Court and the Louisiana Court of Appeals for the Fourth Circuit, on Royal Street in the French Quarter, suffered minor flooding. The main problems for these courts were the buildings' inaccessibility (the city was evacuated, and few people were allowed back in quickly), the lack of utilities (power, in particular), and the effect of the storm on court personnel, all of whom were required to evacuate the city and most of whom suffered their own (often severe) property damage. City and district courts in eight parishes of metropolitan New Orleans were damaged and unusable. Orleans Parish (New Orleans), unlike the rest of Louisiana, has separate criminal and civil district courts, although Hurricane Katrina has led to several efforts to consolidate these into one district court. The district courts handle felony cases and civil cases above the small claims threshold. The Orleans Parish courts—criminal, civil, juvenile, and traffic—handle nonfelony matters and small civil matters. Of the twelve judges on the state Court of Appeals for the Fourth Circuit, nine judges were displaced due to damage to their homes. Still, the court managed to meet once *en banc* in Baton Rouge and resumed operations in Hammond (about sixty miles from downtown New Orleans) in October. In the intervening period, closure orders for the affected courts created legal holidays, thereby extending relevant deadlines. This situation stands in contrast with the New York courts, which extended deadlines and issued continuances on a case-by-case basis only, both to demonstrate the resilience of the court system and to avoid creating a blanket exception for more cases than were necessary. The New York courts aided the bar by making all case documents available to both parties while they sought to reconstruct their records.

After the storm, the civil district court moved to the town of Gonzales[40] and the criminal court moved from its quarters on Tulane Avenue to the Hale Boggs Federal Court Building, which is an a part of the city far less damaged by flooding. The Civil District Court returned to its courthouse in December 2005. The Criminal Court was unable to hold a jury trial until June 2006, and all sections of the court were not able to sit until late October 2006. Before then, a temporary air-conditioning system and other stopgap measures had allowed six and then seven of the thirteen courtrooms to be used at one time.

The Louisiana Supreme Court moved its operations to temporary quarters in Baton Rouge. On October 26, the Louisiana Court of Appeals for the Fourth Circuit moved its operations to the campus of Southeastern Louisiana University in Hammond. The clerk of the Fourth Circuit relocated her home to Lafayette. She was able to borrow space in the law library of the Court of Appeals for the Third Circuit, but still faced a two-hour commute to the court's offices in Hammond.

The federal courts were somewhat better prepared for the storm than were the state courts, in large parts because they had more options for alternative work sites. After the September 11 attacks, the Fifth Circuit Judicial Council met to discuss "terrorism and cyber attacks; chemical, biological and bomb threats; *and the potential of natural disasters*" and to plan for these events.[41] The Court of Appeals for the Fifth Circuit moved its operations to its offices in Houston, where it already had available courtroom space. When federal district courts had to relocate, Congress enacted legislation allowing them to hold court outside their districts. For example, the bankruptcy court for the Eastern District of Louisiana relocated to Baton Rouge, in the Middle District of Louisiana.[42] By November, the federal courts, located in less damaged buildings on higher ground, had begun to return to operation. This relatively quick return reflects the improved capacity of federal courts both to plan for disasters and to implement those plans. The physical damage done by the storm was compounded by the effect of devastation at this scale on New Orleans as a community. Many people had been relocated or had left New Orleans with no clear plan for returning. The storm therefore presented a greater challenge than most court leaders had anticipated. For example:

> For both state and federal courts, the surprising discovery was that the biggest obstacle to gearing up was not court infrastructure as much as finding staff housing and a place to send their children to school.
>
> "We hadn't focused on that but it turns out to be a major consideration," said Chief Judge Carolyn Dineen King of the 5th U.S. Circuit Court of Appeals, from the court's new temporary headquarters in Houston. After the Sept. 11, 2001, terror attacks, federal courts across the country developed contingency operation plans in case of a disaster. King said she learned quickly that the plans did not anticipate that employees would have to move and bring families with them, and also enroll children in school. The original plan called for moving the court to a rural air force base with unused space in Louisiana, but court staff had nowhere to live and no schools nearby, she said.[43]

More than eight thousand prisoners in the Parish "prison" (jail) had to be relocated, a process that was generally handled poorly. Many prisoners were transferred to other facilities out of the region, and misdemeanor or lesser offenders sometimes found themselves in state prisons, with violent offenders. Some prisoners were unable to contact family or friends or to reach legal counsel. In some cases, legal counsel could not find their clients, and prisoners sometimes were incarcerated for longer than they would have otherwise served, such as for traffic violations. Such additional incarceration is ruefully known as "doing Katrina time."[44] In other cases, suspects were released because they had been held too long without charges being filed against them,[45] including one murder suspect.[46] Evidence in approximately three thousand criminal cases pending before the court system was damaged by floodwaters.[47] In interviews, court officials noted that much paper evidence was or is being restored[48] using freeze-drying and other document preservation techniques, and some cases are being tried, often successfully, using "chain of evidence" arguments rather than the actual evidence itself. As well known as the evidentiary problems have become, however, another hindrance to successful prosecutions is that many witnesses and victims have left the city and are difficult to find.

Given New Orleans's poor record of indigent defense, police corruption, and the post-Katrina hardships imposed on incarcerated suspects and detainees, a cynic may find that a crippled criminal justice system in the parish is a potentially good thing. If nothing else, the storm focused attention on problems that existed well before Hurricane Katrina. Before Hurricane Katrina, the public defender's office was poorly funded and poorly led;[49] after the hurricane, the indigent defense system had all but collapsed,[50] due both to the loss of attorneys who evacuated the city (a problem, along with low pay, that also afflicted the district attorney's office) and to the loss of revenue for funding the public defense system from parking ticket revenue and court fees. Meanwhile, the police department, well known to be underpaid, underskilled, and often corrupt before the storm, was crippled by the loss of equipment and personnel during and immediately after the storm.[51]

The Results: Planning and Management Failures

The classic model of disasters suggests that they are very disruptive but that "resilient" communities—that is, communities with the capacity to "bounce back" from disasters—can return, after a fashion, to predisaster functioning. Indeed, some hope that disasters provide opportunities for people to think about improving on the community, yielding improved resilience and lower vulnerability. Thus, in the classic model, a disruption occurs, the community strains to comprehend the disaster and to begin to recover from it, and recovery—driven by prosocial activities of the disaster victims and others in the community and supported by the local, state, and federal government—will begin apace.

That is not what happened after Hurricane Katrina. It cannot be denied that New Orleans has a substantial crime problem, both before and after Hurricane Katrina struck. The claimed outbreak of extreme levels and ferocity of violence in the Superdome and in the Convention Center in the days following Katrina was subsequently found to be grossly exaggerated, however, and the murder rate in Houston only slightly increased, if at all, as a result of Katrina evacuees.[52] On the other hand, what has happened to crime and the overall status of the criminal justice system in New Orleans since Katrina must be critically understood and assessed. This assessment needs to be conducted carefully because Katrina is not the typical disaster in many ways, including the nature and extent of the civil disorder that actually did occur in its aftermath.

At the outset of this analysis, we know that New Orleans city and Orleans Parish were jurisdictions with marginally functional criminal justice systems during normal periods;[53] these systems were then confronted with one of the most damaging events in U.S. history. The question worth asking, then, is to what extent the storm reduced criminal justice capacity in the criminal courts. To assess this question, see figure 4.1. The derivation of this graph, however, should be very cautiously assessed. Uniform Crime Reports (UCR) data posted on the New Orleans Police Department (NOPD) website were used to compute crime rates.[54] The UCR data are the actual number of known offenses, not rates. This difference creates significant challenges for anyone computing crime rates in New Orleans because the selection of a population base to compute them is tricky, at best. Figure 4.1 draws on 2000 census data for 2001 to 2004, a census estimate for 2005, and the Brookings Katrina Index estimate for 2006.[55] To derive a population figure for 2007, the 2006 population was added to the raw population growth of Orleans Parish between June 2006 and January 2007. Because only first quarter 2007 data are available, the crime rate was annualized by multiplying the number of offenses by four. This estimate is very crude, but, as the data show, relatively minor perturbations in population would not fundamentally change the essential story, which is that the New Orleans courts have not been able to keep up with the number of criminal *cases*, much less any "actual" crime above the UCR figures.

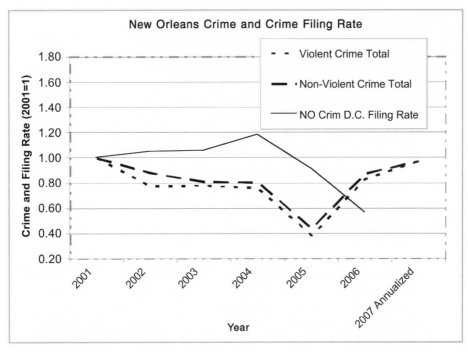

New Orleans Crime and Crime Filing Rate

Figure 4.1

In figure 4.1, the five variables are indexed to each take the value of 1.0 in 2001, which allows the numbers of crimes and filings to be compared on the same scale. The filing rate is based on the actual number of criminal matters filed in the Orleans Parish District Criminal Court. In the figure, the filing rate is compared with the crime rate to see if the criminal courts have the capacity to deal with post-Katrina crime trends in New Orleans, given that (1) the violent crime rate appears to have dropped in 2006 as the city was depopulated, presumably of more likely offenders, and (2) the violent crime rate increased as potential offenders returned to the city, which is what most police officials believe has driven up the crime rate. Presumably, a decline in the number of filings in the criminal courts would decrease or increase in step with changes in the crime rate, but figure 4.1 shows that not to be the case. Between 2001 and 2006, the peak year for the filing of criminal matters in the New Orleans District Criminal court was 2004. During this period, the filing rate exceeds the crime rate, suggesting that there was growing capacity to address crime. The filing rate declines for 2005 at about the same rate as the decline in the crime rate for these years. As the city reopened in 2006 and 2007 and as more people returned to the city, however, the number of filings did not keep pace with the change in crime rates. Indeed, the number of filings continued to decline in 2006 to less than 60 percent of the filings handled in 2001. This decline has occurred even as the murder rate (which is not a large factor in the overall violent crime rate) now appears to exceed pre-Katrina levels by twenty percentage points (although, again, we must use caution in any crime rate calculation in New Orleans) and as nonviolent crime has begun to return to pre-Katrina levels. In fact, the violent and nonviolent crime *rate* in New Orleans is roughly equal now to what it was in 2001. Although data are not available for 2007 filings, the data at least suggest that the capacity of the New Orleans criminal courts, and of the prosecutor's office, as measured by filings, has considerably decayed and remains low.

What explains this slow recovery rate for one of the most important institutions in any city or state? We can divide possible "causal stories"[56] into two broad categories: those things that are directly under the courts' control and those things brought about or managed by external factors about which the courts could do little or nothing. Like most people and institutions in the city and the region, the courts could not control the fact of the storm or influence the steps intended to mitigate it. Responsibility for the maintenance and operation of infrastructure in the city and of civil order rests on city, state, and parish officials (including levee boards). We know that these levels of government as a whole responded poorly to Katrina. In particular, the NOPD was not as effective as such a force should be in an emergency, not measured in terms of crimes or disorder, but measured in terms of how many officers could be fielded in the city.

The courts, however, can and should plan for and influence a number of features of the criminal justice system. Foremost is, unsurprisingly, the management of the court system itself. Courts, like any other institution, need to plan for alternative work sites, alternate means of communication, data and document backup and recovery, and other business and procedural functions. Beyond that, courts must ensure that standard procedural fairness norms apply. Some of these procedural norms are constitutionally mandated, including the Fifth Amendment right to access legal counsel, the Sixth Amendment right to a speedy trial, and the Fifth and Fourteenth amendments' guarantees of equal protection and due process. The courts can directly or indirectly influence the behavior of other aspects of the criminal justice system through their decisions and court orders. That point is particularly important if the other branches are purposefully or otherwise failing to meet their obligations that allow the courts to meet their own obligations. Balancing the two branches or institutions imperatives, however, can be challenging even during normal times. A major source of tension occurs when a court is a tenant in a building operated by another agency. Such was the case in the New Orleans criminal courts, when the city delayed reopening the courthouse several times. Although the city's concerns for the structural integrity of the building were valid, the court's status as a tenant meant that its needs and priorities were subordinate to those of the city.

Given these constraints, how *will* the criminal backlog be handled by the Orleans Parish Criminal Court? Today, it appears that the two most common tools that are or will be used to reduce the backlog are plea-bargaining misdemeanor and some "less serious" felony cases and dismissing charges against suspects whose cases cannot proceed for lack of evidence and lack of witnesses. The courts and the NOPD will also need to come to an understanding, at least in the short run, regarding what cases are most worthy of perusing. Clearly, violent crime will remain a major priority; on the other hand, prostitution, low-level drug crime, and property crimes may not be a priority until the courts and police have returned to a point where they can effectively address these cases.

The difference in interests and tactics among the participants in the criminal justice system must also be considered. There have been allegations that the NOPD, in concert with the criminal sheriff, has sought to arrest more people after Katrina on relatively minor offenses simply to fill beds in the reconstituted (not rebuilt) Orleans Parish Prison, because every filled bed results in revenue flowing from FEMA to the prison.[57] It is not clear whether this practice continues, but from a throughput perspective, one wonders whether many of those cases will ever make it to court or to any sort of adjudication, which raises, of course, the question of whether these arrests were actually worth making as a matter of justice in the beginning.

Thus, the capacity of the courts to handle the volume of business that came before it was significantly degraded by Katrina, and the speed with which the courts recovered from this disruption was slow. Indeed, the return to even an emergency level of functionality was more confusing that perhaps it needed to be. These conclusions are not meant to impugn the efforts of judges and court staff to restore the courts to operation. Rather, they point out that, in the face of an obvious hazard, serious planning should have been undertaken well before Hurricane Katrina so as to lesson the effect of the disaster. With such planning, it is unlikely that the public defense system would utterly collapse, or that people would be held too long without charges in criminal cases.

The Postdisaster Litigation Agenda

There is no doubt that Hurricane Katrina has led to a huge volume of lawsuits against, in particular, the insurance companies that have been slow or nonresponsive in paying claims. Many of these lawsuits are initiated by homeowners, although some have been encouraged to sue by enterprising attorneys.[58] A substantial legal literature has developed about civil liability and insurance matters in disasters in general as well as about Hurricane Katrina in particular, so let us turn to questions of civil litigation in the broader context of court management.

Of course, criminal matters have received more attention than civil matters within the judicial system, for two broad reasons. First, the Sixth Amendment's speedy trial guarantees and the procedural rules that have been implemented to enforce this right work to cause criminal matters to take precedence, but it may be more a rhetorical justification than a real motivation to action on the part of the courts.[59] In any case, the civil court was able to return to work in the Orleans Parish Civil District courthouse in December 2005, earlier than the criminal courts were, whereupon it was met with a remarkable increase in civil suits. Both the federal and state courts experienced increased volume, including insurance claims, bankruptcies, and business disputes.[60] Increased criminal case activity at the federal courts is a function of greater resources in the district, and some movement of cases from state to federal crimes relieved the state criminal courts of their backlog.

A second reason for the focus on criminal matters is the strongly expressed public demand that law and order be "restored" to New Orleans before many evacuees would consider returning to the city. Clearly, the crime rate after Katrina—whether that rate is real or just widely believed—has triggered demand for tougher police and court action against criminal suspects and convicts. If we then accept as a given that the criminal courts will take precedence in recovery and if we consider the problem of assembling a jury in a greatly depopulated parish, we can see a main challenge for the civil courts: finding enough acceptable jurors to allow trials to move forward. Moreover, the demographic composition of that jury pool is likely to be much different (whiter, wealthier) than the pre-

Katrina composition of New Orleans, which may not matter much, but it does raise questions about equitable jury pools in both civil and criminal matters.

With that in mind, what sort of civil suits are the courts in New Orleans facing? Precise data are hard to come by because the number and type of cases constitute a moving target as they move to and from federal court, are or are not treated as class action suits (which may count as one case, but with many claimants), and are appealed by the losing party somewhere in the process. We do know the broad categories of suits, even if we do not know the numbers of cases. The two broadest categories are lawsuits against insurance companies and lawsuits against government agencies that, it is claimed, violated the law by failing to perform some duty delegated to them by the legislative or executive branch.

Because Katrina was a catastrophic event, with concomitant losses, insurance companies became more likely to contest and to deny claims. Arguments made to deny claims include the idea that the storm surge—whether or not it is exacerbated by coastal erosion, structures in water courses, or the failure of levees—is a flood and is not a proper claim because homeowners' insurance policies do not insure against flood. Flood insurance is separately offered and underwritten by the federal government as part of the National Flood Insurance Program. In other instances, insurance companies have claimed that all damage was done by flooding rather than by wind, the latter of which is an insured hazard under many policies. In many cases, it is difficult to discern whether the water destroyed a building before, after, or while the building was ripped apart by either storm surge or wind. In other cases, however, engineering analyses suggest that wind was the major cause of the loss. Because of the delays in paying claims, many policyholders in Louisiana and Mississippi have filed lawsuits.

The constraints on the courts in the aftermath of Katrina could lead to several unusual and perhaps undesirable outcomes in these cases. First, the sheer volume of cases will often cause judges to certify claimants as a class for case disposition. Such class determinations may be easier to come by than they were before the storm, which indeed appears to be what has happened in the consolidated litigation against the United States in *In re: Katrina Canal Breaches Consolidated Litigation*. In an order issued by the U.S. District Court for the Eastern District of Louisiana, the court denied a motion by insurance companies to stay deposition discovery. The court noted that the consolidation of discovery into one case would promote judicial economy and timely justice. The court pointedly noted that the insurance companies are not inconvenienced by the consolidation of the cases because, after all, the consolidation means that the courts and the insurers need not address a bunch of separate cases:

> This fact greatly outweighs any inconvenience that is caused to the Insurance Defendants considering that but for the United States District Court's decision to try and coordinate such discovery, they would be subjected to thousands of individual suits and class actions all operating on different schedules, in different sections of the court, and not subject to this particular Court's oversight. Moreover, if the Court determines that all or some part of this "umbrella" is not operating efficiently, it will sever any category of cases necessary to achieve maximum efficiency.[61]

Furthermore, the court noted that many of the claimants have no insurance and that their only recourse is to the courts for relief against the government.

Second, it is very likely that claimants have had to confront the choice of going to a jury trial or having their claims heard by judges. There are no data available after Katrina to suggest that a no-jury civil trial disadvantages any party disproportionately. On the other hand, the lack of jurors may allow insurance companies to "play out the clock." To avoid these problems and all the other problems—docket backlogs, jury issues, and strategic delay—Mississippi has sought to achieve equity and to reduce demands on the courts by requiring mandatory mediation of insurance claims. Such efforts have led to several settlements. No similar efforts have been undertaken in Louisiana, and it appears that claimants, the state, and the insurers' positions are well entrenched. In some cases, it appears that the interest of Louisiana policymakers is to punish insurance companies for their recalcitrance in paying claims rather than to provide some compensation to policyholders.

There is also likely to be considerable civil litigation—not to mention criminal actions—brought against contractors who swept into New Orleans after the storm, offering to gut houses, remediate mold, and replace damaged and destroyed roofs, plumbing, and climate-control and electrical systems. Given the volume of work, the suddenness with which this volume of work arose, and the mass migration of workers into the city to perform these services, one might believe that fraud, poor workmanship, and failure to fully perform contracted work would become major issues on the courts' dockets. Anecdotally, such cases are important, but the case filing data from the Orleans Parish civil courts are too coarse to determine what types of cases are being brought.

Conclusion

Hurricane Katrina teaches us that *catastrophic* disasters—that is, disasters that severely impede a community's ability to use its own resources to respond and recover—will disrupt the courts for weeks or even months. It appears that planning for a disaster of the scale of Hurricane Katrina was not undertaken by the Louisiana courts, but, in fairness, it should be noted that planning by all institutions at all levels of government was found to be wanting after this disaster. It did not need to be this way, but a combination of official indifference to the hurricane threat at all levels, the continued emphasis on homeland security, and the lack of resources available to do high-quality planning and drilling on emergency plans led to a disaster that was well known to be inevitable. Claims by highest governmental officials, including but not limited to the secretary of the DHS, that this disaster could not be foreseen are at best disingenuous and at worse reflect the current administration's near total abandonment of emergency management and, in particular, hazard mitigation. Instead, the current mantra in Washington is terrorism "prevention" and postdisaster response; the latter has been known for years to be much less effective than preparedness and hazard mitigation.

It is, however, still possible that Hurricane Katrina may serve the same catalytic role, at least for courts along the Gulf Coast, that September 11 served for the New York courts. The extent to which Katrina has actually led to policy or managerial change[62] is an open research question, although suggestive evidence of this change exists broadly, from the enhanced used of mediation in insurance settlements to increasing penalties for contracting fraud.

One thing that Hurricane Katrina did reveal is that many courts remain unprepared to deal with the problems posed by natural disasters or a much less likely but still potentially catastrophic act of terrorism. The sorts of prescriptions contained in various guidance documents are on sound evidence that court leaders are generally inattentive to terrorism or natural hazards and that other branches of government are inattentive to these issues *as they relate to the effective operation of the courts*. Therefore, important resource constraints are created by the dependency of other branches or agencies of government to act, dependencies that range from the simple matter of having the county as the courthouse landlord to more complex questions of interagency and interbranch coordination of emergency planning, provision of resources for planning, and continuity of operations planning.

Although the prescriptive literature on court security is certainly useful, more research needs to be done on key questions on courthouse security, including the following:

1. What are the most common threats to court security?
2. What are the most *consequential* threats to court security?
3. How do these threats vary by jurisdiction?
4. Is planning uniform within or between jurisdictions? What explains the variation in planning? Leadership differences? The nature of the courts' organization in a state?
5. Are "lessons" really "learned" from past events? Or are lessons or aphorisms merely observed, without any fundamental action being taken?

No one scholar or institution can take on these questions, but they do suggest a two-pronged research agenda that addresses the broad questions of what works in the way of emergency planning and how and to what extent are plans considered, drafted, adopted, and implemented. September 11 and Hurricane Katrina are but two very rich cases from which scholars and court administrators could draw to address these questions. In particular, after Hurricane Katrina it is important to understand whether any post–September 11 "lessons" were "learned" in time for Katrina and whether and to what extent the National Center for State Courts's best practices and other guidance tools were applied. Only through this sort of evaluation will we be able to assess progress toward better preparedness for a wide range of threats to the courts.

NOTES

1. See, for example, Ivor Van Heerden and Mike Bryan, *The Storm: What Went Wrong and Why during Hurricane Katrina: The Inside Story from One Louisiana Scientist* (New York: Viking, 2006).

2. Committee on Disaster Research in the Social Sciences, National Research Council, *Facing Hazards and Disasters: Understanding Human Dimensions* (Washington, DC: National Academies Press, 2006).

3. American Institute of Insurance Services, "Disaster Mitigation: What Role Can Insurers Play in the Campaign to Protect Our Communities?" www.aais.org/communications/viewpoint/vpfl982.htm; Robert Olshansky, "Review of Natural Hazard Mitigation: Recasting Disaster Policy and Planning," *Journal of the American Planning Association* 65 (1999): 453; David R. Godschalk, Timothy Beatley, Philip Berke, David J. Brower, and Edward J. Kaiser, *Natural Hazard Mitigation: Recasting Disaster Policy and Planning* (Washington, DC: Island Press, 2000); Diane Steiner, "Mainstreaming Disaster Mitigation:

Challenges to Organisational Learning in NGOs," *Development in Practice* 12 (2002): 473–79.

4. Peter J. May, *Recovering from Catastrophes: Federal Disaster Relief Policy and Politics* (Westport, CT: Greenwood Press, 1985); Philip White and Lionel Cliffe, "Matching Response to Context in Complex Political Emergencies: 'Relief', 'Development', 'Peace-Building' or Something In-between?" *Disasters* 24 (2000): 314–42; Dale J. Roenigk, "Federal Disaster Relief and Local Government Financial Condition," *International Journal of Mass Emergencies and Disasters* 11 (1993): 207–25; Edward L. Lascher Jr. and Michael R. Powers, "September 11 Victims, Random Events, and the Ethics of Compensation," *American Behavioral Scientist* 48 (2004): 281–94; Rutherford H. Platt, *Disasters and Democracy* (Washington, DC: Island Press, 1999).

5. Michael K. Lindell, Ronald W. Perry, and Carla Prater, *Introduction to Emergency Management* (Hoboken, NJ: Wiley, 2007); Frank Thomalla, Tom Downing, Erika Spanger-Siegfried, Guoyi Han, and Johan Rockström, "Reducing Hazard Vulnerability: Towards a Common Approach between Disaster Risk Reduction and Climate Adaptation," *Disasters* 30 (2006): 39–48; Toni Morris-Oswald and A. John Sinclair, "Values and Floodplain Management: Case Studies from the Red River Basin, Canada," *Global Environmental Change Part B: Environmental Hazards* 6 (2005): 9–22; Richard J. T. Klein, Robert J. Nicholls, and Frank Thomalla, "Resilience to Natural Hazards: How Useful Is This Concept?" *Global Environmental Change Part B: Environmental Hazards* 5 (2003): 35–45; Thomas A. Birkland, Raymond J. Burby, David Conrad, Hanna Cortner, and William K. Michener, "River Ecology and Flood Hazard Mitigation," *Natural Hazards Review* 4 (2003): 46–54.

6. Samuel Henry Prince, "Catastrophe and Social Change, Based upon a Sociological Study of the Halifax Disaster" (PhD diss., Columbia University, 1920).

7. Committee on the Alaska Earthquake of the Division of Earth Sciences, National Academy of Sciences, National Research Council, *The Great Alaska Earthquake of 1964: Summary and Recommendations* (Washington, DC: National Academy of Sciences, 1973).

8. Gilbert F. White, "Human Adjustment to Floods: A Geographical Approach to the Flood Problem in the United States," Research Paper no. 29 (Chicago: University of Chicago Department of Geography, 1945).

9. Birkland et al., "River Ecology."

10. Howard Kunreuther, *Recovery from Natural Disasters: Insurance or Federal Aid?* (Washington, DC: American Enterprise Institute, 1973); Howard Kunreuther, "Should Society Deal with the Earthquake Problem?" *Regulation* 15 (1992): 60–63.

11. Raymond J. Burby and Steven P. French with Beverly A. Cigler et al., *Flood Plain Land Use Management: A National Assessment.* (Boulder, CO: Westview, 1985); Raymond J. Burby and Linda C. Dalton, "Plans Can Matter! The Role of Land Use Plans and State Planning Mandates in Limiting the Development of Hazardous Areas," *Public Administration Review* 54 (1994): 229–38; Raymond J. Burby and Peter J. May, "Intergovernmental Environmental Planning: Addressing the Commitment Conundrum," *Journal of Environmental Planning and Management* 41 (1998): 95–111; Raymond J. Burby et al., "Unleashing the Power of Planning to Create Disaster-Resistant Communities," *Journal of the American Planning Association* 65 (1999): 247–58; Philip Berke et al., "Enhancing Plan Quality: Evaluating the Role of State Planning Mandates for Natural Hazard Mitigation," *Journal of Environmental Planning and Management* 39 (1996): 79–96.

12. Ronald W. Perry and Michael K. Lindell, "The Effects of Ethnicity on Evacuation Decision-Making," *International Journal of Mass Emergencies and Disasters* 9 (1991): 47–68; Ronald W. Perry and Michael K. Lindell, "Understanding Citizen Response to Disasters with Implications for Terrorism," *Journal of Contingencies and Crisis Management* 11 (2003): 49–60.

13. Thomas A. Birkland, *After Disaster: Agenda Setting, Public Policy and Focusing Events* (Washington, DC: Georgetown University Press, 1997); Thomas A. Birkland, *Lessons of Disaster* (Washington, DC: Georgetown University Press, 2006); May, *Recovering from Catastrophes*; Peter J. May and Thomas A. Birkland, "Earthquake Risk Reduction: An Examination of Local Regulatory Efforts," *Environmental Management* 18 (1994): 923–39; Peter J. May and Raymond J. Burby, "Coercive versus Cooperative Policies: Comparing Intergovernmental Mandate Performance," *Journal of Policy Analysis and Management* 15 (1996): 171–201; Peter J. May and Robert E. Deyle, "Governing Land Use in Hazardous Areas with a Patchwork System," in *Cooperating with Nature: Confronting Natural Hazards with Land-Use Planning for Sustainable Communities*, ed. Raymond J. Burby (Washington, DC: Joseph Henry Press, 1998); Richard T. Sylves and William R. Cumming, "FEMA's Path to Homeland Security: 1979–2003," *Journal of Homeland Security and Emergency Management* 1 (2004): art. 11, www.bepress.com/jhsem/vol1/iss2/11; Richard T. Sylves, "Adopting Integrated Emergency Management in the United States: Political and Organizational Challenges," *International Journal of Mass Emergencies and Disasters* 9 (1991): 413–24; Richard T. Sylves, "President Bush and Hurricane Katrina: A Presidential Leadership Study," *Annals of the American Academy of Political and Social Science* 604 (2006): 26–56.

14. Michael Griebel and Todd S. Phillips, "Architectural Design for Security in Courthouse Facilities," *Annals of the American Academy of Political and Social Science* 576 (2001): 118–31; Thomas A. Birkland, "Disaster and the Courts' Agenda," *Judges' Journal* 37 (1998): 7–11; Keith O. Boyum, "Understanding Disasters and Other Impacts on Courts: Overview, Comparisons, and Propositions," *Judges' Journal* 37 (1998): 12–16; Theodore B. Pedeliski, "A Case of Judicial Restoration: A Court System Responds to and Recovers from the Red River Flood of 1997," *Judges' Journal* 37 (1998): 17–19; Rebecca Mae Salokar, "After the Winds: Hurricane Andrew's Impact on Judicial Institutions in South Florida," *Judges' Journal* 37 (1998): 26–32; Stephen L. Wasby, "Disruption, Dislocation, Discretion, and Dependence: The Ninth Circuit Court of Appeals and the Loma Prieta Earthquake," *Judges' Journal* 37 (1998): 33–35; Stephen L. Wasby, "The Effect of Disasters on Courts: An Introduction," *Judges' Journal* 37 (1998): 4–5; Oren Root, "The Administration of Justice under Emergency Conditions" (New York: Vera Institute of Justice), www.9-11summit.org/materials9-11/911/acrobat/26/C1TheAftermath/VeraInstituteLessonsFollowingAttack.pdf; Minnesota Conference of Chief Justices, "Court Security Manual," www.9-11summit.org/materials9-11/911/acrobat/26/C6NewThreats/MinnesotaCtSecurityManual.pdf; Workgroup on Emergency Preparedness Florida Supreme Court, "'Keep the Courts Open'—Final Report" (Tallahassee: Florida Supreme Court), www.9-11summit.org/materials9-11/911/acrobat/27/P3%26C10EmergencyPreparednessPlans/FloridaFinalReport; Best Practices Institute National Center for State Courts, "Emergency Management for Courts" (Williamsburg, VA: National Center for State Courts), www.ncsconline.org/Projects_Initiatives/BPI/EmergencyMngmnt.htm#ensure.

15. Thomas A. Birkland, *Emergency Planning and the Judiciary: Lessons from September 11* (New York: Center for Court Innovation, 2004); Root, "The Administration of Justice under Emergency Conditions"; Jonathan Lippman, "September 11th: The New York Experience," www.9-11summit.org/materials9-11/911/acrobat/26/P1LeadingtheCourts/911NYExperience.pdf.

16. The website for this meeting and subsequent discussions is at www.9-11summit.org/.

17. E. L. Quarantelli, "Catastrophes Are Different from Disasters: Some Implications for Crisis Planning and Managing Drawn from Katrina," Social Science Research Council, understandingkatrina.ssrc.org/Quarantelli.

18. William Langewiesche, *American Ground, Unbuilding the World Trade Center* (New York: North Point Press, 2002).

19. See the Government Performance Project page at www.gpponline.org/. This quotation is from the 2005 report on Louisiana.

20. American Judges' Association, "Court Security Survey Report"; Minnesota Conference of Chief Justices, "Court Security Manual"; Florida Supreme Court, "'Keep the Courts Open'—Final Report; National Center for State Courts, "Emergency Management for Courts"; SJI Court Emergency/Disaster Preparedness Planning Project, *Planning for Emergencies: Immediate Events and Their Aftermath: A Guideline for Local Courts* (Washington, DC: Justice Programs Office, School of Public Affairs, American University, 2005); Wisconsin Courthouse Security Resource Center, *Courthouse Security Manual* (Madison: Wisconsin Courthouse Security Resource Center, 2003). All these materials are available at www.9-11summit.org/.

21. National Center for State Courts, "Emergency Management for Courts."

22. Root, "The Administration of Justice under Emergency Conditions," 4.

23. The Third Branch, "Emergency Preparedness in the Judiciary," *The Third Branch*, November (2001), www.9-11summit.org/materials9-11/911/acrobat/26/C1TheAftermath/EmergencyPreparednessinJudiciary.pdf.

24. Supreme Court of Louisiana, *Annual Report 2005 of the Judicial Council of the Supreme Court* (New Orleans: Supreme Court of Louisiana, 2005), 3.

25. Kathleen J. Tierney, "The Red Pill," Social Science Research Council, understandingkatrina.ssrc.org/Tierney/.

26. Federal Emergency Management Agency, "Federal Preparedness Circular FPC 65," www.fas.org/irp/offdocs/pdd/fpc-65.htm; Dan Verton, "Wartime CIOs Alter Security Strategies," *Computerworld* 36 (2002): 14; R. Eric Peterson, "Congressional Continuity of Operations (Coop): An Overview of Concepts and Challenges" (Washington, DC: Congressional Research Service, 2003); R. Eric Peterson, "Continuity of Operations (Coop) in the Executive Branch: Background and Issues for Congress" (Washington, DC: Congressional Research Service, 2003).

27. R. Eric Peterson, "Emergency Preparedness and Continuity of Operations (Coop) Planning in the Federal Judiciary" (Washington, DC: Congressional Research Service, 2003).

28. Roy Harris, "What Price Security?" *CFO* 19 (2003): 54–57; Carl J. Kotheimer and Bill Coffin, "How to Justify Business Continuity Management," *Risk Management* 50 (2003): 30–34; Stephanie Stahl, "'What's Your Disaster Plan?' May Become Newest Refrain," *InformationWeek*, November 26, 2001, 8.

29. Pedeliski, "A Case of Judicial Restoration."

30. Lee Clarke, "Panic: Myth or Reality," *Contexts* 1 (2002): 21–23; Quarantelli, "Catastrophes Are Different from Disasters"; Ira Helsloot and Arnaut Ruitenberg, "Citizen Response to Disasters: A Survey of Literature and Some Practical Implications," *Journal of Contingencies and Crisis Management* 12 (2004): 98–111; Havidán Rodriguez, Joseph Trainor, and Enrico L. Quarantelli, "Rising to the Challenges of a Catastrophe: The Emergent and Prosocial Behavior following Hurricane Katrina," *Annals of the American Academy of Political and Social Science* 604 (2006): 82–101.

31. International Federation of Red Cross and Red Crescent Societies, "World Disasters Report," www.ifrc.org/publicat/wdr2004/; Business Roundtable Partnership for Disaster Relief, "Top Ten Myths of Disaster Relief," www.businessroundtable.org/pdf/20060327002Top10Myths.pdf; Claude de Ville de Goyet, "Stop Propagating Disaster Myths," *Journal of Prehospital and Disaster Medicine* 14 (1999), pdm.medicine.wisc.edu/degoyet.htm.

32. Henry W. Fischer, *Response to Disaster: Fact versus Fiction and Its Perpetuation: The Sociology of Disaster*, 2d ed. (Lanham, MD: University Press of America, 1998).

33. Kathleen Tierney, Christine Bevc, and Erica Kuligowski, "Metaphors Matter: Disaster Myths, Media Frames, and Their Consequences in Hurricane Katrina," *Annals of the American Academy of Political and Social Science* 604 (2006): 57–81.

34. Ibid., 58.

35. Sarah Kaufman, "The Criminalization of New Orleanians in Katrina's Wake," Social Science Research Council, understandingkatrina.ssrc.org/Kaufman/.

36. Tierney, Bevc, and Kuligowski, "Metaphors Matter."

37. New York City Fire Department, "McKinsey Report—Increasing FDNY's Preparedness," New York City Fire Department, www.nyc.gov/html/fdny/html/mck_report/toc.html.

38. Tierney, "The Red Pill."

39. Journalists and some policy analysts continue to bandy about the category rating of Hurricane Katrina based on the Saffir-Simpson scale of tropical storm intensity, with 1 being the weakest hurricane and 5 being the strongest. Unfortunately, the Saffir-Simpson scale only accounts for wind speed. Although wind is a major factor in hurricane damage, particularly some distance inland from where the storm makes landfall, the scale does not account for complex variables that can yield smaller or larger storm surges. In this case, it was the storm surge in Lake Ponchartrain that ultimately led to the failure of the key floodwalls along the drainage canals. See Van Heerden and Bryan, *The Storm: What Went Wrong and Why during Hurricane Katrina*, for a detailed discussion of these dynamics.

40. Laura Parker, "After Katrina, Courts Flooded by Lawsuits," *USA Today*, January 15, 2006, www.usatoday.com/news/nation/2006-01-15-katrina-suits_x.htm.

41. The Third Branch, "Emergency Preparedness in the Judiciary," emphasis added.

42. American Bankruptcy Institute Journal, "Congress Considers Katrina Impact," *American Bankruptcy Institute Journal* 24 (2005): 3.

43. Pamela A. MacLean, "After Katrina: Federal Courts in Gulf Coast States Have Reopened, but Louisiana State Courts Are Still in Disarray," *Broward Daily Business Review*, November 9, 2005, 10.

44. Peter Whoriskey, "In New Orleans, Justice on Trial: Katrina Strains Public Defender's Office," *Washington Post*, April 15, 2006, www.lexis-nexis.com/.

45. Robert Crowe, "One Year Later: Big Easy's Court System Still in State of Emergency; Judge Looking at Releasing Some Prisoners Jailed before Katrina but Still Not Charged," *Houston Chronicle*, August 27, 2006, www.lexis-nexis.com/.

46. Gwen Filosa, "Delay of Trial Lets Murder Defendant Go Free; State's Deadline to Present Case in 2001 Killing Passed, Judge Says," *Times-Picayune*, September 9, 2006, www.lexis-nexis.com/.

47. Whoriskey, "In New Orleans, Justice on Trial"; Patrick Ellard, "Learning from Katrina: Emphasizing the Right to a Speedy Trial to Protect Constitutional Guarantees in Disasters," *American Criminal Law Review* 44 (2007): 1207–37.

48. See also Susan Burgess, "Courting Disaster," *News Media and the Law* 29 (2005): 11–12.

49. Heather Hall, "Hurricane Brings Attention to Long Broken Public Defense System," *Cornerstone* 28 (2006): 15–17.

50. Ellard, "Learning from Katrina."

51. Kevin Johnson, "Engulfed Evidence Puts New Orleans Court Cases in Doubt," *USA Today*, September 22, 2005.

52. Mark Greenblatt, "Crime Wave," *IRE Journal*, March–April 2007.

53. Amanda Ripley, "Crime Returns to the Big Easy," *Time Online*, March 22, 2006.

54. www.nopd.com.

55. See, for example, www.brookings.edu/metro/pubs/200512_katrinaindex.htm.

56. Deborah A. Stone, "Causal Stories and the Formation of Policy Agendas," *Political Science Quarterly* 104 (1989): 281–300.

57. "The Prison Business," *Christian Century* 123, no. 20 (2006): 5.

58. Parker, "After Katrina, Courts Flooded by Lawsuits."

59. Brandon L. Garrett and Tania Tetlow, "Criminal Justice Collapse: The Constitution after Hurricane Katrina," *Duke Law Journal* 56 (2006): 127–78.

60. Tania Tetlow, personal communication, July 2007.

61. *In re: Katrina Canal Breaches Consolidated Litigation*, "Order and Reasons," E.D. La. (2006), Document 3426: 1–2.

62. Birkland, *After Disaster*; Birkland, *Lessons of Disaster*.

5

Environmental Right-to-Know and the Transmutations of Law

KIM FORTUN

Law does more than codify, regulate, and control; it also catalyzes and transmutes, provoking cascading social and cultural effects, particularly when the force of law is informational.[1] Consider the case of Diane Wilson, mother of five, fourth-generation shrimp boat captain in Calhoun County on the Texas Gulf Coast. In 1989, she was forty years old, had more than enough to do, and had more than enough to worry about. Shrimping had never been an easy way to make a living, but it was getting harder. The catch was down and game warden surveillance was up, and there was a brown algae creeping across the surface of San Antonio Bay.[2] The fish suffocated and the shrimpers went further into debt. Environmental regulations were not a shrimper's friend, however. Indeed, a fair amount of energy and creativity went in to efforts to avoid game warden surveillance. Local fish houses where the catch was held for sale had subtle systems for alerting shrimpers if wardens were lingering on the docks or were parked around the corner. Environmental regulations directed at local industry did not have many supporters either. The local chemical industry was the place to work if you really wanted to earn money. Union Carbide had a plant in Calhoun County, as did DuPont, BP, Alcoa, and Formosa Plastics.

On a hot afternoon in 1989, Diane was in her brother's fish house, which she managed with a friend. A shrimper brought in a local newspaper reporting that Calhoun County, population 15,000, was the most polluted county in the United States. (See figure 5.1.) The news was based on the first year of reporting from the U.S. Toxic Release Inventory (TRI), mandated in 1986 as part of the so-called Community Right-to-Know Act, which was bundled into a reauthorization of the Superfund in response to the Bhopal disaster.[3] The TRI is the centerpiece of what has been become known as environmental right-to-know legislation, now considered a criti-

cal part of environmental governance around the world[4] even as it is rolled
back in the United States.[5]

At first, Diane joked about the news, but then it got under her skin,
animating an extraordinary process of discovery and transmutation. With
time, Diane not only learned about the pollution in her beloved San Antonio Bay, but she also learned about the way government and business

Figure 5.1

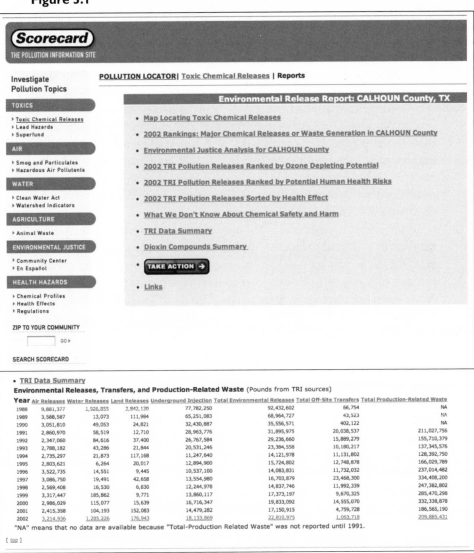

Scorecard

THE POLLUTION INFORMATION SITE

Investigate
Pollution Topics

POLLUTION LOCATOR| Toxic Chemical Releases | Reports

Environmental Release Report: CALHOUN County, TX

TOXICS

› Toxic Chemical Releases
› Lead Hazards
› Superfund

AIR

› Smog and Particulates
› Hazardous Air Pollutants

WATER

› Clean Water Act
› Watershed Indicators

AGRICULTURE

› Animal Waste

ENVIRONMENTAL JUSTICE

› Community Center
› En Español

HEALTH HAZARDS

› Chemical Profiles
› Health Effects
› Regulations

ZIP TO YOUR COMMUNITY

[   ] GO ›

SEARCH SCORECARD

- Map Locating Toxic Chemical Releases
- 2002 Rankings: Major Chemical Releases or Waste Generation in CALHOUN County
- Environmental Justice Analysis for CALHOUN County
- 2002 TRI Pollution Releases Ranked by Ozone Depleting Potential
- 2002 TRI Pollution Releases Ranked by Potential Human Health Risks
- 2002 TRI Pollution Releases Sorted by Health Effect
- What We Don't Know About Chemical Safety and Harm
- TRI Data Summary
- Dioxin Compounds Summary

  TAKE ACTION →

- Links

- **TRI Data Summary**
Environmental Releases, Transfers, and Production-Related Waste (Pounds from TRI sources)

Year	Air Releases	Water Releases	Land Releases	Underground Injection	Total Environmental Releases	Total Off-Site Transfers	Total Production-Related Waste
1988	9,881,377	1,926,855	2,842,120	77,782,250	92,432,602	66,754	NA
1989	3,588,587	13,073	111,984	65,251,083	68,964,727	43,523	NA
1990	3,051,810	49,053	24,821	32,430,887	35,556,571	402,122	NA
1991	2,860,970	58,519	12,710	28,963,776	31,895,975	20,038,537	211,027,756
1992	2,347,060	84,616	37,400	26,767,584	29,236,660	15,889,279	155,710,379
1993	2,788,182	43,286	21,844	20,531,246	23,384,558	10,180,217	137,345,576
1994	2,735,297	21,873	117,168	11,247,640	14,121,978	11,131,802	128,392,750
1995	2,803,621	6,264	20,017	12,894,900	15,724,802	12,748,878	166,029,789
1996	3,522,735	14,551	9,445	10,537,100	14,083,831	11,732,032	237,014,482
1997	3,086,750	19,491	42,658	13,554,980	16,703,879	23,468,300	334,408,200
1998	2,569,408	16,530	6,830	12,244,978	14,837,746	11,992,339	247,382,802
1999	3,317,447	185,862	9,771	13,860,117	17,373,197	9,670,325	285,470,298
2000	2,986,029	115,077	15,639	16,716,347	19,833,092	14,555,070	332,338,878
2001	2,415,358	104,193	152,083	14,479,282	17,150,915	4,759,728	186,565,190
2002	3,214,936	1,285,226	176,943	18,133,869	22,810,975	1,063,718	209,885,431

"NA" means that no data are available because "Total-Production Related Waste" was not reported until 1991.

[top]

"work" and about the way environmental politics is entangled with information politics. She also learned to make connections that others easily miss, moving from Calhoun County, Texas, to Bhopal, India, to Baghdad, Iraq, all the while insisting that she is "nobody in particular."[6]

Diane Wilson's story illustrates how environmental right-to-know legislation works, beyond its effects on corporate behavior and despite problems with information accuracy, completeness, and circulation. My argument responds both to those who applaud and to those who criticize right-to-know initiatives. It also responds to accelerating interest in reducing vulnerability to disaster, evident in response to Hurricane Katrina and the 2006 Indian Ocean tsunami, for example, and among people concerned about global warming.[7]

Critiques of right-to know initiatives tend to focus on problems with the information made available. Analysis reveals that information is often incomplete, unaudited, inaccurate, and delayed in its circulation. This way of thinking about how environmental right-to-know works underestimates the way people actually work with information and around information gaps, often with keen awareness that "transparency" is not the same as "full disclosure." It is thus critical to pay attention to information practices downstream of disclosure as well as to what information—even if imperfect—can reveal and motivate.

Information, it turns out, is not only of substantive value (valuable because of its potential truth content) but also because of what can be called semiotic value. Any piece of information—even if partial or lacking verification—can draw people into processes of inquiry, driven by recognition of potential but unrealized information density, of interests undergirding information gaps, and of varied ways information, even if questionable, can be used, such as for comparisons across space and time.[8] Information thus creates *capacity* to understand and respond to problems, routine and catastrophic.[9]

Those who applaud right-to-know legislation often focus on its effects on the behavior of polluting firms. Right-to-know is said to work because it has a direct effect on pollution outcomes. This critically important point is reason enough to support right-to-know initiatives. This way of thinking about how right-to-know works, however, misses more circuitous social and cultural effects, which dramatically implicate how environmental issues will be dealt with in the future. These social and cultural effects are particularly important to consider when trying to reduce vulnerability to disaster, events that fundamentally destabilize established ways of thinking and acting. Disaster, by definition, deprives people of any star (dis-aster) to orient themselves, overwhelming their ability to make sense of things. Information about "what is going on" is often lacking and is always politically charged. Cultivating critical information practices is thus a key part of disaster prevention and response.

Right-to-know legislation has dramatically increased the quantity and types of environmental risk information in circulation. In what follows, the social and cultural import of such legislation and the practical implications for disaster preparedness in particular are discussed. Enhanced information density does not itself provide answers; it animates rather than dictates activity, propelling people to recognize problems and identify points of intervention. Enhanced information density produces new points of view and draws into visibility the many scales and types of systems in play in the production of risk and in all efforts to reduce it. Initiatives that enhance information density—such as environmental right-to-know legislation—should thus be conceived as critical components of risk reduction and as significant drivers of cultural production and ethical-political movement.

This chapter describes how environmental right-to-know emerged in the wake of the Bhopal disaster, in a context riven by faith that greater access to information would solve a range of social ills. It next provides a brief overview of the informating of environmental policy in the United States and elsewhere. Diane Wilson's story is then used to illustrate what can be thought of as the wayward, transmutational effects of law. This overarching argument returns in the conclusion, emphasizing how right-to-know has prompted information practices, social connections, and political movements that have changed the order of things in the environmental field, in ways that should be protected and leveraged.[10]

Bhopal and the Information Society[11]

An information society, according to Wikipedia, is a society "in which the creation, distribution, diffusion, use, integration and manipulation of information is significant economic, political and cultural activity."[12] Although theorized at least since the 1960s,[13] such a society really began to take shape—and to be popularly recognized as such—in the 1980s. Throughout that decade, the density of information circulation increased exponentially. There were both technical and legal grounds for this expansion. The costs of telecommunications fell dramatically, pushed by a 1984 decision by the U.S. judiciary to break up AT&T. Cell phone networks were established in the United States, and both FedEx and Microsoft reached "tipping points" that led to explosive growth.[14] Home computer use grew, and Pacman fever spread. Information-processing capabilities came to be expected and even to be considered a right. Investment in information circulation as the solution to a range of problems intensified.

The 1980s were also years of crisis. Debt crisis ripped across the developing world. Famine devastated Ethiopia. President Ronald Reagan reigned in the United States. There also was a ripple of industrial disasters: Bhopal in 1984, Chernobyl in 1986, *Exxon Valdez* in 1989. Information deficits were visible aspects of them all.

The story of Bhopal is particularly telling. Poor circulation of information exacerbated the disaster in many ways. Circulation of information between Union Carbide's headquarters in the United States and its Indian subsidiary was problematic, as was circulation of information between workers and managers in the plant. Information systems within the plant did not help, either; many were not functional the night of the gas leak, in part due to lack of maintenance resulting from plans to dismantle the plant and move it to another country as part of a major corporate restructuring intended to prepare the company for a globalizing economy. Indeed, on the very day Union Carbide had to hold a press conference announcing the Bhopal disaster, a press conference had already been scheduled to tell journalists how the company had restructured for a global era.[15]

No alarm announced the release of forty tons of toxic gas over the sleeping city of Bhopal on December 3, 1984. Because there was no evacuation plan, many people ran into the wind. Doctors were told by Union Carbide representatives that methyl isocyanate, the bulk chemical released, could be treated with antacids and water washing of eyes. Up to 10,000 people died within the first few days after the gas leak, and up to 600,000 were exposed. When U.S. Representative Steven Solarz (D-NY) visited Bhopal shortly after the gas leak, he was shocked to find that the mayor of Bhopal had no idea of the potential dangers posed by the plant.[16]

Senator Frank Lautenberg (D-NJ) outlined questions raised by the Bhopal disaster on the first day of the Ninety-ninth Congress: What percentage of the U.S. public lives in close proximity to facilities that produce or use hazardous chemicals? Is it known what these materials are and what hazards they present to adjacent communities? How adequate are emergency procedures established by federal and state governments to respond to environmental disasters? The overarching question was basic:

Can "Bhopal" happen here, in the United States? Union Carbide said that it could not, emphasizing the low probability of simultaneous multiple systems failure as occurred in Bhopal, but skepticism could not be contained.[17]

Representative Henry Waxman (D-CA) emphasized this shift in perspective in congressional hearings ten days after the gas leak in Bhopal:

> We're being told on the one hand that it's a sealed system. But on the other, all these chemicals are leaking into the air on a routine basis. I find that troubling. The federal government doesn't know anything about it and that's outrageous enough. The state government hasn't the ability to regulate. We rely on you to regulate yourself. And if you are regulating yourself, it doesn't seem to me that your own people know why these chemicals are going into the air and what effect they're having on the public.[18]

Waxman argued that it was a discredit to the Environmental Protection Agency (EPA) that it did not know what was going on, pointing out that "EPA didn't mention the fact that there are no standards because EPA hasn't set any. After 14 years it has regulated only eight toxic pollutants. Methyl isocyanate is not considered a hazardous pollutant. . . . Aren't 2,500 deaths enough to convince EPA that methyl isocyanate is hazardous?" Waxman also described the contradictory process by which hazards "count": "EPA doesn't call something a hazard until it's ready to regulate it and it doesn't regulate something until it calls it a hazard. EPA has been chasing its tail for far too long."[19]

Waxman's response to the Bhopal disaster draws out many issues still being worked out today: lack of information about risks both within the companies that produce them and within government agencies; the dependence of government agencies on companies for knowledge about risks; the grave importance of what is officially listed as hazardous. Most basic of all, however, was recognition that the industrial complexes that dot and interconnect the contemporary landscape are open, rather than sealed, systems. In other words, these systems routinely leak and occasionally blow up. "Information strategies" have been a key part of our response.

"Information strategies"—efforts, often led by governments, to increase the availability of information on a particular phenomena—are being instituted around the world as a way of dealing with complex problems within democratic frameworks. Such is the case in the environmental domain, where information strategies are now relied on to address pollution, loss of biodiversity, climate change, and a range of other issues involving entangled social, technical, and natural systems.

Information strategies can be traced historically in various ways: to Kantian constructions of the subject who knows and therein becomes both capable and responsible; to Mill's arguments in *On Liberty* about the need for informed decisions and subsequent need for freedom of the press; to passage of the U.S. Freedom of Information Act and the growth of the consumer rights movement in the 1970s; through rhetorics of "transparency" that have upheld democratization campaigns as well as efforts to build markets since the late 1980s.

Information strategies are structured by ideas about the effects of information circulation and about the (ethical) good of such effects. In short, more information in more hands is assumed to be a good thing. This can imply a rational actor model of behavior and democracy: information strategies increase the knowledge base from which judgments and decisions are derived, resulting in rational actors and rational societies. Other logics, based on quite different constructs of what is real and possible, are also possible. Information strategies can, for example, be perceived as an imperfect but best possible way to respond to high levels of uncertainty about both the present and the future: circulate lots of information to lots of people, hoping that (as connectivity theorists put it) dumb parts become a smart network.

Information strategies were not new in the 1980s, even within the environmental domain. The 1970 National Environmental Policy Act, for example, led to the publication of annual reports on the environment for the president and Congress and mandated that all federal agencies publish environmental impact statements before starting new projects. Belief in such strategies accelerated in the 1980s as the information era intensified. Simultaneously, protection of human health became the explicit goal of environmental legislation for the first time.[20] Efforts to protect environmental health thus became entangled with the beliefs and technologies of information, and the "right to know" became a dominant legislative strategy for protecting human health.[21]

Informing Environmental Policy

"Information strategies" for dealing with environmental risk became the explicit focus of law in the United States in 1986 through passage of the Community Right-to-Know Act, Title III of the Superfund Amendments and Reauthorization Act. Widely regarded as the primary legislative response to the Bhopal disaster in the United States, the act mandated a range of initiatives to support emergency planning and public access to information. High-risk facilities, for example, had to provide the information needed by local rescue personnel to plan emergency evacuations. By the time amendments to the Clean Air Act were passed in 1990, this requirement had evolved into a mandate for "worst-case scenarios" for 66,000 high-risk facilities around the United States.

Another key component of the 1986 Right-to-Know Act was the TRI, the first federal database that Congress said must be released to the public in a computer-readable format.[22] The goal was to allow the EPA as well as citizens to track and evaluate routine emissions. A key effect has been recognition that information itself can be a hazard—to the public image of chemical companies in particular. In response, corporations have "gone green," and control over hazardous information has become almost as important as control over hazardous production itself.

The effects of distributing TRI data in the United States have been enormous, sparking environmental initiatives within corporations, in the communities affected by pollution, and by national and international environmental groups.[23] The first round of U.S. TRI data was submitted in July 1988. The president of Monsanto was so taken aback by the figures disclosed that he pledged to reduce emissions by 90 percent over the next five years. The next year, the Chemical Manufacturers Association initiated its Responsible Care program, a "public commitment" to run safe plants voluntarily beyond compliance with the law. The National Wildlife Federation responded to Responsible Care by denouncing purported progress on emissions reduction as "phantom reductions" attributable to new accounting measures and creative information manipulation.[24] Environmentalism became a struggle over how things would be categorized, counted, and represented, graphically as well as politically.

Initiatives similar to those mobilized in the United States by right-to-know legislation have now been developed around the world, as recommended in Agenda 21, the guidelines for sustainable development agreed to at the 1992 Earth Summit. Informational strategies have become a major focus at the World Bank and within United Nations' programs. In Europe, the right to know is the focus of the Aarhus Convention, a United Nations/European Economic Commission (UN/EEC) Convention on Access to Information, Public Participation in Decision-Making and Access to Justice in Environmental Matters. Originally signed in Aarhus, Denmark, in the summer of 1998, this convention establishes legally binding

instruments guiding the creation of national Pollutant Release and Transfer Registers (PRTRs) in the UN/EEC region as recommended by Chapter
19 of Agenda 21. PRTRs are databases containing information about pollution from industrial facilities, similar to the U.S. TRI.[25] Environmental
organizations such as the WorldWatch Institute consider PRTRs a priority
because they "pinpoint the most affected communities, and the most polluting industries, thereby identifying targets for action."[26]

Right-to-know initiatives raise difficult questions: What information
must be provided to fulfill the right to know about the environment? *How*
must information be provided? Must information be accessible through
the Internet? Has access been realized if information is not organized for
efficient use and correlated with other information that reveals its significance? Is the right to know, in effect, the right to computer models and
interactive, Internet-based maps? Must scientific knowledge be stable and
uncontested to be useful? How much science can "ordinary citizens" take?
What are citizens likely to do with environmental risk information? Will
they remain reasonable?[27]

An Unreasonable Woman

After reading news of the first TRI report in 1989, it was not long before
Diane Wilson called a lawyer and—following his instructions—called a
meeting. To get ready, Diane made a few calls. One plant official told her
to call someone else. "We're not in the information business, lady. We
make chemicals. We build jobs and make better lives for people in this
country," he said. Another plant official acknowledged that they were now
required by law to provide information to local authorities, but "not to every Tom, Dick, and Harry on the telephone." So Diana called the Calhoun
County emergency coordinator. "It's lies!" the coordinator yelled. "That
article's nothing but a twisted pack of lies instigated by people wanting to
make something out of nothing! It's their job to rile up people. That's how
they make their money!" "The Toxic Release Inventory is a national report," Diane replied, "a government report." The emergency coordinator
told her to get her facts straight and joked that Diane did not even know
what a wastewater permit was.[28]

Diane then had to find a new place for a meeting. She had reserved a
room in the Seadrift city hall, but the woman in charge came out to the
fish house one day and told Diane that she would need to find another
place. The woman said that the city was trying to get a grant and that the

meeting wouldn't look good. "It's sending a red flag up in Washington," she said. Someone also called Diane's brother Sanchez and told him to make his sister back off. "But it's just a simple meeting," Diane replied.[29]

Then she got a letter, with a question for a message that read, "Ms. Wilson, Are you aware of this?" The letter was attached to a newspaper clipping with a public notice about a chemical plant Diane had never heard of, Formosa Plastics. Diane did not know how to make sense of it, so she called her lawyer. He ask for the full company name and permit number and told Diane that they could request a copy of the permit from Austin. Then they could ask for a public hearing.

A few days later, Formosa was local news. A television reporter spoke about a Dallas newspaper article that claimed that Formosa was a persistent violator of the Clean Water Act. Then a Formosa representative came on screen and insisted that the allegation was not true and that the company had never dumped into Cox's Creek or any other creek. Diane called the television reporter and asked if it was true that the Formosa did not dump anything. "That's what they say," she was told. Then she called the Dallas newspaper reporter who had written the Formosa story and asked him if the story was true. "Sure," he said. "Can't print it unless it's true." He had copies of EPA documents citing Formosa for wastewater violations, and he would send them to Diane. She could not believe that "they can lie on TV news. And it is alright!"

Such was the beginning of the amazing education Diane has gotten in the wake of environmental right to know.

I first met Diane in the early 1990s, as part of a grassroots and union effort in the United States to commemorate the tenth anniversary of the Bhopal disaster. Already, she was a force to be dealt with and was an incredible resource for her community and an emerging toxics movement. She had forged links between labor and environmental groups and had cultivated contacts in government agencies like the Texas Water Commission. She recognized that Union Carbide's disaster in India was—despite company claims to the contrary—quite close to home. She saw how it all added up.

Disaster in Seadrift[30]

On March 12, 1991, the Union Carbide plant in Seadrift, Texas, Diane's town, also blew up. A year before, the Texas Industry Chemical Council had designated the same plant as the safest in Texas. Just a few days before the disaster, Assistant Secretary of Labor Gerard Scannell announced that Union Carbide's Seadrift plant had been approved for participation in the Occupational Safety and Health Administration's (OSHA's) STAR program, one of the agency's Voluntary Protection Programs for companies with exemplary safety and health programs.

Union Carbide's Seadrift disaster resulted from the explosion of an ethylene oxide production unit. The fireball could be seen ten miles away. John Resendez, a contract worker, was killed, and twenty-six others were injured.[3]

Chemical Week reported that there was a 92 percent satisfaction rate with emergency response by those living within two miles of the Union Carbide plant. Melonie Masih had a different story (see sidebar). So did Diane Wilson, who said:

> People were listening to scanners and all you heard was pure chaos. They didn't know how to stop the fires. There were these big oxide tanks sitting close by. They were sitting there watching them expand; they didn't know what was in them. It was just, you know. Half the people supposed to be in the control room were down in Seadrift, having taken off on a tear . . . but according to the local media the explosion went so well they oughta have another one next year—just to show how great this county is at handling explosions. Yet, the workers who went in to handle it didn't even have protective gear on.

She later obtained internal OSHA documents stating that Union Carbide management had prevented government investigators from questioning workers without company lawyers present. Only one worker was willing to sign a statement.

OSHA proposed a fine of $2,803,500 for 112 willful violations of health and safety regulations.[32] Among the willful violations cited were 106 instances of fire and explosion hazards, three instances of inadequate fire water supply, and three instances of locked gates and blocked emergency exits. OSHA also revoked its approval of the Seadrift plant for participation in the STAR program and said that Union Carbide had a "significant" history of workers' safety violations.

Robert Kennedy, chief executive officer of Union Carbide, said that OSHA should not have "abandoned" the company as a STAR member just because of the accident.[33]

Union Carbide eventually paid $1.5 million to OSHA in fines and agreed to pay $3.2 million to the widow and two children of Resendez.[34] Diane Wilson still had questions, so she made a citizen's request to meet with Union Carbide's Seadrift plant manager as provided for under the industry-wide Responsible Care program.

OUR NIGHTMARE

MELONIE MASIH, *Goliad, Texas*

Our nightmare began early on March 12, 1991. We were awoken from a very sound sleep by a tremendous explosion. The roof of our home appeared to lift several inches from the wall. Later, we would discover cracks in walls, broken windows, and pictures on the floor. The very earth underneath us shook with terrible vibrations. We thought we would be thrown from our very bed. It was shortly after 1:00 AM, but it appeared to be daylight due to the enormous fire resulting from the explosion. In our minds we felt certain an earthquake or the end of the world approached.

We immediately ran to our children ages 10 years and 12 years. Their safety being paramount in our concern. Our 12 year old suffers from a handicapping condition that results in grand mal seizures. Under stress her seizure activity increases.

My husband soon discovered Union Carbide once again was the culprit for disturbing our rest. We had ceased to count the episodes of lost sleep resulting from penetrating odors coming from Union Carbide.

We telephone the emergency number Union Carbide had provided for us at an earlier "near neighbor" meeting. This number had remained posted on our refrigerator for easy access. Following previous instructions given by Union Carbide we asked to speak to the emergency director on call. We were told, "he is busy." Next, we asked what had happened. We were informed, "lady, there has been an explosion." No joking, an idiot could have ascertained that bit of information! Before we could inquire as to what exploded the Union Carbide spokesperson hung up on us.

Then, we dialed the sheriff's department—no answer—dialed again—no answer. During this time we were trying our best to reassure and calm two very hysterical children. The children were literally shaking with fright and crying. It was months after the explosion before they would sleep alone or be free of nightmares. Even today loud noises upset them.

We could see this horrendous, murky cloud approaching our home. Our home was located half a mile from Union Carbide—Seadrift Plant property on the northeast corner of their property. The wind that early morning was from the south-southwest. We smelled a very suffocating, nauseous odor. It seemed to take our very breath away.

During the next few minutes a second and third explosion occurred. We had visions of being completely annihilated. Our decision was made we must evacuate. We telephoned our 80-year-old grandmother, who lived alone and closer to the plant, to inform her we were on our way to get her. Then, we telephoned our parents to let them know we were evacuating. Our daughter began to seizure. It took several minutes to place her in the car. All we could think of was we will be found dead when this nightmare finally ends.

The odor was horrible, terrible, suffocating and terrifying. Our children were begging and crying to put our two dogs in the car. There was no room. The dogs sensed danger; they tried repeatedly to get in the car. Finally, we pulled away from our home and pets not knowing if we would be alive at daybreak.

Our grandmother was waiting at her back door. We hurriedly placed her in the car and drove away quickly. She stated she had been up some time vomiting.

Once reaching the main highway there was tremendous traffic for such an early hour. All types of emergency vehicles were heading toward the Union Carbide Plant. There were numerous vehicles heading away from the plant. We later learned these were employees and neighbors seeking escape.

On the way to our small town of Port Lavaca located 11 miles east of the plant we stopped twice to question sheriff and police personnel. The stops proved futile. They had no information. In fact, they knew less than we did. One policeman even told us he would probably be dead by morning. They could not even tell us how far to go to be considered safe or what we had been exposed to.

During this time our daughter began to seizure again. We had to administer her emergency medication. We decided to seek medical attention and drove to the hospital in Victoria some 30 miles away. We later received knowledge that the explosion had been felt some 85 miles away. While driving to Victoria, I experienced a strong metallic taste in my mouth and some difficulty in breathing.

Upon arriving, we learned that the hospital had received no information. In fact, hospital personnel thought that Saddam Hussein had launched a Scud missile. Soon after our arrival, word came over the radio that ethylene oxide was the chemical involved and that the hospital should expect numerous casualties.

Our children became weak and nauseous and had diarrhea. We gave them Coke to try to settle them. The physician who saw us said that all he could do was treat symptoms and advised us to see our family physician during office hours that day.

Just as we were beginning to recover somewhat from the nightmare, earlier statements and fear again began to enter our minds. A previous statement made at a "near neighbor" meeting by the county judge, emergency management director, and Union Carbide plant manager said that in case of an emergency we would be notified within ninety seconds, but *no one ever came or called!* In addition was a statement by the emergency management director that he could be reached at anytime and anywhere, but he was the last official to report to the courthouse because he was unable to locate his pants! There were statements regarding safety, cancer concerns, fear of chemical plants, and their emission. Why had Union Carbide lied to us?

Today, as I sit here recounting this nightmare of events, we know the answers, answers we have had to learn the hard way. As I recall this information, my heart rate increases, tension develops, fear begins to consume me, and, yes, anger roars up, righteous anger that a company such as Union Carbide can be left to prey upon innocent people without fear of censure. The answers remain simple and point to one all-consuming fact: Union Carbide decided a long time ago that a dollar was more important than human life or planet Earth.

In conclusion, doctors tell us that it may be years before we learn the extent of damage to our bodies resulting from the nightmare of the explosion and our close proximity to the plant. To protect our family from further harm, we have been forced to sell our home, a five-generation farm, and relocate. Our resolve will continue to be to do everything in our power to protect this God-given home we call *Earth*!

On March 16, 1992, a group of eleven local and national environmental activists met at the Seadrift plant to attend the scheduled meeting. The Union Carbide spokesman said that he would not meet with them, saying that he would be prepared later in the week, which would have been after outside experts had left the area. The discussion held just outside the plant gates proceeded in revealing ways:

> *Fred Millar, Friends of the Earth:* Is there a policy about not talking to people from outside the community?
>
> *Union Carbide spokesman:* As I told Diane, we prefer to talk to local people, to keep it local.
>
> *Ramona Stevens, Louisiana Action Network:* The main thing is that Diane has the ability to bring in technical people to go through the documents so that they can discuss them with your technical people.
>
> *Union Carbide spokesman:* I'm local; Diane's local. We'll talk.
>
> *Millar:* When you have the meeting with Diane, will you be bringing engineers and people like that?
>
> *Union Carbide spokesman:* We'll bring the right people.
>
> *Millar:* Experts?
>
> *Stevens:* What about Diane's experts? It's not fair for ya'll to gang up on her. Ultimately, that's what you're doing.
>
> *Reverend Andy Smith, Director of Social and Ethical Responsibilities, American Baptist Churches, USA:* This message is going to shareholders, that Carbide is not willing to allow people to come in that might know what the data you are giving them is, and be able to interpret it. This message is going to go out loud and clear to all the shareholders—that Carbide is not doing what it says it will do under Responsible Care.[35]

Diane remained persistent and creative in her efforts to reduce risk in her community, adroitly working information resources, learning and revealing how information politics are entangled with environmental politics. Her successes were multiple and varied. Her own transmutation literally changed the order of things in Calhoun County, Texas, with ripple effects beyond.

From Politico to Author and Code Pink

In 2005, Diane Wilson published her first book, which chronicles her fight against chemical dumping in Calhoun County, in particular by

Formosa Plastics. The book is titled *An Unreasonable Woman: The True Story of Shrimpers, Politicos, Polluters, and the Fight for Seadrift, Texas* (see figure 5.2).

One reviewer—M. L. Madison, writing for *Feminist Review*—says the book reads "like a fast-paced political novel, and you almost can't believe it's real. Particularly angering is the chapter about Diane's discovering that the Environmental Protection Agency knows about Formosa's illegal dumping, but won't prosecute—despite the fact that many of the chemicals are carcinogenic."[36] The same reviewer describes how

> Wilson creates a memorable cast of characters that include friends, family, local politicos and environmental activists. Her writing is as captivating as the events that shaped the book: You can almost smell the waterfront, see the chemical clouds rising from the towers on the horizon, and hear the truck brakes squeal when one of the local fishermen is on the run from game wardens. You want to cheer her successes and cry for her defeats; her marriage is a casualty of her activism. . . . Despite all, Wilson absolutely *will not* give up. When she can't get hearings, she takes her protests to the streets. When she can't get legislators to return her calls, she befriends reporters. When her pro bono attorney tells her she should quit, she goes on a hunger strike. And she does all of this, amazingly, while being the primary caregiver of her five children.[37]

Another reviewer—William Baue, writing for the Environmentally Responsible Mutual Funds website—describes how Diane's unreasonableness is the book's core subject:

> Reasonable owners, managers, legislators, regulators, judges, and lawyers would hold corporations accountable for their toxic emissions. This book reveals that this is not always the case. Rather, it describes how a single woman must abandon reason to do "unreasonable" acts—hunger strikes and other more direct actions—to hold corporations and their supporters to account. Although it tells an all-too-true story, this book does not read like some nonfiction that bludgeons readers with data. Ms. Wilson focuses on truth over facts—though she does not spurn the latter, as evidenced by descriptions of stockpiling shrimp boxes full of documents acquired by Freedom of Information Act (FOIA) requests. In fact, it is the revelation of data that sets her activism in motion.[38]

Memories of first reading about TRI data for Calhoun County are still sharp for Diane. "It said we were the number one county in the nation for toxic disposal—our county is real small, not known for anything at all, and it was mentioned in this article four times," she explains. "That's not the type of information you can sit on and say, 'I didn't see it'—I moved on it, and so that's where all my work started, right there."

Figure 5.2

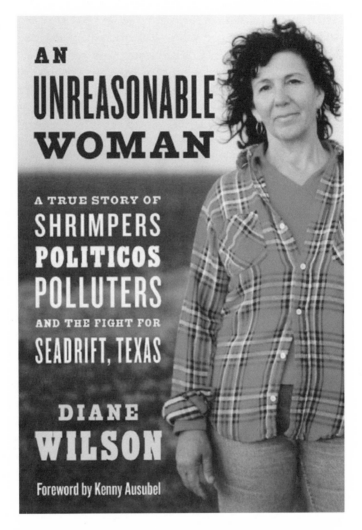

AN
UNREASONABLE
WOMAN

A TRUE STORY OF
SHRIMPERS
POLITICOS
POLLUTERS
AND THE FIGHT FOR
SEADRIFT, TEXAS

DIANE
WILSON

Foreword by Kenny Ausubel

Diane's movement took her in many directions. She founded Calhoun County Resource Watch and eventually won zero-discharge agreements from both Formosa Plastics and Alcoa. She also galvanized passage of zero-discharge resolutions by the Calhoun County Commissioners Court; by Seadrift's city council; and by the Oil, Chemical and Atomic Workers' Union. It took work: hunger strikes, protest speeches, an attempt to sink her shrimp boat on top of an illegal discharge outlet.

She visited Bhopal and became a critical voice in calls for legal accountability for Union Carbide's disaster there. As gas leak survivors demonstrated in Delhi in July 2002, for example, Diane was on a hunger strike in the back of her pickup truck, parked outside the Dow (formerly Carbide) plant in Seadrift. Gas leak survivors were demanding that compensation already awarded to them (roughly US$500 per survivor and US$1,250 to the families of those who died) actually be distributed and that the plant site (which was leaching toxins into local drinking water supplies) be cleaned up. Diane wanted to make sure that their suffering and protests were recognized by Dow. By the time Diane ended her fast, after twenty-nine days, 700 others around the world had joined her, interlinked through www.bhopal.net.

Fasting was not her only strategy. On a steaming day in late August 2002, Diane passed through the entrance gates of Dow's Seadrift plant with chains and a banner under her shirt. Combining skills from shrimping and from years of creative public protest, she climbed a seventy-foot-tall tower, a part of the ethylene oxide production process that had led to disaster in Seadrift more than a decade earlier. Once at the top, she chained herself in and unfurled her banner. The message was simple: "Dow—Responsible for Bhopal." Responsibility for disaster, Diane insisted, was heritable. Dow bought Union Carbide, so Dow now owns Union Carbide's liabilities as well as its assets. Diane was finally pulled down from the tower by a gang of men on a cherry picker and was charged with trespassing. For this act, she served five months in the Victoria County Jail.

Diane was also a founding member of Code Pink and helped organize their many protests against U.S. war in Iraq. An initiative at the Westin Oaks Hotel in Houston in December 2005 was particularly revealing. Code Pink had organized a peaceful protest outside a fund-raising event for Republican Congressman Tom DeLay. By donating $50, Diane was able to join the fund-raiser itself. When Vice President and former Halliburton CEO Dick Cheney took the stage, Diane opened up her black velvet wrap to reveal a banner that read "Corporate Greed Kills—From Bhopal to Bagdad." After being called a bitch and a whore by fellow guests, she was dragged out by police.

Diane's vitality has come from her capacity to make connections between highly technical information, everyday risk, and realpolitik; across the sea and the chemical plants, Seadrift and Bhopal; and across seemingly separate issues such as occupational safety and natural resource management, environmental politics, and the politics of and for war. Right-to-know legislation helped build this capacity. Not in full, of course; clearly,

Diane is an extraordinary person, but the transmutational effects of law deserve note nonetheless.

Conclusion

Law can, of course, directly shape the behavior of people and organizations, reducing risk and injury. The less linear ways law works are also significant.

The argument that law works in wayward ways is certainly not new to cultural and social studies of law. There remains, however, a general need within political and legal arenas to enhance recognition of cultural shifts as drivers and indexes of change. Changes in what is considered robust knowledge, changes in what is considered tractable or actionable, changes in how "fairness" is explicated—all cultural changes—are themselves important outcomes of law. These transmutations—changes in the form or character of things—often escape attention when behavior and performance are at the center of concern. Energy changes into matter and matter into energy through transmutation. Lead turns to gold through transmutation. Biological species differentiate and become distinct through transmutation. Thinking in terms of transmutation thus points to a way that law works beyond its direct effects. Indirect, nonlinear effects are particularly important in evaluating legally mandated disclosure in the environmental arena and in considering ways to reduce vulnerabilities to disaster.

Many commentators emphasize that "empowering the community" and "meeting the needs of ordinary citizens" are key aspects of right-to-know initiatives.[39] How, though, should community needs and empowerment be conceived? What is it that enables communities to protect themselves from risk and injury? What is constitutive of vulnerability, and—by contrast—resilience?[40]

Mike Davis, Charles Perrow, and many others highlight the material conditions productive of disaster.[41] Others highlight social and political conditions that both produce and are capable of deflecting disaster.[42] Amartya K. Sen's thesis about the ways information flow deflects famine is well known, calling attention to the ways the operation of a free press and other democratic institutions decrease the likelihood that available food supplies will be hoarded or diverted for profit.[43] Anthropologist Wadley L. Reed has shown how lateral social connections—supporting information flow, among other things—reduce vulnerabilities to disaster.[44]

The significance not only of having information, but also of being able to critically read and strategically deploy it, has also been considered.[45] Right-to-know initiatives produce these connections and critical practices, even when information is incomplete or faulty.

Indeed, a critical skill in the context of disaster is being able to make effective use of whatever resources—including information resources—are available. Right-to-know initiatives have cultivated this skill. It is this dimension of right-to-know initiatives—the way they cultivate critical information practices and social connections—that is missed in many evaluations of their efficacy, yet here are partial answers to questions about how disaster can be offset.

Disaster—whether creeping or catastrophic—forces and requires change. Initiatives aimed at disaster mitigation and preparedness thus need to be evaluated for the way they produce, or undermine, practices and infrastructure that enhance preparedness for change. Law, as one of many points of entry, should thus attend to the transmutations it permits.

In this way of accounting for things, reducing potentially injurious emissions—that is, changes in firm behavior—would continue to be a key index of the success of right-to-know initiatives. Additional indexes would also be necessary: indexes of evolving ways information available through right-to-know initiatives is triangulated, visualized, and deployed; indexes of the social connections enabled and forged as a result of right-to-know initiatives; indexes of conceptual developments that could make it easier to "recognize" environmental problems and disaster more generally. Recognition, as Elizabeth Povinelli has argued, is profoundly cultural, depending on very specific conceptual, discursive, and technological infrastructures.[46] Right-to-know initiatives have greatly expanded recognition of this order.

Most critical are the connections—both social and conceptual—that information enables. Because of the sheer volume of (environmental) risk information now available and continual innovation of ways to visualize it and connect it to other information, "working knowledge" can emerge, even when findings are not conclusive in a conventional sense. Working knowledge is not comprehensive, nor without error. It has what one of my informants called "requisite precision." Indeed, working knowledge is knowledge that works even when there are known information gaps and less than total confidence in information sources. Working knowledge depends on interpretation and judgment. It permits recognition of the complexity and ever-evolving nature of problems, while also helping people set priorities and mobilize change. Working knowledge works, even when the problems at hand are as complex as most environmental problems. Uncertainty no longer licenses inaction.

The production and sustainability of working knowledge depend on rights and access to information. They also depend on cultural transmutations that grant legitimacy to modes of thinking often censored in legalistic and technocratic arenas. Thinking comparatively rather than conclusively, with the goal of setting priorities rather than resolving all differences of perspective, for example, begins to make sense. Entanglement between social, technological, ecological, economic, and other kinds of systems begins to seem obvious, and people become adept at recognizing many pressure points where systems are subject to change. People—like Diane Wilson—who index and further propel such transmutations begin to seem eminently reasonable because the process and character of reason itself has shifted.[47] The transmutations of law can thus be quite significant indeed.

The implications for disaster preparedness and response are clear and are not particularly complex. People need risk information of many kinds, and they need it in advance of catastrophe. Concerns that people will misinterpret information are not unfounded, but they should not dominate decision making about information availability. People are interpreting creatures, and this needs to be cultivated by law, leveraged rather than suppressed. And practice does make more robust, if not perfect. It is through exposure to information that people develop the critical sensibilities that are needed for right-to-know initiatives to work.

Right-to-know legislation thus anticipates transmutation of its subjects (both human and informational) rather than assumes readiness in advance. It does not directly provide answers or solutions, but builds the infrastructure—technical, social, and cultural—that supports recognition of and response to risk, in routine as well as in catastrophic times. Risk and disaster are thus mitigated through the production of actors, like Diane Wilson, who have the capacity to reason beyond what convention denotes as reasonable and beyond what information itself reveals. It is transmutation rather than transparency in itself that it critical.

NOTES

1. My research on these issues began in 1989, when I went to Bhopal for ethnographic fieldwork. I have followed the Bhopal case and figures like Diane Wilson since then, trying to understand the cultural, social, and political-economic dynamics that shape efforts to reduce environmental health risks. I am currently working on a book that examines how the development of information culture and technology since the late 1980s has shaped knowledge and governance of the environment.

2. Diane Wilson, *An Unreasonable Woman: A True Story of Shrimpers, Politicos, Polluters and the Fight for Seadrift Texas* (White River Junction, VT: Chelsea Green Publishing, 2005), 37.

3. The TRI is a database of information about legal releases of approximately 650 chemicals by industry in particular sectors, now including manufacturing, metal and coal mining, and electric utilities. The list of substances subject to reporting has expanded over time (from about 300 at the outset), although there have also been controversial "delistings." The EPA provides electronic public access to the information in the TRI, allowing it to be downloaded and configured by organizations like OMB (Office of Management and Budget) Watch, which maintains RTKNET.org, and Environmental Defense, which launched the now-famous scorecard.org website in 1998. Scorecard links TRI information to health information to enhance users' understanding of risk, risk distributions, and opportunities for risk reduction.

4. Economists Tom Tietenberg and David Wheeler explain that "disclosure strategies form the basis of what some have called the third wave in pollution control policy—after legal regulation [emissions standards], and market-based instruments [tradable permits, emissions charges]." Tietenberg and Wheeler argue that first-phase approaches were excessively costly or incapable of achieving stipulated goals, especially in developing countries, where legal and regulatory institutions are weak. Market-based approaches are said to have done better, but even in industrial countries have not been able to handle the sheer number of substances to be controlled. To counter these problems, Tietenberg and Wheeler explain that third-phase pollution control policy "involves investment in the provision of information as a vehicle for making the community an active participant in the regulatory process. . . . The timing seems to emanate from a perceived need for more regulatory tools in the regulatory community, from a demand for environmental information from communities and markets and from falling costs of information collection, aggregation and dissemination." Tom Tietenberg and David Wheeler, "Empowering the Community: Information Strategies for Pollution Control," paper read at Frontiers of Environmental Economics Conference, Airlie House, VA, October 23–25, 1998, 1.

5. In late 2006, despite enormous opposition, the EPA weakened reporting requirements for the TRI. Previously, facilities had to provide detailed information about listed chemical releases of more than 500 pounds. The rule change allows facilities to resort to a short, much less detailed form (Form A) for releases of most TRI chemicals of up to 5,000 pounds, as long as 2,000 pounds or less are directly released to the environment. Twelve states have sued the EPA, arguing that the changes are a violation of the Emergency Planning and Community Right-to-Know Act because the EPA neither justified the changes nor even had the authority to make them. OMB Watch is a leading organization tracking this controversy and others related to environmental right to know. See http://www.ombwatch.org/article/archive/97.

6. Many people and organizations have insisted that Wilson is indeed special, even if "nobody particular." Wilson has won a number of awards, including the National Fisherman Magazine Award, Mother Jones's Hell Raiser of the Month Award, Louis Gibbs's

Environmental Lifetime Award, Louisiana Environmental Action's Environmental Award, the Jennifer Altman Award, and the Bioneers Award. Graphic artist Molly Bang has told and illustrated Wilson's story for young people in the book *Nobody Particular: One Woman's Fight to Save the Bays* (New York: Henry Holt, 2000).

7. See, for example, W. Neil Adger, "Vulnerability," *Global Environmental Change* 16 (2006): 268–81; Carl Folk, "Resilience: The Emergence of a Perspective for Social-Ecological Analyses," *Global Environmental Change* 16 (2006): 253–67; and Gilberto Galloping, "Linkages between Vulnerability, Resilience and Adaptive Capacity," *Global Environmental Change* 16 (2006): 293–303. See also the glossary of disaster risk reduction terms posted by the U.N. International Strategy for Disaster Reduction project: http://www.unisdr.org/eng/library/lib-terminology-eng.htm.

8. Michele Murphy aptly describes how information gaps can be understood as part of "regimes of imperceptibility." My argument is that bits of information can draw people into these regimes, as into a funhouse. They see the distortions of mirrors, bump into walls, and try to navigate unstable ground—learning how such regimes are configured, sliding out of them a bit more in the know. See Michael Murphy, "Uncertain Exposures and the Privilege of Imperception: Activist Scientists and Race at the U.S. Environmental Protection Agency," in *Landscapes of Exposure: Knowledge and Illness in Modern Environments*, ed. Gregg Mitman, Michelle Murphy, and Christopher Sellers, special issue of *OSIRIS* 19 (2004): 266–82.

9. The incremental learning process I describe here is not unlike the process of learning to do feminist semiotics as taught by figures like Teresa de Lauretis, emphasizing the need to understand what systems say as well as what they do not and cannot say. Understanding the gender effects of a social system, de Lauretis argues, demands "a movement back and forth between the representation of gender (in its male-centered frame of reference) and what that representation leaves out or, more pointedly, makes unrepresentable." The analyst must find or invent a way to move "between the (represented) discursive space of the positions made available by hegemonic discourses and the space-off, the elsewhere, of those discourses: those other spaces both discursive and social that exist, since feminist practices have (re) constructed them, in the margins (or 'between the lines,' or 'against the grain') of hegemonic discourses and the interstices of institutions, in counterpractices, and in new forms of community." Teresa de Lauretis, introduction to her *Technologies of Gender: Essays on Theory, Film and Fiction* (Bloomington: Indiana University Press, 1987), 1–30, quotations on 26.

10. My argument is not that environmental regulation should be limited to information disclosure, depending on "voluntary compliance." Old-fashioned "command-and-control" regulation remains critical and can be justified with increasing precision because of continuing developments in environmental health science. Consider, for example, advances in understanding the health effects of fine particulates and subsequent justification for tightening air quality standards. For details on 2007 revisions to the National Ambient Air Quality Standards, see http://www.epa.gov/oar/particlepollution/naaqsrev2006.html.

11. The background provided here and in the following section is drawn from my essay "From Bhopal to the Informating of Environmental Health: Risk Communication in Historical Perspective" in *Landscapes of Exposure: Knowledge and Illness in Modern Environments*, ed. Gregg Mitman, Michelle Murphy, and Christopher Sellers, special issue of *OSIRIS* 19 (2004): 283–96.

12. http://en.wikipedia.org/wiki/Information_society.

13. See, for example, Peter Ducker, *The Age of Discontinuity* (London: Heinemann, 1969); Daniel Bell, *The Coming of Post-Industrial Society* (New York: Basic Books, 1976); Jean-François Leotard, *The Postmodern Condition* (Manchester, UK: Manchester Univer-

sity Press, 1984); and Manuel Castells, *The Rise of the Network Society*, vol. 1, *The Information Age: Economy, Society and Culture* (Malden, MA: Blackwell, 1996).

14. Kevin Kelly, "New Rules for the New Economy," *Wired*, September 1997. 4, http://www.wired.com/wired/archive/5.09/newrules.html?pg=4&topic=&topic_set=.

15. Wil Lepkowski, "The Restructuring of Union Carbide," in *Learning from Disaster: Risk Management after Bhopal*, ed. Sheila S. Jasanoff (Philadelphia: University of Pennsylvania Press, 1994).

16. Janice Long and David Hanson, "Bhopal Triggers Massive Response from Congress, the Administration," *Chemical and Engineering News* (February 11, 1985), 59.

17. Ibid., 53.

18. Wil Lepkowski, "Bhopal Disaster Spotlights Chemical Hazard Issues," *Chemical and Engineering News*, December 24, 1984, 20.

19. Long and Hanson, "Bhopal Triggers Massive Response," 56.

20. Through passage, in 1976, of the U.S. Resource Conservation and Recovery Act (RCRA), in particular. This legislation required "cradle-to-grave" tracking of hazardous wastes and controls on hazardous waste facilities. The RCRA was amended in 1984, partly in response to the problems at Love Canal, which gained media attention in 1978.

21. The right to know is also part of the development of rights discourse since World War II to encompass human and civil rights as well as patients' rights, animal rights, and the right to a clean environment (Carl Wellman, *The Proliferation of Rights: Moral Progress or Empty Rhetoric?* (Boulder, CO: Westview, 1998).

22. John Young, "Using Computers for the Environment," in *State of the World 1994*, ed. Lester Brown (New York: W. W. Norton, 1994).

23. The literature on the TRI and environmental right to know is now fairly expansive. See, for example, James Hamilton, *Regulation through Revelation: The Origin, Politics and Impacts of the Toxic Release Inventory Program* (Cambridge: Cambridge University Press, 2005); Peter H. Sand, " The Right to Know: Environmental Information Disclosure by Government and Industry," in *Proceedings of the 2002 Berlin Conference on the Human Dimensions of Global Environmental Change: Knowledge for the Sustainability Transition. The Challenge for Social Science*, ed. Frank Biermann, Sabine Campe, and Klaus Jacob (Amsterdam, Berlin, Potsdam, and Oldenburg: Global Governance Project, 2004), 292–301; Anne Platt McGinn, "From Rio to Johannesburg: Reducing the Use of Toxic Chemicals Advances Health and Sustainable Development," *World Summit Policy Briefs* (WorldWatch Institute: June 25, 2002, e-mailed edition), 3; S. Dasgupta, B. Laplante, and N. Mamingi, "Pollution and Capital Markets in Developing Countries," *Journal of Environmental Economics and Management* 44 (2001): 310–35; Elisa Morgera, "An Update on the Aarhus Convention and its Continued Global Relevance," *Review of European Community & International Environmental Law* 14, no. 2 (2005): 138–47; J. C. Terry and B. Yandle, "EPA's Toxic Release Inventory: Stimulus and Response," *Managerial and Decision Economics*, no. 6 (1997): 433–43; Shameek Konar and Mark Cohen, "Information as Regulation: The Effect of Community Right to Know Laws on Toxic Emissions," *Journal of Environmental Economics and Management* 32 (1997): 109–24; Don Sherman Grant II, "Allowing Citizen Participation in Environmental Regulation: An Empirical Analysis of the Effects of Right-to-Sue and Right-to-Know on Industry's Toxic Emissions," *Social Science Quarterly* 78, no. 4 (1997): 859–73; S. Afsah, B. Laplante, and D. Wheeler, "Controlling Industrial Pollution: A New Paradigm," Working Paper no. 1672 (Washington, DC: World Bank, Policy Research Department, May 1996); Sidney M. Wolf, "Fear and Loathing about the Public Right to Know: The Surprising Success of Emergency Planning and Community Right-to-Know Act," *Journal of Land Use and Environmental Law* 11, no. 2 (Spring 1996): 217–325; Susan L. Santos, Vincent T. Covello, and David B. McCallum, "Industry Response to Sara Title III: Pollution Prevention, Risk Reduction and

Risk Communication," *Risk Analysis* 16, no. 1 (1996): 57–66; Susan Hadden, "Citizen Participation in Environmental Policy Making," in *Learning from Disaster: Risk Management after Bhopal*, ed. Sheila Jasanoff (Philadelphia: University of Pennsylvania Press, 1994).

24. Gerald V. Poje and Daniel M. Horowitz, *Phantom Reductions: Tracking Toxic Trends* (Washington, DC: National Wildlife Federation, 1990).

25. E. Petkova with P. Veit, "Environmental Accountability." For current information about PRTRs in different regions, see http://www.prtr.net/prtr/index_e.cfm.

26. McGinn, "From Rio to Johannesburg," 3.

27. For more on concern that exposure to risk information will provoke hysteria, see my "From Bhopal to the Informating of Environmental Health."

28. Wilson, *An Unreasonable Woman*, 47.

29. Ibid., 58.

30. This section is excerpted from my book *Advocacy after Bhopal: Environmentalism, Disaster, New Global Orders* (Chicago: University of Chicago Press, 2001).

31. The explosion and fire at Seadrift was caused by overpressurization of an ethylene oxide production unit. When the oxide unit column blew, a large piece of shrapnel hit the pipe rack and ruptured lines containing methane and other products.

32. The figure here for the proposed fine was drawn from George Draffen, *Research Compendium on the Union Carbide Corporation* (Seattle: Institute on Trade Policy for Communities Concerned about Corporations, 1994), 254. Louis Ember reports that OSHA announced proposed penalties against Union Carbide of $2,817,500 (Ember, "Responsible Care: Chemical Makers Still Counting On It to Improve Image," *Chemical and Engineering News*, May 29, 1995, 10–18). OSHA levied these fines under its egregious policy, which allows $25,000 for each violation. In 1986, Union Carbide was the first facility cited by OSHA under its egregious policy, for violations at their facility in Institute, West Virginia (the "sister plant" of the Bhopal plant because of its similar design).

33. Gregg LaBar, "Citizen Carbide?" *Occupational Hazards*, November 1991, 33–37. OSHA again awarded the Seadrift plant "star" status in its Voluntary Protection Program in 2007. OSHA's announcement of the award describes the Seadrift facility as having "706 employees who operate the plant's 14 production units. An additional 646 contractor employees are on site performing maintenance, capital projects, and guard and janitorial services. The chemical plant produces more than 40 products for use in everyday household, business and consumer products, such as plastic for wire and cable applications, automotive parts, toys, diapers, roofing materials, antifreeze, and health and beauty products." Electronic version of press release, http://www.osha.gov/pls/oshaweb/owadisp.show_document?p_table=NEWS_RELEASES&p_id=14276).

34. Draffan, *Research Compendium on the Union Carbide Corporation*, 254.

35. Exchange filmed by Chris Bedford for *Out of Control: The Story of Corporate Recklessness in the Petrochemical Industry* (Boulder, CO: Oil, Chemical and Atomic Workers Union, 1992).

36. Book review, *Feminist Review* (February 2007), http://feministreview.blogspot.com/2007_02_01_archive.html).

37. Ibid.

38. William Baue, "Book Review: An Unreasonable Woman: The True Story of Shrimpers, Politicos, Polluters, and the Fight for Seadrift Texas," Environmentally Responsible Mutual Funds website (September 27, 2005), http://www.socialfunds.com/news/article.cgi/1816.html.

39. See, for example, Archon Fung, Mary Graham, and David Weil's new book *Full Disclosure: The Perils and Promise of Transparency* (New York: Cambridge University Press, 2007). Promotional text for the book reads as follows:

Which SUV's are most likely to rollover? What cities have the unhealthiest drinking water? Which factories are the most dangerous polluters? What cereals are the most nutritious? In recent decades, governments have sought to provide answers to such critical questions through public disclosure to force manufacturers, water authorities, and others to improve their products and practices. Corporate financial disclosure, nutritional labels and school report cards are examples of such targeted transparency policies. At best, they create a light-handed approach to governance that improves markets, enriches public discourse and empowers citizens. But such policies are frequently ineffective or counterproductive. Based on an analysis of eighteen U.S. and international policies, Full Discourse shows that information is often incomplete, incomprehensive, or irrelevant to consumers, investors, workers and community residents. To be successful, transparency polices must be accurate, keep ahead of disclosers' efforts to find loopholes, and, above all, focus on the needs of ordinary citizens.

40. Increasingly (particularly in the emerging community of researchers and practitioners focused on human adaptation to climate change), "vulnerability" is the term used to describe what puts particular social groups at risk, increasingly the likelihood of the incidence of disaster and decreasing the capacity to respond to and survive disaster. "Resilience" is the opposing term and is created by social, cultural, political, economic, and technical infrastructures that reduce the risk of disaster and enable people to deal relative effectively with crisis events. How these concepts are worked out will dramatically shape policy and life chances in coming years.

41. Mike Davis, for example, describes how

> the extreme events that shape the Southern California environment tend to be organized in surprising and powerfully coupled causal chains. Drought, for example, dries fuel for wildfires which, in turn, remove ground cover and make soils impermeable to rain. This increases the risk of flooding in areas where earthquakes may have already exposed new surfaces to erosion and increased steam power by raising land elevation. In such conditions, storms are more likely to produce sheet flooding, land slides, and debris flows that result in dramatic erosion and landform change. Vast volumes of sediment rapidly realign river channels, and before the advent of twentieth-century flood control engineering, even switched river courses between alternate deltas. Sedimentation can also create sandbars that temporarily cut off tidal flows to coastal marshes –initiating a 50–75 year-long cycle of ecological readjustment. . . . This is not random disorder, but a hugely complicated system of feedback loops that channels powerful pulses of climatic or tectonic energy (disasters) into environmental work. The Southern California landscape epitomizes the concept of nonlinearity where small changes in driving variables or inputs—magnified by feedback—can produce disproportionate, or even discontinuous, outcomes.

Mike Davis, *Ecology of Fear: Los Angeles and the Imagination of Disaster* (New York: Vintage Books, 1998), 18–19. See also Charles Perrow's very influential *Normal Accidents: Living with High Risk Technologies*, 2d ed. (1984; repr., Princeton, NJ: Princeton University Press, 1999), and his more recent *The Next Catastrophe: Reducing Our Vulnerabilities to Natural, Industrial, and Terrorist Disasters* (Princeton: Princeton University Press, 2007).

42. See Charles Briggs with Clara Mantini-Briggs, *Stories in the Time of Cholera: Racial Profiling during a Medical Nightmare* (Berkeley: University of California Press, 2003); and Paul Farmer, *Pathologies of Power: Health, Human Rights, and the New War on the Poor* (Berkeley: University of California Press, 2003).

43. Amartya K. Sen, *Poverty and Famines: An Essay on Entitlement and Deprivation* (Oxford: Clarendon Press, 1981).

44. Wadley L. Reed, "Coping with Crisis—Smoke, Drought, Flood and Currency: Iban Households in West Kalimantan, Indonesia," *Culture and Agriculture* 24 (March 2002): 26–33.

45. Fortun, "From Bhopal to the Informating of Environmental Health"; Fortun, *Advocacy after Bhopal*.

46. Elizabeth Povinelli, *The Cunning of Recognition: Indigenous Alterities and the Making of Australian Multiculturalism* (Durham, NC: Duke University Press, 2002); Elizabeth Povinelli, "Radical Worlds: The Anthropology of Incommensurability and Inconceivability," *Annual Review of Anthropology* 30 (2001): 319–34.

47. There is now a wealth of scholarship that critically assesses conventional, "Enlightenment" constructs of reason, the best noting how alternatives are both coded by and must be worked out within governing norms and discourses. Jacques Derrida, for example, explains that "since the revolution against reason, from the moment it is articulated, can operate only *within* reason, it always has the limited scope of what is called, precisely in the language of a department of *internal* affairs, a disturbance." Jacques Derrida, *Writing and Difference*, trans. A. Bass (Chicago: University of Chicago Press, 1978), 36. Diane Wilson, in my reading, is a compelling example of this type of disturbance. For overtly feminist critiques of conventional constructs of reason (and objectivity), see Donna Haraway, "Situated Knowledge: The Science Question in Feminism and the Privilege of Partial Perspective," *Feminist Studies* 14, no. 3 (Fall 1988): 575–99; Evelyn Fox Keller, "Dynamic Objectivity: Love, Power and Knowledge," in *Reflections on Gender and Science* (New Haven, CT: Yale University Press, 1985), 115–26; and Gayatri Spivak's essays in *In Other Worlds: Essays in Cultural Politics* (New York: Methuen, 1987).

6

Reintegration, or the Explosive Remnants of War

Peter Redfield

Edward B. Rackley

The categories used to situate and analyze humanitarian issues in policy are far cleaner than most events on the ground. Perhaps nowhere does this truism grow clearer than at the end of emergencies, when exceptional suffering fades into normal misery. Whereas crises and catastrophes suggest the decisive lucidity associated with urgent need (however superficially or inappropriately applied), their aftermath remains deeply ambiguous and rarely featured in media reports. The "postemergency phase" identified by policy documents substitutes bland generalization for the patchwork of local and international uncertainties that accompany the end of crises, particularly conflicts that enter what anthropologist Carolyn Nordstrom describes as the time of "not-war-not-peace."[1] Although shooting may have lessened or even stopped, neither guns nor alliances simply disappear. In addition, international systems developed to respond to sudden events confront the longer-term effects of upheaval on political and economic ties as well as on individual lives. The medical and legal edges of the humanitarian tradition grow unclear.

In this chapter we examine the problem of defining the "end" of a crisis state when would-be humanitarians include the larger symptoms of social disruption within their purview. We will focus on recent concerns about child soldiers and efforts to reintegrate them into society in the aftermath of conflict. Deploying a technical euphemism for unexploded ordnance—"explosive remnants of war"—we consider how figures such as child soldiers disrupt simple definitions of a postemergency phase in both medical and legal terms. For empirical specificity, we refer to contemporary cases in the Democratic Republic of Congo (DRC) and in Uganda. We also describe the trajectory of an influential, crisis-oriented humanitarian organization with which we are directly familiar: Médecins Sans Frontières (MSF), otherwise known as Doctors Without Borders.

Observing that neither humanitarian organizations nor the medical or legal traditions they draw on are particularly well suited to the problems and contexts they now seek to confront, we suggest that current efforts represent a potential redefinition of international crisis in practice. Issues such as sexual and gender-based violence, mental health, and child soldiering suggest long potential time frames and reveal elements of inertia amid the volatile dynamic of crisis. Although organizations like MSF have typically shied away from chronic crises and development work, fearing the lack of a clear exit strategy, the growing range of humanitarian expectations and scope of humanitarian projects returns them to similar, unstable ground. By recognizing the extended effects of crisis states, humanitarian actors put themselves in a position in which it is increasingly difficult to limit their responsibility or withdraw. When they do so, it is amid a greater sense of uncertainty and incompletion than that which accompanies more immediate acts of "saving lives."

Crisis and Emergency Tools

The first step in our argument is a brief review of the significance of catastrophic moments of human suffering for the humanitarian tradition. Concepts of crisis have played a foundational role in humanitarianism, from the formation of the Red Cross and the initial Geneva conventions in response to war to the standardization of emergency medicine in response to natural disasters. Like older traditions of charity, humanitarianism frames the ethics of action in terms of a response to pre-existing conditions. Rather than individual misery or a general category like "the poor," however, the modern humanitarian focus has rested on populations defined by particular misfortunes: wounded soldiers on a nineteenth-century battlefield, say, or the shocked survivors of a tsunami. In this sense, the history of the Red Cross movement connects with the practice of missionary medicine amidEuropean empire and the rise of the welfare state in modern governance, all of which connected actions with institutions beyond personal virtue. At the same time, however, the Red Cross lineage of humanitarianism conceived of suffering as an exceptional state and its response as an attempt to re-establish normal conditions appropriate for human dignity. Even if the Red Cross movement created lasting institutions and norms of expectation related to warfare and disaster, it cast its activity in emphatically temporary terms.[2]

Focused on the short-term needs of suffering people, humanitarianism has thus long oriented itself toward the present and the necessity of urgent action. Unsurprisingly, humanitarian fund-raising appeals feature dramatic moments when the line between life and death looms large and an immediate response promises continued survival. Although such iconography simplifies the less certain terrain of actual humanitarian practice, it appeals to concerns about life in contemporary moral discourse and retains the force of an essential medical truth: undeniably, there are moments when prompt action saves lives. The concept of crisis itself has a long medical history, marking a turning point and hence the decisive moment for intervention. The standardization of emergency medicine in the second half of the twentieth century only sharpened this medical sensibility as it produced the technical means to quickly stabilize and treat a patient requiring urgent care. The "second wave" of humanitarianism—cast at a global scale, shaped in response to televised images, and marked by the rise of nongovernmental organizations (NGOs)—emerged in conditions in which it had become possible to imagine both immediate knowledge and rapid response.[3] The machinery of contemporary relief efforts thus concentrates on matters of human survival, the limited sense of life defined by existence.

Perhaps no organization better embodies the emergency ethos of global humanitarianism than MSF.[4] Established as a nongovernmental alternative to the Red Cross in 1971, the group initially positioned itself around emergency interventions, suggesting something along the lines of a universal hospital emergency room. Although adopting a role of self-appointed gadfly, the group framed its complaints in relation to action. Amid many other NGOs and state and interstate organizations, MSF slowly developed the material and conceptual basis for a mobile humanitarian apparatus, one that could intervene quickly in a variety of settings, largely in response to displaced populations. Over time, however, even MSF's purview widened alongside its reach. Like other actors in the aid, the group expanded its field of concerns well beyond emergency medicine, addressing a variety of health conditions such as HIV-AIDS. Even when responding to emergency settings, humanitarians increasingly worried about issues such as mental health and sexual violence. Although survival remains of crucial concern, the sense of life that contemporary humanitarianism seeks to defend includes a larger range of well-being. The response therefore exceeds the parameters of emergency medicine associated with immediate, urgent care.

To clarify the distinction involved, let us turn first to a recent fund-raising letter from MSF. "Dear Friend," it begins. "People shouldn't die of cholera, but they do. Simple things like clean water, proper sanitation, and good hygiene can prevent an outbreak of the disease and immediate rehydration can save a person's life when they are infected." Having established the basic medical facts of the disease, the letter continues to recount a recent cholera outbreak in Zambia and the difference that MSF was able to make by providing rapid response. "Your support," it concludes, "enables Doctors Without Borders to respond to outbreaks of cholera and many other deadly diseases with the speed and resources necessary to save lives. Please help us today."The choice of cholera for this purpose is not arbitrary. In many respects, it is the classic outbreak disease, one closely associated with catastrophe. From the perspective of public health, a primary danger associated with both warfare and natural disasters of any sort is that of sudden population movements, when masses of displaced people in unsanitary conditions quickly lead to outbreaks of infectious disease. As the letter indicates, however, cholera is relatively easy to treat, posing more of a problem of logistics than science for contemporary biomedicine. Based on years of experience working in refugee camps, MSF has developed a packaged "kit" of equipment and guidelines to respond to cholera, one that can be deployed anywhere in the world on a few days' notice. Provided all systems operate and local actors cooperate, cholera response—essentially containment and hygiene—can be highly effective; death rates fall precipitously, and in a relatively short time span all patients who survive can return to ordinary life. For all the mess involved, cholera response is clean and neat. This sort of humanitarian action produces tangible results of the sort easily incorporated into fundraising materials. Action, in the form of speed and resources, will indeed save lives.

Even in classic emergency settings, however, the end of any crisis is often less clear than the moment of its identification and initial response. People who recover from cholera often return to unsanitary conditions where they can become infected again. On a grander scale, the "postemergency phase" of any humanitarian operation remains uncertain even in its definition. According to MSF's authoritative volume, *Refugee Health Care: An Approach to Emergency Situations,* by one common criterion a postemergency phase begins when the crude mortality rate of a population falls below one death per 10,000 per day, taken to be the norm. "However," the guidebook quickly adds, "the border between these two phases is not that clearly defined and the evolution from emergency to postemergency is not unidirectional." Moreover, "the post-emergency phase ends when a permanent solution is found for the refugee problem (repatriation, integration into the host country or re-settlement in a third country). The duration cannot therefore be defined."[5] As the reference work goes on to note, some refugee crises persist for years, if not decades. A humanitarian health response therefore must shift from a concentrated focus to infectious diseases to include a wider range of chronic concerns, including such things as reproductive health, tuberculosis programs, and psychosocial and mental health. At some point, the problems facing the population no longer appear exceptional, however significant they may be. At that juncture, humanitarian action grows indistinguishable from more general concerns about development and public health.

By pursing this quick translation of catastrophe into population movements and potential epidemics, then, there is both a field for decisive action and a much larger terrain of uncertainty. What seems like a clear, well-defined response to a sharply defined problem grows fuzzy at a wider angle. Once a sense of immediate urgency fades, longer-term questions return to view. Survival momentarily ensured, people return to the endless task of living. From the perspective of humanitarianism, then, come three general observations:[6]

1. Crisis defines and justifies a milieu for action. An emergency is an exceptional state, one in which time concentrates into an instrumental sense of the present, "where every second counts." This situation invites technical response, in which knowledge compresses into decision.
2. Claims of crisis extend well beyond immediate moments of urgent action. They emerge from and recede into political contexts. Within these contexts, an exceptional state can have effects and can serve as resource.
3. Crises do not simply end as much as fade from view, often displaced by other dramas elsewhere. In fading, they reveal a more complicated topography of time beneath the concentrated present of action. Here an event lives on, affecting the continuing present of everyday life in its aftermath.

We will concentrate on this third observation for the remainder of the chapter. Unsurprisingly, even though humanitarian organizations like MSF have broadened their scope of action, their public image remains deeply attached to moments of crisis, particularly those covered by international media. Emergency response remains central to fund-raising efforts (where it reliably provokes generosity), implicit in much of the technical apparatus such organizations use, and a key component of the humanitarian esprit de corps. The newer activities and concerns, however, lend themselves even less well to a clean and surgical end. The contemporary problem of child soldiers illustrates the broader problem.

The Problem of Child Soldiers

Amid the circulation of international media and advocacy in the wealthier parts of the world, the problem of child soldiers has emerged as a topic of growing concern for members of the public and organizations alike.[7] Children have, of course, long personified the innocent victim, and, by the norms of childhood in wealthy countries, the participation of children in armed conflict appears an unthinkable violation. To situate contemporary concern, however, any anthropologist must first emphasize that both conceptions of childhood and warfare are hardly timeless universals. The definition of who counts as a child and who can count as a legitimate member of a fighting force has varied, and the ethnographic and historical record is more complex than contemporary advocacy movements might imply.[8] At least two features of the contemporary phenomenon appear relatively distinctive, however. First, the military use of children is now a part of conscious strategy rather than an initial stage in a longer career. Children are recruited as children, not as future adults. Second, the conflict experience does not represent a legitimate form of coming of age for surrounding communities. Being a child soldier, in other words, is no longer an acceptable rite of passage into adulthood, but rather a detour and possible dead end.

Thus, transnational sentiment of humanitarian concern, however parochial in its assumptions, does converge with a very real problem. Contemporary child soldiering represents a sort of living crisis, one that violently detaches an individual child from a given community into a new association shaped by conflict, without offering a clear path of return. To examine responses in relation to humanitarianism, let us examine two areas: the quasi-legal realm of policy and the efforts of specific humanitarian projects, including MSF. Although the result remains a sketch, it indicates the wider tensions revealed by humanitarian efforts to address the issue.

The Policy View on Children in Armed Conflict

"Postconflict reconstruction," a neologism employed by political analysts and humanitarian workers, aims to capture the daunting nexus of immediate and medium-term social, economic, and security needs facing a country emerging from years of conflict. Recovery from war is a long-term process, however, and it often exceeds the scope and expertise of relief agencies, which typically limit their involvement to services tailored to women and children directly affected by conflict: survivors of sexual violence and rape, former child soldiers, war orphans, populations returning from exile or long-term displacement, and the like.

As fighting now increasingly involves civilian targets, armed conflicts have a devastating effect on children. From direct observation, humanitarian policymakers know that thousands of children are killed or die as a result of warfare, and others take part in combat. Moreover, because schools and health facilities are targeted for attack, children often lack both for education and medicine while being denied essential humanitarian aid. Although the increasingly documented phenomenon of child soldiers receives particular attention, it is but one way children are manipulated and exploited by adults as cannon fodder, munitions mules, spies and scouts, camp minders, cooks and porters, and sex slaves.

P. W. Singer's book, *Children at War*, describes how conventions on wartime conduct, both cultural traditions and those born of nineteenth-century humanitarianism, have deteriorated to the point where children are abducted and reprogrammed to kill and be killed while their adult overlords watch from a safe distance.[9] Youth are attracted by the military's apparent exit from the destitution and vulnerability wrought by the war raging around them, and a chronic absence of economic opportunities in many contemporary conflict settings means that militias and armed groups need to conduct little active recruitment to fill the ranks. At the same time, the political ambitions of military forces relying on child soldiers remain limited in an institutional sense, a matter of sequential raids more than comprehensive conquest and enduring rule. The temporal scope of action on the battlefield thus mirrors that of the larger social issue, emphasizing a continual present rather than an expansive future.

Looking more closely at the child soldier phenomenon, or "children associated with armed conflict" (CAAC), two approaches have emerged for humanitarian agencies to engage the problem: (1) disarmament, demobilization, and reintegration (DDR) programming and (2) United Nations Security Council (UNSC) resolutions, combining legal instruments with "evidence-based advocacy," most recently and visibly in the 2005 UNSC Resolution 1612. The first approach recognizes the long-term implications of child soldiering, although successful outcomes lie beyond control of relief agencies. The second concentrates on establishing a legal framework for official recognition of the problem, implying a more general and ongoing monitoring and reporting of grave violations against children by parties to conflict. We will examine each briefly in turn as they pertain to two neighboring countries in Africa.

Disarmament, Demobilization, and Reintegration (DDR) in the DRC

The proliferation of United Nations' peacekeeping operations coincides with an increase in UN-led programs to disarm and disband warring parties as well as reintegrate ex-combatants into civilian life. DDR programs have featured in postconflict reconstruction from Afghanistan to Haiti, but the bulk of DDR interventions—twenty-four since 1992—have occurred in Africa. The failure of early DDR programs in Somalia and Liberia, partly attributed to their vague mandates, prompted a shift in recent years toward more focused interventions, now codified in a new set of policy guidelines developed in 2005.[10]

In the disarmament phase, weapons belonging both to combatants and the civilian population are collected, documented, and disposed of (in most cases, destroyed). This process includes the assembly of rebel combatants, often in an area guarded by government forces; collection of personal information; collection of weapons; certification of eligibility for benefits; and transportation to a demobilization center. During demobilization, armed groups are formally disbanded. At this stage, combatants are generally separated from their commanders and transported to cantonments, or temporary quarters, where they receive basic necessities and counseling. Eventually, they are transported to a local community where they have chosen to live permanently. "Reinsertion" is the transitional assistance offered to ex-combatants during demobilization before longer-term reintegration begins. Such assistance can include cash payments, in-kind assistance (goods and services), and vocational training. Despite the logistical challenges of disarmament and demobilization, reintegration—the acquisition of civilian status and sustainable employment and income—is considered the most difficult phase of any DDR process.

Because DDR originally focused on short-term disarmament, reintegration is the least developed phase, in some cases confined to vocational training in one or two fields. In most postconflict countries, particularly those in Africa, job opportunities are scarce, and ex-combatants have little occasion to apply their newly acquired vocational skills. In a survey of ex-combatants in Sierra Leone, more than 75 percent said that the training component of DDR had prepared them well for employment; the most common complaint about the program was that it should have lasted longer.[11] By contrast, in the Democratic Republic of Congo, the reintegration process was "chaotic and problematic," according to a 2007 Amnesty International report.[12] "We risked our lives to hand in our weapons," said a former fighter interviewed for the report. "We are incapable of feeding our families and cannot even pay the rent. The solution is for these people to give us our weapons back." Both responses highlight a common tension within the DDR approach: by defining the issue through the military status and equipment of combatants, the sequence overlooks the extent of social and economic rupture surrounding them. The "crisis" in this sense is not one of militarization alone.[13]

A snapshot from the ground provides a better sense of the ambiguities of such policy initiatives. In early 2006, one of the authors (Ed Rackley) evaluated large-scale DDR programs for the World Bank and UNICEF across the DRC. His team was hired to assess the effect of a number of projects to secure the release of child soldiers from an array of military groups and to return them to their families and communities. The projects were designed to provide children with the means and mental wherewithal to resist the pressures of rerecruitment. Such pressures remain constant. Combat continues, and children are attractive soldiers—so the logic runs—because they rarely disobey or run away, do not require a salary, and have more malleable minds than adults and older adolescents. It is no accident that the DRC's richest mineral regions were also the scene of its most intense combat and its highest concentration of child soldiers. During Mobutu Sese Seko's reign (1965–1997), mineral resources and mining industry in the southeastern Katanga province, for example, generated more than 50 percent of the country's gross national product; by 2004, following a decade of war, Katanga festered in a state of aggrieved destitution. From a humanitarian policy perspective, the province lagged at least two or three years behind the rest of the country in terms of the peace process. Ethnic militias and Mai Mai warlords still roamed the interior, and disarmament and demobilization of key military factions had barely begun.

Evaluating DDR programs in rural areas wavering between war and peace reveals the specific conditions and economic constraints facing the demobilized child soldier, his or her family, and the wider community of return. From Kalemie on the shores of Lake Tanganyika, the team took a motorcycle trip out to a village where a number of children had been reunited with their families. The same trip had been attempted the day before by jeep, but insurmountable mud had forced a return to town, where the team visited a local transit center for recently released children awaiting reunification while their families were traced and contacted. In the village and in the transit center, the situation was disturbingly similar. The boys were mostly under ten years old. Prepubescent children held by Katanga militias typically served mostly ritualistic roles and rarely bore arms; these boys had transported fetishes and various magic effects for Mai Mai militia leaders, who believed their bodies were bulletproof. In similar fashion, prepubescent girls had been made to wash the naked bodies of adult combatants with potions before and after battle. Many were daughters of the Mai Mai officers and commanders, so any prospect of securing their permanent release from military servitude was scant. In the interim, they would be treated as immediate family members of adult combatants, the team was told by DDR officials. The children would be incorporated into the DDR process only when and if their fathers decided to surrender and disarm. Although clearly affected by war, these children did not easily fit into the DDR framework.

After six weeks of such encounters, the team drafted its report. A major finding of the evaluation concerned the difficulties of ensuring successful reintegration for former combatants, children and adults alike. The absence of economic opportunity meant that even skilled manual laborers could find few avenues for income generation. Lack of alternative livelihoods had been the primary motivator behind many children's initial decision to flee their families and join militias. The same pressure threatened to prove the primary cause of their rerecruitment. At the same time, material and psychological needs of former child soldiers remained urgent. Aid agencies had established programs to address these needs during the initial transition phase from militia to communities and families. Once reunited, however, finding both self and livelihood without the aid of a gun remained a primary challenge. Although aid agencies could provide training programs and try to match trainees with apprenticeships in urban areas with a prospect of permanent employment, such a trajectory was far rarer in the commercial desert of the Democratic Republic of Congo.

Evidence-Based Advocacy in Northern Uganda

To provide a parallel with the DDR evaluation in the DRC, we now turn to one of its neighbors to the east, Uganda, and to the UNSC resolution and advocacy approach. Although much of Uganda stabilized following Yoweri Museveni's ascension to power in 1986, the northern region of the country experienced continuing unrest. The conflict has most recently pitted government forces against the Lord's Resistance Army (LRA), a religious insurgency now based in southern Sudan and the northeast of the DRC. From the late 1990s, LRA campaigns began devolving into a "war of children against children" featuring episodic skirmishes, massacres, mutilations, and abductions of local children by LRA combatants, often children themselves. The LRA thus found itself a ready-made subject for the more lurid strains of international journalism. The combination of continuing insecurity and government policies produced large-scale displacement of the civilian population, sending approximately 1.67 million people into more than two hundred camps for internally displaced persons (IDPs), eighty percent of whom were children and women. The five worst affected areas in the north have been Apac, Gulu, Lira, Kitgum, and Pader districts. As of April 2007, the official DDR process had not begun and a political settlement with the LRA was still pending. Aid agencies have nonetheless been running rehabilitation programs for children who had been released or escaped from armed groups.

The sense of "rehabilitation" in this context contained poignant gender and sexual undertones and could involve more than one generation of children. Among the approximately 15,000 formerly abducted children who escaped from the LRA between mid-2002 and 2006, approximately 1,000 girls returned with children of their own as a result of forced sexual relations during captivity.[14] Fear of a similar fate disrupted the lives of a far larger number of people. At the peak of hostilities in mid-2004, an estimated 44,000 children and adults were moving each night from peri-urban squatter camps to shelters in towns and hospitals, thus minimizing the risk of abduction. By October 2006, in response to improving security conditions in the countryside, the official figure had declined to 5,778 such child "commuters" (including 2,962 girls), yet both mobility and vulnerability remained facts of everyday life. The continual search for cooking fuel, wild foods, and livelihood options forced children and women to visit isolated areas outside camp security zones, exposing them to potential attack.

From the perspective of child soldier advocacy, the LRA was the primary but not the only danger confronting northern youth. Although the government of Uganda had no conscious policy to recruit children, children were present among the Local Defence Units (LDUs) and the Uganda People's Defence Forces (UPDF). During a 2006 visit of the UN Special Representative for Children and Armed Conflict to Uganda, the government agreed to enter into an "action plan" and strengthen the implementation of existing legal and policy frameworks on the recruitment and use of children by the national army and its paramilitary forces, particularly the LDUs. As of early 2007, however, the 1,128 children reportedly mobilized into LDUs around Kitgum, Pader, and parts of Teso more than two years earlier were still awaiting release.

Such bilateral action plans are part of the UN approach to monitoring and reporting on grave violations against children, particularly on sexual violence and child soldiers. Beginning with Resolution 1261 in 1999, the Security Council has produced a series of documents to enhance the protection of children in situations of conflict. As part of this process, in 2003 the secretary-general issued a list of fifty-four countries in which the rights of children were systematically violated as a result of armed conflict. Significantly, Uganda was featured on that list and remains on more recent iterations of this resolution. Specifically, the Security Council requested that the secretary-general order UN agencies on the ground to devise

> an Action Plan for a systematic and comprehensive monitoring and reporting mechanism, which utilizes expertise from the United Nations system and the contributions of national governments, regional organizations, non-governmental organizations in their advisory capacity and various civil society actors, in order to provide timely, objective, accurate, and reliable information on the recruitment and use of child soldiers in violation of applicable international law and on other violations and abuses committed against children affected by armed conflict, for consideration in taking appropriate action.[15]

Six core grave violations were identified as a guide for reporting and monitoring in the listed countries: killing and maiming of children, abduction of children, attacks on schools and hospitals, sexual violence perpetrated against children, recruitment and use of children as child soldiers, and denial of humanitarian access to children.

A central component of the UN advocacy approach involves the establishment of a research framework and the generation of documented incidents of the above violations. Given Uganda's status on the secretary-general's list of countries violating the rights of children, the Office of the High Commission for Human Rights (OHCHR) and UNICEF began working with the national government on an Action Plan. As part of this process, a Uganda Task Force on Monitoring and Reporting, comprising OHCHR, UNICEF, Save the Children, and the Uganda Human Rights Commission, was set up and given the mandate of designing and implementing a working mechanism to comply with the Security Council's requirements. The task force developed a reporting and documentation mechanism, beginning with extensive training for human rights and child protection practitioners at the local level. Initial data collected on an ad hoc basis by the task force during the first half of 2006 provided evidence of the six violations across the northern districts.[16] Perpetrators came from within the government armed forces and groups (UPDF/LDU) as well as the LRA. In addition, the secretary-general's resulting report on children in armed conflict confirmed that children continued to be recruited and used by the UPDF and by LDUs.[17]

On the basis of resolutions and evidence generated by expanding surveillance and monitoring structures, the United Nations and associated agencies acquired a body of evidence with which to advocate against the use of child soldiers. Although the success of such an approach depends largely on informal pressure and secondary effects amid the larger tides of diplomacy, in the context of Uganda it has produced tangible results. At the point of most recent assessment in early 2007, the number of night commuters continued to decline and aid agencies began to shrink their programs. The UPDF and its auxiliary forces, the LDUs, had largely complied with international standards prohibiting the use and recruitment of child soldiers, although other abuses against children continued, particularly on the side of the LRA. A full DDR process in northern Uganda remained on standby, pending a political settlement to the war. Peace negotiations and an International Criminal Court (ICC) investigation continued to drag on, while some 3,000 women and children were thought to remain in LRA captivity. Things did look better, particularly in comparison to the DRC, but where negotiations with the LRA would lead remained uncertain.

Finding an End?

What, then, to say about the child soldier phenomenon at the level of policy? Following concerted advocacy and direct engagement of the Security Council, the problem of child soldiers is now a part of the UN horizon, formally recognized in UNSC Resolutions 1539 and 1612. In addition to this legal armature, humanitarian organizations have a general model (DDR) for the long-term process of returning former soldiers to civilian life. Together they constitute a strategic framework through which to imagine an end to this form of crisis. Actual implementation of this framework has proved difficult however. In impoverished settings like the Democratic Republic of Congo, the "reintegration" phase of DDR remains particularly elusive, to the extent that a former fighter might suggest reversing the process and returning to arms. The situation in Uganda appears brighter in economic terms, and yet any final resolution remains on hold, awaiting formal conflict settlement. The civilian population may venture back to the countryside, feeling more secure, but the larger threat remains. In neither case does the crisis appear to end cleanly; the aftereffects of child soldiering are hard to contain in resolutions or three step plans.

What these policy efforts undoubtedly produce is a framework defining the problem of child soldiering as currently constituted and outlining its ideal trajectory. Such a framework can function as a resource for both intergovernmental and nongovernmental advocacy projects, which, in turn, reinforce and refine it. At points, the political equation in a given context may yield substantive results and may benefit particular individuals and communities. At the same time, however, the very conceptual framing of the policy approach elides central aspects of everyday experience in conflict settings: poverty, fear, uncertainty, and the litany of small compromises people make to survive. Terms like "reintegration" assume a stable social and economic order, and plans and legal instruments leave open the challenges of their implementation. Overall, as urgency diffuses into a mass of more common complaints, the endgame of crisis lends itself poorly to management and the various technologies of humanitarian intervention.

The Project View: MSF in Uganda

Having approached the issue of child soldiers through a broader policy perspective, let us now look at a specific humanitarian project, one assembled less from plans than improvisation and more directly focused on embodied forms of suffering. Turning from international law back to clinical medicine shifts the scope of expectation as well as the scale of action. Because health conditions have varying timelines and therapies varying effects across a population, clinical work is necessarily individuated, specific, and potentially recurring. Thus, an additional layer of background about Uganda is helpful. Although the conflict in northern Uganda only recently received significant international attention, it has flared off and on for at least two decades. As anthropologist Tim Allen notes, in a longer view its roots extend back over a century to the travels of armed traders, amid the jostling of rival European forces for influence in the wider region.[18] Regional differences and ethnic rivalries lie beneath the surface conflict between the LRA and the UPDF. The conflict itself is far less of a conventional "war" than a sporadic campaign of fear in which the LRA (and some suspect the UPDF) have managed to incite and perpetuate a state of instability. On its end, the LRA pursues small-scale terror tactics, famously featuring abductions, amputations, and the liberal use of child soldiers. For its part, the national army has failed to provide consistent protection and has been accused of its own atrocities. The result is the ongoing IDP crisis, with most of the displaced population living in squalid camps. The population in the camps, although fearful of the LRA, remains suspicious of the national government and its army, whose power base lies in the south. Further complicating the situation is the fact that this conflict intertwines with the long-simmering war in southern Sudan and a patchwork of alliances through which the two governments have helped sponsor insurgencies against each other. The border itself—like many in Africa—is an artifact of colonial rule rather than a reflection of cultural divides. Although governments, intergovernmental agencies, and NGOs may all work through national boundaries, experiences on the ground are more local, heterogeneous, and interconnected than such units might imply.

MSF has been active in Uganda since 1980. Its most recent ventures in the northern conflict zone, however, only took shape following an upsurge in violence in 2003, when several sections of the organization opened projects addressing the large masses of people living in displacement camps.[19] Here we the focus on one such project, undertaken by MSF Switzerland in the town of Gulu. As well as offering a variety of health services to people living in neighboring camps, in response to events on the ground the MSF mission unexpectedly found itself helping administer a night-commuter center on the grounds of St. Mary's Hospital Lacor (the site of an Ebola virus outbreak several years before). Here several thousand children crowded into the gates every night, afraid of the possibility of abduction, and during the day they would return home. While at first they huddled in the open, the aid agency soon built a hygienic environment for them, with tents and latrines, within the hospital compound. MSF also offered basic clinical care and psychological counseling, particularly aimed at those who had experienced violence firsthand, including abductees and former members of the LRA. Although many elements of the center were classic features of any refugee camp, the total assemblage represented a new variant, and the addition of psychosocial services was a hallmark of the expanded humanitarian project.

The night-commuter centers quickly achieved a relatively high degree of publicity, helping place the Ugandan crisis on the international map. Although MSF included the country on its annual list of top ten "underreported crises" for 2004, the IDP problem there finally entered media circulation that year, and the beginning of the ICC investigation and UN agency fact-finding missions increased political attention. Child "commuters" fearing for their safety became a vivid symbol of continuing security problems and instability, and that some children had experienced or participated in violence directly, with wrenching personal stories, made good copy. One shelter would host five or more journalists a night. Although MSF refused most requests, believing that the children were becoming overphotographed and overinterviewed, the organization nonetheless deployed its own images freely for advocacy and fund-raising purposes.

By the time one of the authors (Peter Redfield) visited in late 2004, the Lacor center was operating far below peak levels and under its capacity of 4,250 persons. Where once some 6,000 had massed inside, regular numbers now ran one-third of that. Children ran through and around the orderly row of tents (several of which had been shifted from a cholera project just down the road). Some were young, perhaps six or seven years old, but many were older, if all officially under sixteen. The MSF project coordinator outlined the basic features of the center while leading an impromptu tour and inspecting the latest work. Although officially in charge of MSF's side of the enterprise, he evinced some skepticism about its long-term effects, noting that the organization had a weakness for "committing to things we can't or don't want to do." Although MSF could improvise something like the commuter shelter in response to specific need, it was not the group's core mission, and the group was already searching for another entity, perhaps local authorities or an international organization like War Child, to step in and take over operations.

Beyond tents, the water system, the latrines, and the health clinic, MSF also helped sponsor a counseling center, where the tour inevitably led. The therapy tent emitted a glow of neon light. Inside, the decor was sparse, other than a poster outlining the Convention of the Rights of the Child hanging on one wall. Four Ugandan counselors sought to meet the varying needs of the young population. As well as group sessions, they also offered talks to both the center residents and members of neighboring communities to discuss topics such as sexual violence and its aftermath. The community visits presented a special challenge, one counselor noted, not only due to the sensitivity of the topic, but also because leaders expected tangible returns for attendance. In this poor setting, if a meeting did not offer food, attendance was guaranteed to be low. The counselors focused more on girls than boys, especially those age fourteen and over. As well as the threat of rape (incidents of which had occurred just outside the hospital walls), girls navigated a wider field of potential problems, including harassment, pregnancy, risky abortions, and suicide attempts. They also were thought to be more emotional than the boys and to have greater difficulty talking. In cases in which it seemed warranted, the counselors would try to follow up with home visits, but beyond the center itself, the children had few available resources. The focus of their kin groups lay with immediate subsistence, not long-term therapy, and unless they could achieve official classification as a category of current international donor interest—former soldiers or AIDS orphans—few organizations would help. As an MSF doctor noted with irony, in this sense they might have been materially better off having HIV.

At the end of 2004, the war was in a lull and the rate of abductions slowing. MSF's mission director, less enamored with the project than his colleagues at the organization's Geneva headquarters, believed that the night-commuter center would not last long. If demand kept shrinking, MSF would surely shift its resources to other projects in Uganda or elsewhere, ones with a clearer medical focus and definable outcome. On a return visit in mid-2006, however, the center was still in operation and still run by MSF Switzerland. By now, the overall security situation appeared to be improving, although local optimism remained guarded. MSF Switzerland had a new team in place, and its members puzzled over why, now the war seemed to be winding down or at least growing dormant, a large group of children in the Lacor shelter were not going home. Why weren't they reintegrating? Over drinks at a bar, members of the project team discussed the issue. On the one hand, a small number of children clearly had nowhere else to go or had been deeply scarred by violence. Many more, however, defied such a diagnosis. Although poor and needy, they were not former child soldiers and did appear to have living kin. Some staff speculated that other members of their household may have grown accustomed to their absence and rather enjoyed the baby-sitting service, or perhaps the children themselves preferred the experience of staying with a fluid group of their peers rather than facing more restrictive social roles at home. At the same time, there was the larger question of the change in the social landscape. If communities had altered as a result of conflict and displacement—kin groups scattered and under economic stress—then where was their home? One team member argued forcefully against "reintegration," suggesting that it was an illusion. Although aware that the local residence patterns did not conform to European norms, the MSF project possessed only a limited sense of the ethnographic terrain and was uncertain the degree to which it might have altered. Had norms changed? Was the "general atmosphere of violence" that an MSF psychologist noted earlier that year now dissipating?[20] Just as the surrounding crisis faded but did not end, this specific project resisted any easy resolution. MSF would clearly move on to another frontline, but it was unclear what the organization would leave behind.

The project-level perspective both confirms the degree of uncertainty involved in finding and recognizing humanitarian endpoints and underscores the extent of disruption worked by war. Beyond the figure of the child soldier stretches a larger set of childhoods affected by conflict, their educational trajectories curtailed, social networks reworked, and energies diverted. To grasp and engage with this wider context requires both local knowledge and a deeper sense of history than most international organizations afford. As a sense of crisis fades, however, it becomes increasingly visible, a reminder that events and emergencies never stand completely apart from everyday life and that effects of war reverberate like unexploded ordnance, long after the fighting is over. Here humanitarian action faces structural inequity and lack of basic infrastructure, blending into development. It has no contained, portable toolkits it can simply apply.

Conclusion

In a 2006 collection of essays addressing humanitarian issues, Veena Das explores the complex relationship between a disruptive event and the continuing practice of everyday life. She suggests a more subtle and contingent relation between language and self than the framework of trauma might imply.[21] The effects of a catastrophic event such as the partition of India can ripple through an extended family over time, affecting not only individual psyches but also the very fabric of its sociality. A rape or a disappearance alters lives for a generation. From this perspective, it is an illusion to assume that an event is simply contained in time. In another recent work concerned with the experience and politics of suffering, Didier Fassin examines controversies surrounding AIDS in South Africa at the intersection of colonial history and biomedicine.[22] Bodies, he suggests, remember violation; they carry the past along with them like scars. Thus, a current crisis, like HIV-AIDS, cannot escape the shadow of earlier struggles against apartheid. A given social order does not simply vanish with the fall of a political regime, and any world remade remains fragile. Beneath the shared commonality of species biology lies the raw inequality of differing conditions. From such a perspective, the aftermath of violence is a very public problem, not reducible to individual therapy.

These truths are, in a sense, old truths, but easily lost amid the language used to describe crisis. The title of this chapter alludes to both the hope of "reintegration" and the problem of unexploded ordinance. From the perspective of humanitarianism, child soldiers present a more complex challenge than cholera. Whereas the classic apparatus of public health, once translated to a local setting, can resolve the immediate threat of certain epidemics, the larger field of psychosocial problems is far harder to bind in time. Child soldiers are more akin to land mines, long-lasting remnants of war that disrupt the social landscape. Deactivating them not only requires delicate and patient technical work, however, but also a milieu in which their postexplosive lives can be sustained. Neither law nor medicine can offer a quick or simple cure for poverty, political uncertainty, or social fragmentation. Unlike the codification of abstract rights or the promotion of immediate survival, war's aftermath is particular and flows through lifetimes. The "crisis" described here remains true to the classic medical etymology of the term, marking only a potential turning point, one that appears decisive from the present, but whose longer-range outcome remains unclear.[23]

NOTES

1. Carolyn Nordstrom, *Shadows of War: Violence, Power and International Profiteering in the Twenty-first Century* (Berkeley: University of California Press, 2004).

2. See John F. Hutchinson, *Champions of Charity: War and the Rise of the Red Cross* (Boulder, CO: Westview Press, 1996), on the manner in which the Red Cross came to play an medical auxiliary role for European military forces by World War I.

3. Luc Boltanski, *Distant Suffering: Morality, Media and Politics* (Cambridge: Cambridge University Press, 1999); Michel Fehr, Gaëlle Krikorian, and Yeates McKee, eds., *Nongovernmental Politics* (New York: Zone Books, 2007).

4. MSF is actually a loose assemblage of nineteen national sections that share a common charter and ethos, but often squabble among themselves. For the purposes of this chapter, we treat it as a single organization and foreshorten the historical complexity involved. The kit system referenced in the cholera example below stabilized in the later 1980s and continues to exemplify MSF's mode of emergency response. For more on kits, see Peter Redfield, "Vital Mobility and the Humanitarian Kit," in *Biosecurity Interventions: Global Health and Security in Question*, ed. Andrew Lakoff and Stephen Collier (New York: Columbia University Press, 2008), 147–71. For more on MSF as an organization, see, for example, Peter Redfield, "Doctors, Borders and Life in Crisis," *Cultural Anthropology* 20, no. 3 (2005): 328–61; or, more comprehensively, Anne Vallaeys, *Médecins Sans Frontières: la biographie* (Paris: Fayard, 2004).

5. MSF, *Refugee Health Care: An Approach to Emergency Situations* (London: Macmillan, 1997), 243.

6. For general orientation, see recent work addressing the topic of humanitarian emergencies, for example, Didier Fassin and Paula Vasquez, "Humanitarian Exception as the Rule: The Political Theology of the 1999 Tragedia in Venezuela," *American Ethnologist* 32, no. 3 (2005): 389–405; and Mariella Pandolfi, "Contract of Mutual Indifference: Governance and the Humanitarian Apparatus in Contemporary Albania and Kosovo," *Indiana Journal of Global Legal Studies* 10 (2003): 369–81.

7. For example, University of North Carolina–Chapel Hill's Student Movement to End Child Soldiering, campus-y.unc.edu/index.php/component/content/95?task=view.

8. See, for example, David Rosen, *Armies of the Young: Child Soldiers in War and Terrorism* (New Brunswick, NJ: Rutgers University Press, 2005).

9. Peter Singer, *Children at War* (New York: Pantheon, 2005).

10. www.unddr.org/iddrs/.

11. www.stanford.edu/~jweinst/docs/manuscripts/humphreys_combatantsurvey.pdf. For a more vivid account of the ambiguities of disarmament on the ground, see Danny Hoffman, "Violent Events as Narrative Blocs: The Disarmament at Bo, Sierra Leone," *Anthropological Quarterly* 78, no. 2 (2005): 329–54.

12. web.amnesty.org/library/Index/ENGAFR620012007.

13. For more on the general figure of African crisis, see Achille Mbembe and Janet Roitman, "Figures of the Subject in Times of Crisis" *Public Culture* 7, no. 2 (1995): 323–52.

14. Over the period from January 2005 to July 2006, local reception centers facilitated the return home of 2,163 newly escaped or released children. These and other statistics in this section derive from Edward B. Rackley's evaluation visit to Uganda in 2007.

15. United Nations Security Council Resolution 1539, April 22, 2004.

16. Uganda Task Force on Monitoring and Reporting, Report contributing to the Preparation of the 6th Report of the Secretary General to the Security Council on Children in Armed Conflict, Developments in Uganda 1 January 2005 to 31 July 2006.

17. United Nations Secretary General, 6th Report to the General Assembly on the status of Children in Armed Conflict, 2006.

18. For additional historical background, see Tim Allen, *The International Criminal Court and the Lord's Resistance Army* (London: Zed Books, 2006); Sverker Finnström, "'For God and My Life': War and Cosmology in Northern Uganda," in *No Peace, No War: An Anthropology of Contemporary Armed Conflicts*, ed. Paul Richards (Athens: Ohio University Press, 2005), 98–116; Heidi Behrend, *Alice Lawena and the Holy Spirits, War in Northern Uganda, 1986–97* (Oxford: James Curry, 1999); and Mark Leopold, *Inside West Nile* (Santa Fe, NM: School of American Research Press, 2005).

19. Four of MSF's main operational sections—MSF France, MSF Holland, MSF Switzerland, and MSF Spain—were active in Uganda between 2001 and 2006. MSF Belgium ran projects in neighboring countries but not in Uganda itself.

20. www.doctorswithoutborders.org/news/2006/03-07-2006.cfm.

21. Veena Das, *Life and Words: Violence and the Descent into the Ordinary* (Berkeley: University of California Press, 2006).

22. Didier Fassin, *When Bodies Remember: Experiences and Politics of AIDS in South Africa* (Berkeley: University of California Press, 2007).

23. "'The crisis' according to the Hippocratic treatise *On Affections*, 'occurs in diseases whenever the diseases increase in intensity or go away or change into another disease or end altogether.'" Randolph Starn, "Historians and 'Crisis,'" *Past and Present* 52 (August 1971): 4. See also Reinhardt Koselleck, "Crisis," *Journal of the History of Ideas* 67, no. 2 (April 2006): 357–400.

Contributors

Thomas A. Birkland is the William T. Kretzer Professor of Public Policy at North Carolina State University.

Michele Landis Dauber is an associate professor at Stanford Law School.

Kim Fortun is an associate professor in the Department of Science and Technology Studies, Rensselaer Polytechnic Institute.

Javier Lezaun is University Lecturer in Science and Technology Governance at Oxford University.

Edward B. Rackley is a consultant researcher for Transition International.

Peter Redfield is an asssociate professor of anthropology at the University of North Carolina.

Austin Sarat is the William Nelson Cromwell Professor of Jurisprudence and Political Science at Amherst College.

Peter Schuck is the Simeon E. Baldwin Professor of Law at Yale Law School.

Susan Sterett is a professor of political science at the University of Denver.

Index

KF 3750 .S27 2009

Catastrophe

DATE DUE
